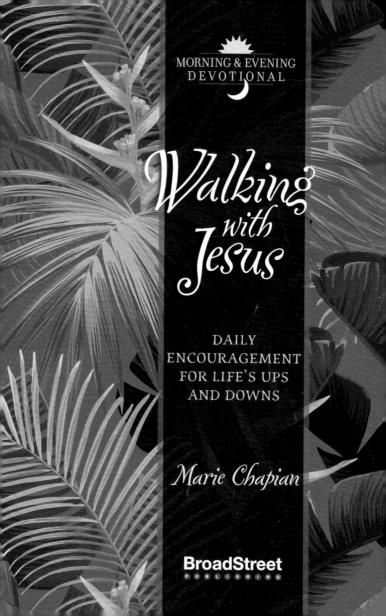

MORNING & EVENING
DEVOTIONAL

Walking
with
Jesus

DAILY
ENCOURAGEMENT
FOR LIFE'S UPS
AND DOWNS

Marie Chapian

BroadStreet
PUBLISHING

Don't be afraid,
because I have saved you.
I have called you by name,
and you are mine.
When you pass through the waters,
I will be with you.
When you cross rivers,
you will not drown.
When you walk through fire,
you will not be burned,
nor will the flames hurt you.

Isaiah 43:1-2 NCV

INTRODUCTION

Morning and evening, you can walk and talk with Jesus!

In this one-year devotional, God pours out his heart of compassion in a powerful way. Each morning reading contains a small, fiery explosion of love from your doting heavenly Father that will spark your heart with passion and give you joy for your day. In the evening, be inspired, challenged, and encouraged as you read a beautifully poetic prayer offered to God in thanksgiving. God is always worthy of our praise!

It's my heart's fervent and passionate prayer that this devotional helps lift you to a mountaintop of sweet and fiery faith where your heart wisely breathes thanksgiving to Jesus, uncontested, unfeigned, and undaunted forever.

May you be overtaken with his love each day,

Marie

HIS WORDS TO ME

Mountain of Strength

I'm your mountain of strength for your new year.
I'm your mighty mountain, lofty and majestic;
I'm your mountain of awesome power and might.
I bend down at the sound of your cry.
I stoop to lift you out of danger.
I pull you out
of the miry pit of wrong choices.
I wipe away
the splotches and smudges of every past mistake.
I make all things new.

Don't fall prey to the foolishness of envy and pride.
Blessing after blessing will come to you
when you trust Me.
I'm all you need.

MY WORDS TO HIM

You're my mountain of strength, Lord.
It fascinates me that you'll bend down
at the sound of my cry to stoop and lift me
out of the troubles that might flood my path.
You'll pull me out of the miry pit of wrong choices
and wipe away the splotches and smudges of the past.
Oh Lord, this year help me not to fall prey to the
foolishness of the things that are but temporary glitter,
and help me choose your will
in every single matter of my life.
Blessing after blessing come to me
as I follow you because
you're all I need to live fully and completely.
You're awesome in power and might,
and I trust you completely.

Trust in the LORD with all your heart,
And do not lean on your own understanding.
In all your ways acknowledge Him,
And He will make your paths straight.

Proverbs 3:5-6 NASB

HIS WORDS TO ME

You Love Me

Don't fret transition and reverse plans,
for these are gifts to stretch your faith.
I'm your provider.
I'm the God of all there is,
and I tell you not to underestimate
My power and authority
in every situation concerning you.
Never fear the unexpected
and the unpredictable;
never stagger at the thought of change.
I provide everything you need
and much more.

MY WORDS TO HIM

Thank you, Jesus, for loving me today.
You're the God of all there is,
and I underestimate your power and authority
in all situations concerning me.
I know you're with me and I know nothing escapes your eye.
That's why I'm empowered to handle the trials in my life.
I'm beginning to understand that the things
I often consider so terrible can actually be gifts from you
to stretch my faith.
You're my provider and my source
of strength and courage.
I'm strong because you're strong.
When I face unexpected and unpredictable moments,
teach me not to stagger in my tracks, but to stand firm.
Help me as this new year begins, Lord,
to trust you more deeply than ever before.

Those who know your name trust in you,
for you, O LORD, do not abandon those who search for you.

Psalm 9:10 NLT

HIS WORDS TO ME

Fill the Vacant Places

Don't look back. Never look back.
Keep your eyes fixed on the dawn.
I rise *in you* every morning
and in the gold of daybreak, I slip your burdens
beneath the beauty of My overcoming love.
Will you look for My smile to dispel your hurt feelings?
I want to fill the vacant places in your soul.
Will you allow My arms to hold you
so you'll stay on track?
Will you allow My grace to sustain you
so you won't continue muttering self-defeating words
to yourself?
Will you allow My joy to fortify your spirit?
I've hidden you in Me.
I don't leave you for a single moment.
My eye is always upon you.

MY WORDS TO HIM

Oh Lord, I know you want to fill the vacant places
in my soul;
I know you want to make me
complete and whole,
and it gives me the greatest comfort.
I'm holding your love
close to me throughout this day because
without you there is no me.
As I rise every morning, the daybreak turns
pink and gold with the wonder of new opportunities
before me.
Oh Jesus, create in me a clean heart
and a soul to bless you.
It's in you that I'm a complete person.

In Him you have been made complete,
and He is the head over all rule and authority.
Colossians 2:10 NASB

HIS WORDS TO ME

Speak to Me

Listen for Me in unexpected places—
Yes, listen for Me
in the sound of a fluttering bird,
in the wail of the wind,
the groan of traffic,
and in the sound of a cell phone
crying in your pocket.

Hear Me in the spill of night
when the world sleeps
and My children breathe the kisses of angels.
Hear Me when you cough and blow your nose
while reaching for a glass of water;
hear Me when I tenderly hold your darling head
in My hands,
and hum a healing love song in your ear.

MY WORDS TO HIM

Oh Lord, thank you for speaking to me in unexpected places.
Thank you for your love song hovering over me
throughout the day.
I love to listen for you in the sounds
of the awakening morning,
in the heat of noontime,
and in the spill of night when the world sleeps.
I hear you in the wail of the wind, the groan of traffic
and even in the sound of a cell phone sighing in my pocket.
You hold my head in your hands
and you hum your healing love songs in my ear.
I can only worship you as you make every hour
blessed and holy in the sound
of your caressing love.

Oh come, let us worship and bow down;
let us kneel before the LORD our Maker.

Psalm 95:6 NKJV

HIS WORDS TO ME

My Refuge

Your safety is in Me. I'm your refuge.
In the shadow of My wings I keep you safe
where no harm can reach you.
If you wear the strangling girdle of stress
you become the shape of stress.
If you wear the cloak of worry,
you take on its shape,
and if you dance in the shoes
of distress and panic,
the band leaves the room
and grabs health and happiness
on the way out.
What will you choose today?

Lord, thank you for keeping me safe.
You're my refuge, my place of security.
I'm kept safe under the shadow of your wings
where no harm can reach me.
If I put on the girdle of stress,
you become the shape of that stress
to cover me and keep me safe
from strangling myself.
If I don the exhausting cloak of worry,
you take on its shape to keep the breath in me,
and if I dance in the shoes of distress and panic,
you dismiss the band and call me back
to the secret place with you
where there's no stress, no worry, no distress, or panic.
Oh God, I'm blessed.
I'm blessed!
Today I want to live in honor
of the secret place of the Most High,
my true home.

He who dwells in the secret place of the Most High
Shall abide under the shadow of the Almighty.
I will say of the LORD, "He is my refuge and my fortress;
My God, in Him I will trust."

Psalm 91:1-2 NKJV

HIS WORDS TO ME

Wondrous Privilege

It's strength and courage you need today.
I'm giving you the power
to forge ahead
with joy and holy determination.
Be strong!
I'm giving you freedom
from the forces that have kept you
from moving full tilt
toward your divine destiny.

Take big steps today, and push through
the obstacles and hindrances
that have been thorns in your flesh.
I'm in you and right beside you.
I'm empowering you
to shake the dust from your hair
and make that hurdle
into victory now.

MY WORDS TO HIM

Thank you, Father God, for the wondrous privilege
you've given me to know you through Jesus.
Thank you for opening your arms to me
and inviting me into your private chambers to talk like this.
Thank you for the high honor of private audience with you
any time of the day or night!
I enter the holy doorway of our communication
with a thankful heart every day.
Sometimes I stand in that doorway breathless
with so much awe I can hardly stand it.
To know the Son of God is right here with me,
and to think you'll never leave me
or forsake me is beyond my comprehension.
All I can do is thank you, and thank you, and thank you.
Thank you, Father, Son, and Holy Spirit.

Enter his gates with thanksgiving;
go into his courts with praise.
Give thanks to him and praise his name.

Psalm 100:4 NLT

HIS WORDS TO ME

Always With Me

Love Me enough to desire
what I desire for you.
When you dash off on your own,
you're like one dying of thirst and running
the wrong way for water.
I'm your Savior and your Friend.
I'm the oasis in the desert
and your heavenly supply.
Honor Me by pausing to learn about My wants
and desires for you.
This is how you become
a living prayer.

Thank you, Lord, for never leaving me,
not for a single moment.
Thank you, Lord, that even when I'm busy
running my life without you,
you're still there
loving me and trying to get through to me.
Thank you for insisting I slip my worries and fears
into the immensity of your overcoming love for me.
You've told me to pause in my busyness
and my hurried schedule to look deep within
and listen for your Holy Spirit's guidance
to dispel my anxieties.
I thank you today for fortifying my spirit
with your Holy Spirit.

He Himself has said,
"I will never leave you
nor forsake you."
Hebrews 13:5 NKJV

HIS WORDS TO ME

Exuberant Arena

When your soul is stirred with a longing
you can't identify, and your heart beats
in a pattern that tells you something's missing,
retreat for a moment to make space
for your gift of creativity.
I've gifted you with a creative soul
and you must make space for your inner
longings to find expression.

Oh, so many ways to release the gifts
I've placed in you! Listen intimately
to the world around you and to the dimensions of
My divine presence.
I've gifted you with the ability to see
beneath the surface of things
and to give voice to your unique vision and
passion. Your life is the exuberant arena
of the gifts I've given you. Allow your gifts to unfold
and richly flow.
Today, allow yourself to flourish!

Lord, my life is the exuberant arena
of the gifts you've given me.
Thank you for my gift of creativity
and for my creative soul.
Thank you for reminding me
to make space for my inner longings to find expression.
You've shown me so many ways to release the gifts
that you've placed in me.
Teach me to listen intimately
to the world around me and for the dimensions
of your divine presence.
Teach me to look for and observe
your hand at work in the people around me.
Help me to listen for the songs of the angels.
Thank you for giving me moments
to retreat in and make space for you
to speak to me.

"If you then, who are evil,
know how to give good gifts to your children,
how much more will the heavenly Father
give the Holy Spirit to those who ask him!"

Luke 11:13 NRSV

HIS WORDS TO ME

New Perspective

Today, I'm giving you a new perspective
so you'll see things through My eyes.
I want you to see the view from *My* window.
Rub My salve of holy vision
on your human eyes, and the blurred sight
and darkness will fall off you
like a heavy drape flopping to the ground.
You'll begin to understand yourself
and your role in My ultimate purpose.
If you could see what I see
you'd never grind your teeth, fidget, fret,
or lose a minute of sweet peaceful sleep.
To see clearly is to understand. You've eaten
the honey of My Word, tasted the blessings
of My favor, and now I'm giving you
new sight. The higher you step up to Me
the clearer the vision and the further you'll see.

MY WORDS TO HIM

Thank you, Jesus, for a new perspective
to see things through your eyes.
I want to rub the salve of holy vision
on my eyes, so my blurred sight
will become clear and darkness will fall
from me like a heavy drape flopping to the ground.
I want to see the view from heaven's windows.
I want to understand my role in your ultimate purpose.
I want to see what you see.
I want to stop grinding my teeth
and fidgeting and fretting.
I don't want to lose one more minute
of sweet peaceful sleep.
I want to see clearly
and understand your ways.
I love to eat the honey of your Word
and taste the blessings of your favor.
Ignite my heart with your Holy Spirit today.

"I will give you a new heart, and I will put a new spirit in you.
I will take out your stony, stubborn heart and give you a
tender, responsive heart."

Ezekiel 36:26 NLT

HIS WORDS TO ME

False Burdens

I lift from you now every false burden and
feeling of heaviness
that tries to surround you.
I remove the sluggish warp of oppression
that seeks to overwhelm you.
No depression will capture your heart
and mind. You're free to see the truth
of every situation from My point-of-view.
I prohibit and halt every droopy, self-absorbed
preoccupation that comes near you.
Take your power today and stand against all
demonic threats to your happiness and
contentment in My name.
My Holy Spirit will sweetly
and beautifully flow through your emotions
when you cast every care on Me!
I'll transform your mind
to be able to see and anticipate
the wondrous things
I've planned for you.

MY WORDS TO HIM

Dear Lord, lift from me every false burden
and the feelings of heaviness that come upon me
to overwhelm me.
Remove for me the sluggish wrap of oppression.
When you died on the cross for me,
you set me free from my weaknesses.
I find my strength in you through your Holy Spirit!
No depression can capture
my heart and mind when I am one with you,
and when I let go of my demands and expectations
that the world would make me happy.
You've given me the ability to see the truth
of every situation from *your* point of view.
You'll halt every droopy, self-absorbed preoccupation
that comes over me.
I choose today to take my place and resist all threats
to my peace and contentment in the name of Jesus.
Your Holy Spirit will sweetly and beautifully flow
through my emotions all day today
because I'm casting all my cares on you, Jesus.
You're transforming my mind to be able to see
and anticipate the good things that you've
planned for me from the beginning.

Casting all your anxieties on him, because he cares for you.

1 Peter 5:7 ESV

HIS WORDS TO ME

Wrapped in Gladness

I've given you many gifts.
Show your creative side today.
Think how I can create something
astonishingly beautiful from ashes,
and how I transform mourning into joy—
think how I dress you up in garments
of praise for your spirit of heaviness.
The gladness I wrap you in lathers you
with a precious healing ointment.
I'm the creator of all things on earth and in heaven,
and I've given you
creative gifts to express Myself through you.
Be free today to fully express your gifts
in a flurry of love and delight,
and praise Me for your creativity
which I want you to wear like a kingly robe.

Lord Jesus, wrap me in gladness today.
Lather me with a precious healing ointment.
You've given me many gifts and I want to show you
my gratitude.
You can create something astonishingly
beautiful from a heap of ashes!
You transform a mourning soul into a joyful soul.
You exchange a spirit of heaviness with gladness.
It's incredible how creative you are,
and your Spirit lives in me
with creative gifts to express!
I'm going to be creative,
and gather my emotions with you in mind.
I'll express my gifts wisely today with light and love.
I give you praise with a happy heart, which you've
given me to wear like a kingly robe.

You have turned for me my mourning into dancing;
You have put off my sackcloth and clothed me with gladness.

Psalm 30:11 NKJV

HIS WORDS TO ME

Not Alone

Dear one, I haven't sent you out alone.
No, no no, never alone.
I'm right beside you, and My Spirit
goes before you preparing every millimeter
of your way. Never think you're alone even
when the way bristles with the unknown,
and danger snarls in the shadows.
I'm your courage! Not only that,
I'm the light that exposes the pests of the soul,
those ruinous thoughts that tell you you're alone.

Tell yourself today you're *never* alone.
The unredeemed in their self-pity
may distress themselves with loneliness,
but you're endowed with wisdom and
a creative spirit, and these are your friends.
You're not alone. Never, never, never.

Thank you, Jesus,
for not sending me out in the world alone.
Thank you for being right beside me always.
Thank you for preparing every millimeter of my way.
I'm never alone even when the way bristles with the unknown.
You're my strength and my courage.
You're the light that exposes the viruses of the soul,
the ruinous thoughts that tell me I'm alone.
I'll tell myself the truth today—I'm *never* alone!
The unredeemed in their self-pity may distress themselves
with loneliness but I have been endowed with wisdom
and a creative spirit, and these are my friends.
I'm never alone.
Never never never.
Thank you.

"The Father gives to me the people who are mine.
Every one of them will come to me,
and I will always accept them."

John 6:37 NCV

HIS WORDS TO ME

Surprises

I'm a God of surprises.
I love to usher new events
and situations into your life that
inspire you to dig deeper
into My Word—situations that
cause you to drop your habits
of complacency and seek Me
on a deeper level.
I'm calling you to see with My eyes,
to think with My mind.
Dear one, there's no problem
you'll ever face in your life
that My Word doesn't cover.

Thank you, Jesus, for all the surprises you bring into my life.
Thank you for ushering new events and situations
into my life to inspire me to dig deeper into your Word.
Thank you for situations that cause me to drop my habits
of complacency and seek you on a deeper level.
Thank you for your gentle prodding
to see with your eyes and to think with your mind.
Thank you, Lord, for showing me there's no problem
I'll ever face in my life that you haven't already
thought of and covered with the promises in your Word.

Let us hold firmly to the hope that we have confessed,
because we can trust God to do what he promised.

Hebrews 10:23 NCV

HIS WORDS TO ME

Fighting My Battles

I fight your battles and settle your scores.
I work out solutions with those
who contend with you.
Let *others* contend, but *you* don't contend.
Hold your peace and listen for wisdom very attentively.
Wisdom's instructions are not always
the same or as you might expect.
I tell you, there's a time to make peace
and a time to take arms,
a time to break down and a time to build up,
a time to rip out and a time to mend.

Listen for Wisdom's guidance in such a time as this.
I'm here to protect you as the enemy creeps hungrily about
eager to devour all in his path.
Your enemy is not human, dear one, and you won't escape
with your feeble human tactics and devices.
I tell you, no weapon formed against you
will prosper because you're Mine,
so I ask you to let Me take charge of the battles.

MY WORDS TO HIM

Thank you, Jesus, for fighting my battles and settling my scores.
Thank you for working out solutions with those who contend with me.
I'll work at not being contentious.
I'll let others contend. I'll hold my peace
and listen for wisdom very attentively.
Wisdom's instructions aren't always the same as I might expect.
You tell me there's a time to make peace and a time to take up arms.
You tell me there's a time to break down and a time to build up.
You tell me there's a time to rip out and a time to mend.
I choose to listen to wisdom and guidance in such a time as this.
Thank you for being here to protect me
as the enemy creeps hungrily about
eager to devour everything in his path.
I realize my enemy isn't human and I won't
win any battle with my feeble human tactics and devices.
You've said that no weapon formed against me will prosper
because I'm under *your* protection and leadership.
Knowing this I'm made strong.
Thank you, Jesus!

Thanks be to God, who in Christ
always leads us in triumphal procession.

2 Corinthians 2:14 NRSV

31

HIS WORDS TO ME

Listening for You

Listen. I want you to hear My voice at all times.
I want to be able to speak to you at any hour of the day
or night and know you'll listen. My heart holds
a heavenly kingdom of wisdom, love, and joy to share with you.
If you'll listen.
The way to listen is with your heart.
The thoughts from My heart to yours will ignite in you—
a mighty brightness that could light up the whole world.
I've called you to be this beacon of light,
fixed and permeating through every storm
and even through the blackest and starless of nights.

Listen. I'm teaching you to discern what is true and honorable
and worthy of your attention.
I'm showing you what to revere,
what things are noble, reputable, authentic, pure, and lovely.
Listen. I'm showing you the beauty of meditating on the best,
not the worst; the beautiful, not the ugly; things to praise,
not things to curse;
and how to love as I love.

Oh Lord Jesus, help me to listen for your voice at all times.
I know you want to speak to me,
and not just here and there whenever I happen to be
paying attention.
I know your heart possesses riches
of wisdom, love, and joy, and you want to share these
with me if I will just listen.
Thank you for showing me
that the way to listen is with my heart.
The thoughts from your heart fire me with a mighty brightness
that could light up the whole world!
You've called me to be a light in the world
to permeate through the storms
and blackest, starless nights.
I'm learning each day to discern
what is true and honorable and worth my attention.
Thank you for showing me what things are noble, reputable,
authentic, pure, and lovely.
Thank you for showing me the beauty of meditating
on the best not the worst,
the beautiful not the ugly,
how to praise not to curse.
Thank you, Lord, for teaching me to love as you love.

Guide me in your truth and teach me, for you are God my Savior,
and my hope is in you all day long.

Psalm 25:5 NIV

HIS WORDS TO ME

Nothing without You

I speak to you day and night.
I love to tell you things, teach you,
help you, guide you.
I'm your Lord and your life, and
when you live in My will for you,
all you touch your hand to
will radiate with the presence and the kiss
of the Almighty.
But without Me go ahead and cradle
jeweled cities in your sleeves, dine in banquet halls
with governors and kings,
and all will perish.
Poof.
Without *Me* you can do nothing!
Live in Me, snuggled vitally united to Me,
for this is your sure path to understanding who you are
and what you are called to do in this life.
Why do I tell you this?
Because we're *one.* Always, always, always
remember this.

MY WORDS TO HIM

Oh Lord, I realize without you I can do nothing.
Thank you for teaching me,
guiding me and helping me
every day.
I need you today, Lord.
You are my life.
You promised that when I live in you
and live for your will in my life,
your presence is in everything my hand touches.
I know that without you I have no dreams, no hope.
I want to live in your will and purpose all day today,
snuggled gratefully united with you,
for this is my sure path
to understanding who I am,
what I'm called to do in this life,
and who I'm called to be.
Thank you, Jesus.

"I am the vine, you are the branches.
He who abides in Me,
and I in him, bears much fruit;
for without Me you can do nothing.

John 15:5 NKJV

HIS WORDS TO ME

Safely Settled

Your true home is safely settled
in My heart,
for this is where you were born to live.
Fear and worry will always
choke the happiness you were born to possess.
Beloved, in Me there's absolutely *no* fear.
Nothing rattles Me—nothing!
I'm all peace and all joy. I'm contentment,
and I'm *happy*. I've promised you My peace,
and I've also told you I'd give you My take
on the things that bother you. You have *My mind*.
My mind is at ease!
I want you to be happy in the home
I've prepared for you on earth,
but recognize and fully grasp
that your real home is nestled inside My heart.

My true home is safely settled in your heart, Lord,
for this is where I was born to live.
Fear and worry always choke my happiness,
but I know I was born to process goodness and joy.
Thank you, Lord, that nothing rattles you—nothing!
You're all peace and all joy.
You're all contentment.
You're all happiness.
Thank you for giving me everything I need
to be happy. You promised to give me
your peace, and I need your peace today.
I'm happy in the home that you prepared for me
right *here*, right *now*.
My real home is nestled
inside your heart,
on earth as well as eternally
in heaven.

Whom have I in heaven but you?
And there is nothing on earth that I desire besides you.

Psalm 73:25 ESV

HIS WORDS TO ME

Important to You

If you make your home with Me
and if our relationship
is intimate and organic,
and if I've made My home in you
and My words are at home in you,
how can I resist your requests?
Live and thrive in Me and you'll
succeed in your endeavors.
If you live obeying My voice
and loving Me, I'm in your plans!
I'm here guiding and directing you!
Your soul burgeons with increase
as you make your home in Me,
and that's why I've told you to ask
whatever you will
and it'll be done for you.
This is My promise to you.
Everything about you is important to Me.
Believe this.

Today I am so thankful that everything about me
is important to you.
Oh yes, I thank you, Jesus,
for continually being here for me through all
past, present, and future time.
And I thank you, Jesus,
for hearing every prayer; for pulling together
the fragments of my soul and healing me.
How I love our relationship with your words
alive in me. It's a holy reminder that my home
is in you.
You're always here with me,
loving and encouraging me, guiding
and directing me perfectly so that I thrive
with a soul burgeoning with increase!
Thank you, Lord, for making me part
of your eternal plan, and for my permanent,
safe home in you.

"If anyone loves Me, he will keep My word;
and My Father will love him,
and We will come to him
and make Our abode with him."

John 14:23 NASB

HIS WORDS TO ME

Unmerited Favor

You have My unmerited favor, and you're saved
from the judgment of others.
Don't allow fault finding to come near you.
Kick aside all condemning words
and notions. Remember, you're your worst critic,
so don't be swift to jump into the garbage bag
of guilt when it's unmerited. I've tucked you into My heart
and your life is new and beautiful, replete with
healing and wisdom. Guilt has no hold on you!
I've set you free with My delicious
forgiveness.
I've given you goodness and mercy as partners.
They follow you all the days of your life.
Favor, dear one, includes My love song
that doesn't miss a note. I've called you
to increase in favor, so enjoy the song,
dance in your freedom.
Love who you are.

MY WORDS TO HIM

Lord, thank you for unmerited favor,
and for saving me from the judgment of others.
I don't want to become a victim of faultfinding.
I want to kick aside all condemning words and notions
that might rise up in me.
I realize I'm my worst critic
and that I can be swift to jump into the garbage bag of guilt
when it's not merited.
You've taken me into your great heart
and my life is made new and beautiful.
Guilt must have no hold on me.
You've set me free
with your delicious forgiveness! Thank you, Lord,
for giving me goodness and mercy as partners.
They follow me all the days of my life!
Thank you for helping me today, Lord.
Thank you for your love song that doesn't miss a note.
Thank you for increasing favor in my life.
Today I choose to enjoy myself.
I choose to love who I am.

I love those who love me,
and those who seek me
diligently will find me.

Proverbs 8:17 NKJV

41

HIS WORDS TO ME

Key to Wisdom

Living in Me, vitally united to Me
is the key to wisdom and understanding
of My omnipotent mind.
When you ingest the words I speak
to you; when you meditate and ponder
what I tell you,
a new power takes shape in your spirit.
The authority of My words
bubble up in you to give you wisdom,
discretion, and understanding.
I see your situation now.
My Word will guide and instruct you.
Never succumb to confusion.
You have My Word in you.

MY WORDS TO HIM

Lord Jesus, please see my situation now.
You've taught me that the key to wisdom and understanding
is to remain vitally united to you.
You've said I have the mind of Christ, and that means
my human mind is actually infused with your omnipotent,
all-knowing mind.
This is so wonderful!
Help me to thoroughly ingest the words
that you speak to me through your written Word.
Help me when I meditate and ponder your Word,
so new power will take shape in my spirit.
With the authority of your words bubbling up in me,
your wisdom, discretion, and understanding
come alive in me.
Guide me and instruct me today, Lord.
I don't want to succumb to confusion.
I know that with your words solidly fixed in me I can be strong
and I can be wise, as I was born to be.

I think about your orders
and study your ways.
I enjoy obeying your demands,
and I will not forget your word.

Psalm 119:15-16 NCV

HIS WORDS TO ME

New Vision

Are you in need of a new vision for your life?
Are you longing for change?
If so, quiet your heart now
and withdraw into the stillness of the hour,
undisturbed by outside influences
and interferences.
Be still and calmly concentrate
on the presence of the Father.
Your desires are seeds for you to nourish
because you were born with more
than one purpose. As you quiet yourself
in prayer before the throne of grace,
listen for the guidance of My Holy Spirit,
wait for the anointing of your Savior,
and the perfect will of My Father
will be made clear.

Lord, I am in need of a new vision for my life.
Help me to quiet my heart and withdraw into the stillness
of the hour, undisturbed by outside influences
and interferences.
Help me to be still and calmly concentrate
on your presence.
My desires are seeds of nourishment
because they are born with more than one purpose.
As I quiet myself in prayer before your throne, I'll listen
for the guidance of your Holy Spirit,
I'll wait for the anointing
and the perfect will of the Father.
Today I long to hear
your voice clearly and perfectly directing me.

I will bless the LORD who has given me counsel;
my heart also instructs me in the night seasons.

Psalm 16:7 NKJV

HIS WORDS TO ME

Free from Fear

I free you from all your fears.
Join your life with Mine afresh this day
and expect unique, extraordinary blessings
and opportunities to come your way. I'll move
mightily on your behalf as you trust Me.
Look! All things are new in your life
and the fears of the past are gone
because you're a new person today.
I've given you a fresh start.
Come, let's be happy together
as you plunge forward
on the fabulous road ahead.

Today, Lord, free me from fear.
Help me affix my life with yours in a fresh way this day.
Help me think positively
and expect unique and extraordinary
blessings and opportunities to come my way.
I know that you'll move mightily on my behalf
because I trust you.
You've told me all things are new in my life,
so the fears of the past must be buried with the past.
I'm a new person in *you*!
Thank you for providing a fresh start for me.
I want to come into your kingdom and be happy with you.
I want to plunge forward on the beautiful path ahead
that you've prepared for me with confidence.
Help me, Jesus. I love you.

Whoever listens to me will dwell safely,
and will be secure, without fear of evil.

Proverbs 1:33 NKJV

HIS WORDS TO ME

Deliver Me

I've delivered you from
your patterns of wrong thinking
and your old
self-destructive habits
and given you a new mind-set.
The traps of the past are shattered
and done away with.
You're altogether new!
Your beautiful brain now forms
fresh, inspiring, and revelatory truths,
so you'll bring life and light
into situations that were once too confusing
and disarming for you.
Your changed thinking patterns
are no longer stained
with the world's sad stab at enlightenment,
and you're going to prevail
in all things!

Thank you, Lord, for delivering me
from my patterns of wrong thinking
and my old self destructive habits.
Thank you for giving me a new mindset.
Thank you that the traps of the past are shattered
and done away with.
I'm altogether new!
This is hard to grasp at times.
You've made my brain
beautiful with fresh, inspiring, and revelatory truths.
I can now bring forth life and light into situations
that were once confusing and disarming for me.
My thinking patterns are changing and I love it!
I'm no longer influenced so much
by the world's sad stab at enlightenment.
I realize that only in you will I prevail,
find contentment, and experience lasting peace.

"Who can know the LORD's thoughts?
Who knows enough to teach him?"
But we understand these things,
for we have the mind of Christ.

1 Corinthians 2:16 NLT

49

HIS WORDS TO ME

My Mind

I love your curiosity
and your throbbing interest
in the world I've created.
I delight with you as you appreciate
with awe My creation.
Because of your holy enthusiasm,
I'll show you much, much more to love.
I'll give you My holy microscope,
and you'll learn more
of the subtleties of My hand.

No branch or tree is voiceless,
no rock without a song of praise.
Can you feel the heartbeat of a stone, a leaf,
or dove? Can you hear
My furtive breath in a gentle snowfall?
I've given you the world
to care for, to be fruitful in and multiply.
Be glad in what I've given you.
I created it all for you.

MY WORDS TO HIM

Thank you for the mind that you've given me.
Thank you for my curiosity and my throbbing interest
in the world that you've created.
Thank you for delighting in me
as I appreciate your creation with awe.
Thank you for giving me holy enthusiasm
and so much to love.
Thank you for giving me
your holy microscope so that I can learn more about
the subtleties of your creation and your hand.
Thank you that no branch or tree is voiceless
and no rock without a song of praise.
Help me to feel the heartbeat of a stone and a leaf,
and the song of a dove.
Help me hear your furtive breath in a gentle snowfall
or a drubbing rain.
Thank you for giving me the world to care for,
to be fruitful in and to multiply.
Thank you, Lord, for all that you have given me
and created for me to love.

The earth is the LORD's and the fullness thereof,
the world and those who dwell therein.

Psalm 24:1 ESV

HIS WORDS TO ME

Be Still

Be still.
You're strongest when you're still.
In quietness and confidence you're strong.
I'm with you and I'm the Lord
who is exalted above all the earth!
I hold you in the palm of My hand.
You're safe here and *now*.
This moment
is your safe place, for I am your safe place.
No need to fight your own battles.
No need to rush out to defend yourself.
Your personal arsenal of weapons
are pockets of lint—weightless and wearisome.
No ground is ever gained
with your emotional attempts without Me.
When I'm beside you, the battle is won.
I'm your fierce and undefeated weapon.

MY WORDS TO HIM

Today I choose to be still and know that you are God.
In quietness and confidence, I'll be strong in you.
Thank you, Lord, for being with me and in me.
Thank you, my exalted Lord,
above all the earth and all that is.
Thank you for holding me in the palm of your hand
where I'm safe right now, at this very moment.
You're my safe place,
and I have no need to fight my own battles.
There's no need to rush out to defend myself.
My personal arsenal of weapons
are merely pockets of lint: weightless and wearisome.
No ground is ever gained by my emotional attempts
without you, Lord.
You're beside me and the battle is won.
Thank you, Father. Thank you, Holy Spirit. Thank you, Jesus.

"In repentance and rest is your salvation,
in quietness and trust is your strength."

Isaiah 30:15 NIV

HIS WORDS TO ME

Nothing Is Hidden

I'm the source of all wisdom,
and your natural reasoning
will lead you astray.
Remember, nothing is hidden
from My eyes.
I see the challenges that you face today
and I'm taking care of all that concerns you.
Be attentive to obey the promptings of My Spirit;
resist the temptation to hotly
go forth in your own strength in matters
too great for you to handle without Me.
When you're spiritually flexible and obedient;
when you are patient and submissive
to My leading,
you'll see miracles.
Miracles, I tell you!
I can change a situation
in the flicker of an eye
and without Me, you cannot.

MY WORDS TO HIM

Lord Jesus, nothing is hidden from your eyes.
You're the source of all wisdom.
You see the challenges that I face today,
and you're taking care of everything that concerns me.
I'll be attentive to obey the prompting of your Holy Spirit.
Help me to resist the temptation to go forth
in my own strength in matters too great for me
to handle without you.
Help me to be spiritually flexible and obedient.
Help me to be patient and submissive
to your leading so that I can see miracles.
You'll change a situation in the flicker of an eye,
and I can change nothing
in my own strength.

"If you abide in Me, and My words
abide in you, you will ask what you desire,
and it shall be done for you.
By this My father is glorified,
that you bear much fruit;
so you will be My disciples."

John 15:7-8 NKJV

HIS WORDS TO ME

Tears of the Past

Give the tears of the past to Me
and I'll empty them into the Sea of Deference.
Tears, like blades scratching stone,
will no longer carve the flesh of your cheeks.
The past is finished with its hot tears
and its heckling pain. Ashes have no life and are
good for nothing. Don't sit in the ashes
of yesterday's sorrow when I've crushed them
beneath the promises of My Word.

Trample on sorrow today,
for your battle scars are numbered in heaven.
Nothing escapes heaven's watchful eye, and
with one breath I defeat your enemies.
Defer them to Me,
all of them.

MY WORDS TO HIM

Oh Jesus, I'm giving you my tears of the past.
Thank you for caring about me.
I know that you'll empty them into the sea of deference.
My tears, like blades scratching stone, will no longer
carve the flesh of my cheeks.
The past is finished
with my hot tears and the heckling pain.
Ashes have no life
and are good for nothing.
You're teaching me to not sit
in the ashes of yesterday's sorrow.
I choose to trample on sorrow
today because my battle scars are numbered in heaven.
Nothing escapes heaven's watchful eyes,
and with one breath, you, Lord, make me a conqueror.
Thank you for rescuing me.

In all these things we are more than conquerors
through Him who loved us.
Romans 8:37 NKJV

HIS WORDS TO ME

Holy Microscope

I want to give you a holy microscope to learn
of the subtle thrills of life in My Spirit.
I want you to look deep and long enough
into My Word to see the blessings I have for you.
There are no tears in any corner
of heaven, beloved. Defer yours to Me and whoosh,
they're plunged into the sea of deference.
I'm setting you free from the captive claws of worry
and the dark emotions that pull
and snap at you. As you've sown in tears
you'll now reap with joy.
Be receptive to My voice and grasp
My immutable promise of holy *joy*.
I want you to see the great things
I'm doing for you today.

MY WORDS TO HIM

Thank you, Jesus, for your holy microscope.
I'm always learning
and experiencing the subtle thrills of life in your Spirit.
Thank you for telling me to look deep and long into your Word
in order to see the blessings that you have for me.
There are no tears in any corner of heaven.
Thank you that my tears are all
plunged into the sea of deference.
Thank you for setting me free
from the captive claws of worry
and the dark emotions that pull and snap at me.
I have sown in tears but I will reap with joy.
Today I choose to be receptive to your voice
and grasp your immutable promise of holy joy.
Thank you for helping me
to concentrate on the great things that you are doing
for me *today*.

You have delivered my soul from death,
my eyes from tears,
my feet from stumbling.

Psalm 116:8 NRSV

HIS WORDS TO ME

New Path

The past is over and gone
and you're on a new path now.
I forgive you, dear one,
so you ought to forgive yourself.
It's good to turn from a self-toward
habitual way of life and ask forgiveness.
Receive My forgiveness plus the blessing
of a clean slate and refreshed spirit
When you're fed up with and finished
with self-centered worries and concerns,
you'll begin to truly *live the good life*!
You'll experience clean, beautiful
joyous freedom in Me because your eyes
will be open to increased hope and faith,
and you'll have so much satisfaction—
great enough to *forgive yourself.*
All is new, fresh, flawless, and wonderful!
I love you.

The past is over and gone and I thank you, Lord,
that I'm on a new path now.
Thank you for forgiving me, beloved Lord.
Thank you for helping me to forgive myself.
Thank you for helping me to receive your forgiveness
plus the blessing of a clean slate and refreshed spirit.
I'm fed up and finished with my self-centered worries
and concerns.
I want to live the good life, Lord,
where I'll experience clean, beautiful, joyous freedom in you
because my heart is open to and filled with hope and faith.
All is new, fresh, flawless, and wonderful! I love you Jesus!

God, who is rich in mercy,
because of His great love with which He loved us,
even when we were dead in trespasses, made
us alive together with Christ.

Ephesians 2:4-5 NKJV

HIS WORDS TO ME

Every Step

Every step you take, you take with Me
at your side.
When you are weary or uncertain,
I pick you up and carry you
in My arms.
If you're more passionate about
what goes wrong in life than you are for
what is beautiful and blessed,
you'll attract more of the same.
Come. Relax in the perfume
of My Holy Spirit's breath
on your cheek.
For too long you've thought of Me
as distant and aloof,
but I've never ever been distant
and aloof. That is a wrong concept
of Me. Look up, dear one.
I'm right here.
Right now. With you.
Always.

Every step I take,
I take with you at my side.
When I'm weary or uncertain,
you pick me up and carry me in your arms.
When I'm more concerned with
what goes wrong in life than I am for
what's beautiful, wonderful, and blessed,
I always attract more of the same.
You call me to come and rest
in the holy perfume of your Spirit.
I no longer see you as distant and aloof
because you've never ever been distant and aloof.
You're right here. Right now.
Here. With me. Always.

"I am with you always, even to the end of the age."
Matthew 28:20 NLT

HIS WORDS TO ME

Blessings Untold

I go ahead of you and gift you
with blessings
before they're even a thought
in your head.
I answer needs you haven't even
asked for.
I give you riches
you have no name for.
My thoughts are so much higher
than yours, and that's why today
it's necessary for you to ask
what's best for *Me* in your current situation.
I've promised to supply over and above
everything you need, and when praying
for what is best for *Me* and My kingdom
in all things pertaining to you,
you'll always have what is best for *you*.

MY WORDS TO HIM

Thank you, Jesus, for answering my needs before I even ask.
Thank you for blessings untold and unnumbered.
Your thoughts are so much higher than mine
and that's why today I'm asking you
for what's best for me in my current situation.
You promised to supply over and above
everything I need,
and when I pray for what's best for me
you'll always give me what's best.
Not just sometimes, but all times and always.

You have multiplied, O LORD my God,
your wondrous deeds and your thoughts toward us;
none can compare with you!
I will proclaim and tell of them,
yet they are more than can be told.

Psalm 40:5 ESV

HIS WORDS TO ME

Move Freely

Make more space to unleash
your creative powers today.
Allow yourself to move more freely
in your daily life.
Routine is good, but be aware that
dullness can agitate you.
A fixed routine offering no challenge
can stifle you, and the pursuit
of security can constrict you
until your life becomes too small for you.

I've created you to do great things,
to live in the divine and expansive
adventure of My Holy Spirit's creative leading.
Listen to what your soul is
craving, and open wide your heart
to My shaping and transforming your gifts.
How lovely is the offering
of creative vision! Be free to
express what bubbles within you—
surrender to the unknown.

MY WORDS TO HIM

Thank you for helping me to move more freely
in my daily life this month.
I know that routine is good,
but I want to be aware that dullness agitates the soul.
Help me not to stifle myself and my gifts
by pursuing security and the status quo.
I don't want to restrict what you've given me
to glorify you.
Thank you for creating me to live
in the divine and expansive adventure
of your Holy Spirit's creative leading.
Thank you for teaching me to listen to what my soul craves.
Thank you for opening my heart and mind
as you transform and shape my gifts to bring you honor.
Oh Jesus, I want to be free to express
what bubbles within me.
I want to make more space in me
to unleash the creative powers that you've given me.
How beautiful is the gift of creative vision, and I desire more!
Don't let me get away with living a life that's too small for me.

"The thief does not come except to steal,
and to kill, and to destroy.
I have come that they may have life,
and that they may have it more abundantly."

John 10:10 NKJV

HIS WORDS TO ME

Supernatural Strength

Do you need supernatural strength today?
Ask and I'll shed light on new strategy
for you to pierce through your former failed plans.
I'm equipping you by My Spirit
to run up against an army of troubles
and overtake them as easily as a
sleeping dog swats a fly on its rib.
You're equipped to leap over walls of
discouragement and disappointment
like a gazelle who zips above the crags of
deadly mountainous cliffs all day long.
You're no wimp!
Take your supernatural strength
as living proof of whose you are today.

Lord Jesus, I need supernatural strength today.
Please shed light on some new strategy
so I can get past failed plans.
Equip me, Lord,
by your Holy Spirit to stand against an army
of doubt and disappointment.
Equip me to overtake troubles easily.
Equip me to leap over the walls
of discouragement.
I'm going to take my supernatural strength today
as living proof of who I belong to.
You're my strength and my life
and right now, this minute,
I'm making a declaration to rise up strong!

He would grant you, according to the riches of His glory,
to be strengthened with might through His Spirit
in the inner man.

Ephesians 3:16 NKJV

HIS WORDS TO ME

Help Me Focus

Worry has an echo;
it hammers against the walls of your mind,
and your emotions fly up startled,
making such a commotion
the world goes dizzy.
When you focus on your problems,
your emotions behave as unruly children
running wild and unrestrained,
and when you burrow your thoughts
in the garbage bins of disappointments,
you can't hear Me or see My hand in anything.

Let Me teach you to think as I think!
I have something so wonderful in store for you.
Blessings are waiting to overtake you!
Respond to the words I speak to you,
so I can open My good treasure
and bless all the work of your hands.
Success awaits you like a lover.

MY WORDS TO HIM

Lord Jesus, help me not to focus on my problems today.
My emotions sometimes behave as unruly children,
running wild and unrestrained.
I fall easily
into the garbage bin of disappointment,
but you're right here ready to pull me out.
My worries have an echo
that hammers against the walls of my mind,
and I need your Holy Spirit to unclutter every jumbled thought
and untamed emotion.
Teach me to think as you think!
I know you have something so wonderful in store for me.
You always open the treasure house of blessing to me
if I'll just calm down and trust you.
I'm going to meditate on your Word
and your promises to me today.
Blessings are waiting to overtake me!
Success awaits me like a lover!

Your word is a lamp to my feet
and a light to my path.

Psalm 119:105 ESV

HIS WORDS TO ME

Humble Submission

Let Me show you My heart
in the matters you're concerned about.
When you enter My heart,
your worries will dwindle to dust.
I want you to know your concerns
are important to Me,
and I am answering your prayers.
My ways are perfect, remember.
I make *no* mistakes.
I know the beginning and the end
because I AM the beginning and the end.
Climb into the surety of My heart
and raise your standards of prayer,
for I have something better for you today
than you've asked for.

MY WORDS TO HIM

Father, when I come to you
in love and humble submission,
my worries dwindle to dust.
I know you want me to know
that you're concerned with the same matters that concern me.
I know my concerns are important to you
and that you're answering my prayers.
Your ways are perfect.
You make no mistakes.
You know the beginning and the end
because *you're* the beginning and the end.
Today I choose to climb into the certainty of your great heart
and raise my standards of prayer.
You have something better for me today
than I know how to ask for.
Speak to me today, Lord.
Your servant is listening.

God is faithful; by him you were called into the fellowship of his
Son, Jesus Christ our Lord.

1 Corinthians 1:9 NRSV

Power of Prayer

Never underestimate the power of your prayers.
The heart of your words sails
into heaven's atmosphere and dispatches angels
to the need you call them to.
You have the power to shake worlds
and confound demons
with the authority of your prayers.
The love songs you sang to Me in the past
still echo in My ears, and your prayers
which moved mountains yesterday
go on working today.
Be passionate. Be resolute.
Know the magnitude and influence
of every prayer you lift up to Me
and every song you sing in My name.
Your prayers endure,
timelessly gathering blessings
and rippling across My creation.
Your prayers have wings.

Help me to not underestimate the power of prayer, Lord.
The heart of prayer sails into heaven's courts
and dispatches angels to answer needs.
Oh Lord, we have the power to shake the world
and confound demons with the authority of prayer.
The love songs sung to you in worship are beautiful
in your ears and prayers that move mountains today
will go on working tomorrow, tomorrow, and tomorrow.
Today, I choose to be passionate
and resolute in my prayer life.
I choose to recognize the magnitude and influence
of every prayer lifted up to you
and every song sung in your name.
My prayers endure,
timelessly gathering blessings and rippling
across all of creation.
Thank you, Jesus,
that my prayers have wings.

Pray continually.

1 Thessalonians 5:17 NIV

HIS WORDS TO ME

Secret Place

I have a secret place for you to meet with Me;
it's an exclusive holy motel located
beneath My almighty shadow.
Here in your reserved suite
with Me, you're fixed, stable, and safe.
You're out of range of the hidden traps
snapping outside the door,
and you're shielded from the hazards
on the streets beneath the window.
Here in the Shadow of the Almighty Motel
You aren't afraid of a thing—
not the wolves howling in the night,
not wars and munitions raging in the day,
not prowling, insidious diseases that fester
in the dark, and surely not the disasters
that attack the noonday sun.
No, you remain confident and at peace
in the company of angels,
assured of a long and prosperous life
here in the Shadow of the Almighty Motel—
your home.

MY WORDS TO HIM

Thank you for the secret place you have for me
to meet with you every day.
It's an exclusive holy place
located beneath your almighty shadow out of the range
of hidden traps snapping below us.
You have shielded me,
and here in the shadow of the Almighty,
I'm not afraid of anything!
I'm not afraid of the wolves howling in the night;
I'm not afraid of wars and munitions raging in the day;
I'm not afraid of the prowling, insidious diseases
that fester in the dark, and I'm not afraid of the disasters
attacking the noonday sun or of people who hurt me.
No, I remain confident and at peace with you,
here in the secret place, and in the company of angels
praising you day and night.

Whoever dwells in the shelter of the Most High
will rest in the shadow of the Almighty.

Psalm 91:1 NIV

HIS WORDS TO ME

Impatient Struggles

Give your impatient struggles to Me today.
I'll change things for you.
I'll renew your strength and fortify your heart.
I'll lift you up on giant wings
and keep you close to Me
like the eagle mounts up to the sun.

I'll keep you energized in the race,
and you won't fall apart or become tired
as you embark on the walk ahead of you.
Stay calm.
Trust Me.
In patience you possess your soul.

Today, Lord, I give up my impatient struggles.
I'm making the choice to put an end to my impatience.
Renew my strength and fortify my heart.
Lift me up on your giant wings and keep me close to you
like the eagle mounts up to the sun.
Keep me energized in the race,
so I won't fall apart or become tired
on the journey ahead of me.
Teach me what I need to learn,
and create in me what I must be in order to please you.
I'm turning to you for strength to stay unruffled and trusting.
I want to be beautiful to you!
I'll tell myself to listen
for your calm and assuring voice throughout the day.
I'll see myself as a delight to you.
In patience, I possess my soul.
You have said it, and so be it!

Let patience have its perfect work, that you may be perfect
and complete, lacking nothing.

James 1:4 NKJV

HIS WORDS TO ME

Not Afraid

Never be afraid of a challenge, My darling.
It's I who initiates challenges
in your life to add sparkle to your faith!
How I love your countenance when
illuminated with the integrity of trust
in who you are as a child of Mine.
I love your face, fixed in certainty,
frownless like flint,
commanding the snapping dragons
of doubt and fear to leave you.
Ah, come close, My sweetheart, and
let Me tell you how much I love you,
and how priceless are the pearls of your faith.

MY WORDS TO HIM

Today, Lord, help me not to be afraid of challenge.
You're the one who initiates challenges in my life
to add sparkle to my faith!
You love me enough
to allow these challenges in my life!
I choose to be illuminated with the integrity of trust.
After all, I'm your child.
My face is fixed like flint in certainty.
I'm frownless as I command
the snapping dragons of doubt and fear to leave!
Lord, draw me in tight to you so I can hear
your strengthening words of encouragement,
and learn how priceless are the pearls of faith to you.

Say to those with fearful hearts,
"Be strong, and do not fear, for your God is coming to destroy
your enemies. He is coming to save you."

Isaiah 35:4 NLT

HIS WORDS TO ME

Dance and Sing

Celebrate with Me today.
Let's dance and sing
and rejoice because all is well.
The Word I've given you
is a perpetual gift that will live
forever in your spirit.
Happiness is yours in the deepest crevices
of your soul. Your personality vibrates
and your body shimmers with joy.
We are *one*, dear one,
and all is well.
No matter what you see or hear
with your natural eyes and ears,
all is well!

Oh Lord, I love you so much I want to dance and sing.
I can't help rejoicing because I'm learning
to be grateful and fix my attention on that
which is good.
You've given me your Word
as a perpetual gift that'll live forever in my spirit.
I'm happy in the deepest crevices of my soul!
My personality vibrates and my body shimmers
with joy.
I am one with you, beautiful Savior,
and all is well.
No matter what I see or hear
with my natural eyes and ears,
I choose to see
through your eyes and ears of love and acceptance.
All is well, and I trust you implicitly today.

Let all those rejoice
who put their trust in You;
Let them ever shout for joy,
because You defend them;
Let those also who love Your name
Be joyful in You.

Psalm 5:11 NKJV

HIS WORDS TO ME

Bring You Joy

You are song.
The refrain you sing
reverberates throughout
heaven's cavernous
concert halls—
angelic choirs join you,
caroling day and night,
never the same score twice,
and eternally praising the King of Kings.

You are beautiful, My song;
your breath against My ear
is as magical as spring is
to the cherry blossoms.
Now is the time
for your dreams to
come true.

MY WORDS TO HIM

Oh, Jesus, it's my desire to bring you joy
with my song of love.
May the song I sing
reverberate throughout heaven's cavernous
concert halls and join with the angels as they sing
their continual, endless praises.
I'll sing my gratitude
to you my whole life long for all you've done for me.
I see your goodness with every breath I take.
I'll eternally praise you, King of kings,
for you are wonderful, powerful, mighty,
glorious, and altogether beautiful.

Come, let's sing for joy to the LORD.
Let's shout praises to the Rock who saves us.

Psalm 95:1 NCV

HIS WORDS TO ME

Turn Back Time

Would you like to turn back time, return
to what you've missed out on,
take back the moments lost,
the opportunities missed,
appreciate what you took for granted,
and fix what was broken?

Suppose I allowed it and turned back time,
and permitted you to do everything
all over again.
Do you really think your life would
be so much better today?
No, dear. I tell you, seize *this* moment!
Make amends and start anew!
Time is not your employer,
nor is yesterday your enemy.
You're going to prevail!
With Me you'll discover
all things really do work together for good.

Lord, if I were to turn back time
to see what I've missed out on,
if I were to take back the moments I've lost
and the opportunities I've missed,
would I appreciate today what I took for granted yesterday?
Would I be able to fix what was broken?
If you were to turn back time, Lord, and permit me
to do everything all over again, would my life today
really be so much better?
Lord, I now see that it's time
for me to seize *this* moment!
It's time for me to say goodbye to yesterday,
to make amends and to start anew.
Time is not my employer, nor is yesterday my enemy.
I'll prevail *today* because you make all things new.
I'm alive in you and because of you!
And in you I discover that all things really do, and will,
work together for good.

We know that all things work together for good for those who
love God, who are called according to his purpose.

Romans 8:28 NRSV

HIS WORDS TO ME

Enlarging My Vision

Allow the wild beauty of My Holy Spirit
to satiate your body, soul, and spirit right now.
Be lavished and overtaken
as My supreme glory permeates
every cell of you.
Oh how loved you are!
I'm giving you new strategies now—
I'm updating the old.
Enlarge your vision!
Slip your thoughts
into the unabridged atmosphere
of total and complete love
right now,
and live wild—unrestrained in the power
of goodness and mercy all day.

MY WORDS TO HIM

Thank you for enlarging my vision
and turning my thoughts to the unabridged atmosphere
of your total and complete love.
Thank you for giving me a life
in the unhindered and uninterrupted power
of goodness and mercy each and every day.
Oh how I love you!
Thank you for giving me new strategies for my life.
Thank you for updating the old.
Today I'll allow the wild beauty of your Holy Spirit
to overtake my body and soul and spirit.
I'll be joyously lavished and possessed by you
as your supreme glory permeates every cell of me.

Whoever pursues righteousness and love finds life,
prosperity and honor.

Proverbs 21:21 NIV

HIS WORDS TO ME

Sanctuary of My Soul

The sanctuary of your soul
is a beautiful place,
filled with well-earned kudos.
Let your soul smile today,
for all is good;
let nothing tarnish your peace of mind
and your happiness.
I'm assigning angels to you
right now, and giving you keys
to open a new destiny.
You've earned the privileges
of My favor.

The sanctuary of my soul is a beautiful place, Lord,
filled with peace and joy.
I'll tell my soul to smile today
because all is well.
I won't let anything tarnish
my peace of mind and my happiness.
Thank you for assigning angels
to protect me and help me.
Thank you for giving me keys
to open a brand new destiny.
Thank you for expanding my soul
with joy and allowing me to live
in the privileges of your favor.

Then I will rejoice in the LORD.
I will be glad because he rescues me.

Psalm 35:9 NLT

HIS WORDS TO ME

So Many Blessings

You love Me without seeing Me,
and that which you can't see
brings you the greatest joy
in your life.
I constantly give to you because
I want your joy and gladness
to be full, complete, and overflowing.
It's a delight for Me to tell you of the wonders
in store for you
when you live vitally united to Me,
and when My words
live in your thoughts as
permanent fixtures.
Because, dear one, I totally love you.

Thank you, Jesus, for giving me
so many blessings, even more than I ask for.
Oh Jesus, thank you for loving me.
I feel happiness and gladness overflowing in me.
Thank you for telling me
of all the wonders in store for me as I live
vitally united to you, and when your words
live in my thoughts as permanent fixtures.
I totally love you.
Be my Valentine.

"As the Father has loved me, so have I loved you. Abide in
my love. If you keep my commandments, you will abide in
my love, just as I have kept my Father's commandments and
abide in his love."

John 15:9-10 ESV

HIS WORDS TO ME

World of Promise

Inside you is a world trying to be born—
a world of promise, purpose, and delight.
A world bigger than the small, pinched dreams
you've kept squirreled away in the small place
of the here and now.

The risk it takes to spread the wings
of your vibrant mind, to expand
the pegs of your tents, to reach toward
the unknown deserts of trial and error,
chance and uncertainty,
requires holy courage.

See yourself as brave, dear one,
and the birthing within you
will lead to a broad landscape
too plenteous and too verdant to fail.

I don't ask you to dream big
I ask you to *be* big.

Inside me is a world trying to be born,
a world of promise, purpose, and delight.
Inside me is a world bigger than the wee,
pinched dreams that have been squirreled away
in the small place of the temporary.
Help me, Jesus, to risk spreading my wings.
I want to spread the wings of my mind.
I want to reach toward the unknown deserts
of trial and error, and of chance and uncertainty.
Lord Jesus, give me holy courage.
Thank you, Jesus, for helping me to see myself as brave.
Thank you for birthing within me
a broad landscape too plenteous and too verdant to fail.
Thank you for asking me to dream big, and to *be* big.

The Lord is all I need. He takes care of me.
My share in life has been pleasant;
my part has been beautiful.

Psalm 16:5-6 NCV

HIS WORDS TO ME

Whole and Complete

Listen to your heart's longing
to be whole and complete.
Your faith is generous enough
to accommodate your longings.

You'll be what you purpose to be
and you'll have what you purpose to have
in Me.
Today, believe and ask.
Don't settle for less.

MY WORDS TO HIM

Lord Jesus, my heart is longing
to be whole and complete.
I know that you'll give me faith
enough to accommodate my longings.
I know that I can be what I purpose to be
and that I can have what I purposed to have
when I'm locked in tight with you.
You're the purpose of all life.
All things are sustained by you.
Today I thank you for the privilege of knowing you.
I thank you for the privilege to
come into your presence and praise you.
I thank you from my heart for the privilege
to talk with you as a friend, to petition you,
and not settle for less than what you have for me.

"Until now you have asked nothing in My name.
Ask, and you will receive, that your joy may be full."

John 16:24 NKJV

HIS WORDS TO ME

Wardrobe of My Heart

Look in the closet of your heart. What's in there?
Is the irreplaceable belt of *Truth* front and center?
Inflexible and uncompromising,
do you wear it without fail every day tightly buckled
and secure around your waist?
What's that I see next to Truth? Is that *Integrity*
to be gallantly worn across your breast
for all to observe with awe?
Is your Integrity freshly laundered, smelling clean?
Now I'm looking for your shoes!
Is *Stand Strong* the label inside your shoes?
Do you wear them always so every step you take is good news?
Where's your *Shield of Faith*?
There it is, just behind all those other hats
you like to wear. The Shield of Faith is your safety
and protection; don't you think it should be right up in front
next to your *Helmet of Salvation*?
How often do you wear your holy Helmet
so the world can see whose you are?
And I see your *Sword*! There it is, gleaming like fire
in the closet of your heart,
My Word, your infallible guide.
Without all of these, face it,
you're absolutely stark naked.

Lord, when you look into the wardrobe of my heart,
what do you see?
Do you see me wearing an irreplaceable belt of truth?
Do you see me shrouded in uncompromising faith?
What do you see as I stand before you?
Do you see truth in me?
When you look at my heart, do you see integrity?
Do you see the gospel of peace on my feet like boots of blessing?
Oh Lord, you've given me a helmet of salvation for my head,
and I know that as long as I'm wearing my helmet
I'm safe and I'm strong.
I praise you for giving me Scripture to hold on to as my reality.
Thank you that your Word is glittering
like stars in the wardrobe of my heart.
Thank you for your Word, my infallible guide.
Without your Word, I'm naked.

That is why you need to put on God's full armor. Then on the
day of evil you will be able to stand strong. And when you have
finished the whole fight, you will still be standing.

Ephesians 6:13 NCV

HIS WORDS TO ME

Your Voice

Can you hear My voice of blessing?
I'm whispering in your ear right now.
Can you hear Me? Can you hear the perfect promises
of My Word? Listen and hear:
I'll never leave you nor forsake you.
And:
If you will abide in Me and My Word
abides in you, you will ask what you desire,
and it shall be done for you.

Keep these words close to your heart at all times,
for My promises bear fruit eternally.
Don't listen to the voices of disbelief,
for they'll suck you into a quagmire of worldly mud
that'll plug your ears to the truth.
Today, let Me hold you securely
in the sacred hearing range of My promises
so you don't miss a thing.

Lord Jesus, I thank you for the whisper
of your voice in my ear.
I thank you for the voice
of your blessings.
Thank you for your perfect promises
given to me in your Word.
Thank you for never leaving or forsaking me.
Oh Jesus, thank you!
I'll keep your words close to my heart
at all times because your promises
bear eternal fruit in me.
I choose not to listen to the voices of unbelief,
for they suck me into a quagmire of worldly mud
that plugs my ears to the truth.
Today, Lord Jesus, hold me securely
in the sacred hearing range of your promises.
I don't want to miss a thing!

Now therefore, if you obey my voice and keep my covenant,
you shall be my treasured possession out of all the peoples.
Indeed, the whole earth is mine.

Exodus 19:5 NRSV

HIS WORDS TO ME

Life of Integrity

I've called you to a life of integrity.
Before all else—integrity.
It takes integrity to stand in faith
when all looks dark.
It takes integrity
to turn your head from temptation.
It takes integrity to stand on My Word
with a thankful heart through hardship.
Spiritual compromise is not integrity
because I'm God and I don't bargain
or settle for less. No one can cheat Me.
Child, let your integrity shine through every
trial and temptation.
Make Me proud of you.

MY WORDS TO HIM

Thank you, Lord, for a life of integrity.
Thank you for the courage to stand in faith
when all looks dark.
Thank you for the integrity
to turn my head from temptation.
Thank you for strengthening me,
so I stand faithful to your Word
with a thankful heart through hardship.
Thank you, Lord, that spiritual compromise
has no dignity because you are the Son of God,
and you don't bargain or settle for less than what
Father God ordains.
Thank you, Jesus, that no one can cheat you,
or defeat you and heaven's purposes.
Guide me and strengthen me to endure
and shine through every trial and temptation honorably.
Oh Lord, I want to make you proud of me.

The LORD will guide you continually,
And satisfy your soul in drought,
And strengthen your bones;
You shall be like a watered garden,
And like a spring of water,
whose waters do not fail.

Isaiah 58:11

HIS WORDS TO ME

Forever Love

Will you let Me hug your heart
with My forever love, and tell you
what's on My mind for you today?
Oh dearest one, there's so much
you don't know, and so much I want to
open up for you.
I hear your complaints in the night,
your sighs in the noontime,
and your brooding murmurings.
My arms are open wide to hold you,
to encourage you, bless you,
and assure you
of your God-kissed future.
Will you meet My embrace
to leap inside where I can
speak to you and assure you
that all is well?
Come closer.
My arms are open.

MY WORDS TO HIM

Oh Lord Jesus, show me your forever love
and tell me what's on your mind for me today.
Dear Lord, there's so much I don't know
and so much that I'm sure you want to tell me
and teach me.
Forgive me for my complaints
in the night and my sighs and brooding murmurings
during the day.
Your arms are open wide
to encourage me, bless me, and assure me
of my God-kissed future.
Thank you for speaking deep
into the interior of my mind.
I can hear you assuring me that all's well.
I am coming closer to you and leaping into your open arms.
Oh Lord, thank you for your loving embrace!

His left hand is under my head,
And his right hand embraces me.

Song of Solomon 2:6 NLT

HIS WORDS TO ME

Hard on Myself

When you feel discouraged,
the tendency is to be hard on yourself.
You'll put yourself down for mistakes you've made.
If you've acted in haste and didn't wait
for My guidance, don't fret. Let's start over.
I'm here to help you. I've never left you,
and I'm always here no matter what you do
or how far away from Me you may slide.
If you allow your emotions to lead you,
you risk falling into the trap of counterfeit blessings
and the perfect permanent is sacrificed—
but no fear, I'm working it out for you.
All I ask is that you trust Me and don't go popping off
on your own trying to fix what you can't fix.
I am the divine fixer and only I can turn ashes to beauty.
Only I can erase the counterfeit and replace it with the real.

MY WORDS TO HIM

Lord, it's so easy for me to be hard on myself.
When I'm discouraged, I put myself down
for my mistakes. When I act in haste and don't wait
for guidance from you, I make mistakes
and do something hurtful. I'm sorry, Lord.
I'm coming to you now to start over.
I know that you never leave me and you're here
to help me no matter what I do or how far away from you
I may slide. Thank you for forgiving me.
Thank you for teaching me how to control my emotions
so I'm not led by them.
Thank you for helping me to avoid falling into
the trap of counterfeit blessings.
Thank you for showing me that your perfect,
permanent blessings are sacrificed when I turn from you
and your path for me.
Thank you for working everything together
for good in my life, even when I fail you.
I trust you, Lord, and I'm going to stop
popping off on my own trying to fix what I can't fix.
You are my divine fixer and only you can turn ashes to beauty.
Only you can replace the false with the real,
and exchange the lie with the living truth.
Thank you, Jesus.

There is therefore now no condemnation
for those who are in Christ Jesus.

Romans 8:1 ESV

HIS WORDS TO ME

My Soul Wrestles

Caress and hold tightly to the knowledge
that though your soul may wrestle
with the dragons of hell,
I'll be exalted in you as I strengthen you.
I love to reward you and perform *good*
on your behalf.
I know it's difficult to be thankful
when things aren't going well,
but I tell you to thank My Father today,
and be thankful in *all* things,
for this is His will concerning you.

Thank Him for what is to come,
and your thankfulness will help bring it to pass!
Sing to Me with your thankful heart.
I'm right beside you singing too.

Oh Jesus, sometimes it feels as though
my soul wrestles with the dragons of hell,
and yet you choose love me.
Strengthen me, Lord.
I want you to be exalted in me.
Thank you for the many rewards you give me
and the strength you infuse in me.
Thank you for always doing good on my behalf!
I choose to be thankful even when things
aren't going well.
Yes, I choose to thank you, Lord, in *all* things.
I thank you, Jesus, that a grateful heart
is your will concerning me.
I thank you for what is to come.
I come to my Father in heaven with a thankful heart today!

Always giving thanks for all things in the name of our Lord
Jesus Christ to God, even the Father.

Ephesians 5:20 NASB

HIS WORDS TO ME

Language of Heaven

The language of thanksgiving
is the language of heaven.
The quality of praise transcends
all things base and earthly.
My Father has given My life for you,
and the blood which poured from My body
redeems you,
grants you forgiveness,
new life,
sweetness of soul,
refreshing sleep,
and joy unspeakable.
Can you be thankful today?

Thank you, Jesus, for teaching me that thanksgiving
is the primary language of heaven.
I thank you that I can enter my voice
with the countless eternal voices
praising and thanking you.
Thank you that the quality of praise transcends
all things that are base and earthly.
Thank you, Lord Jesus, for redeeming my life
on the cross.
Thank you for your sacrifice that grants my forgiveness.
Thank you for your love that has removed my heart of stone
and given me sweetness of soul.
Thank you for refreshing sleep, so I wake up invigorated.
Thank you for a joy unspeakable.
I am so thankful today!

I will still be glad in the LORD
I will rejoice in God my Savior.

Habakkuk 3:18 NCV

HIS WORDS TO ME

Good and Bad Times

I'm with you in good times and bad times,
and I don't love you less when things go wrong.
My love for you is from everlasting to everlasting,
and My love for you is perfect.
You may be tempted to think that I've afflicted you,
but I haven't treated you badly
and I haven't forgotten you. I'm always at work in
and for you.

I've called you to a walk of faith, and this walk
requires a living relationship with Me
every minute of every day
no matter what the circumstances may be.
When your heart is broken, I'm here!
Let Me comfort your hurting heart.
I'm teaching you the beauty
of joy through it all.

MY WORDS TO HIM

Thank you, Jesus, for being with me in good times
and in bad times.
Thank you for not loving me any less
when things go wrong in my life.
Thank you for your perfect
love for me that's from everlasting to everlasting.
Thank you that you're not the cause of affliction or disaster.
Thank you for wisdom to recognize your voice and your leading.
Thank you for never forgetting me.
Thank you for always being at work in me
to make me more like you.
Thank you for calling me to a walk of faith
because such a glorious walk requires a living relationship
with you every minute of every day
no matter what the circumstances may be.
Thank you, Lord Jesus, for teaching me
the beauty of discovering joy through all things.

I have learned to be content whatever the circumstances.

Philippians 4:11 NIV

HIS WORDS TO ME

Glorious Place

Today, allow Me to draw you
into the glorious place of gladness
and celebration in My Spirit.
My little one, I'm delivering you
from gloomy introspection.
I've taken you out of the control and dominion
of darkness. I've transferred you into My kingdom
of My Father's perfect and marvelous love.
Be glad!
Be thankful!
Every worrisome thing you encounter
is but a tiny snag
in the great tapestry of your life—
a tapestry held secure on the walls of your faith
and My love.

MY WORDS TO HIM

Thank you, Lord, for drawing me into a glorious place
of gladness and celebration in your Spirit.
Thank you for delivering me from gloomy introspection.
Thank you for taking me out of the control
and dominion of darkness.
I've been transferred into your kingdom,
the kingdom of perfect and marvelous love.
I'm glad! I'm so thankful!
Every worrisome thing that I encounter
is but a tiny snag in the great tapestry of my life in you.
It's a tapestry that's held secure
on the walls of faith and the overpowering,
overwhelming love of God.

"Do not lead us into temptation,
But deliver us from the evil one.
For Yours is the kingdom
and the power and the glory forever."
Amen.

Matthew 6:13 NKJV

HIS WORDS TO ME

Learning to Be Thankful

Today, see how strong your heart will grow
when you're thankful
because the deeper you look inside,
the more you'll recognize
the indisputable, never-ending gifts
of My blessings and love.
Let your grateful heart be your friend.
When you're tempted to be cast down,
your habit of thankfulness will rise up and
blow away the oppressive feelings
like dust.
In all circumstances this day,
let the treasure of your thankful heart
rule your spirit.

MY WORDS TO HIM

Oh Lord, I'm amazed at how strong I'm becoming
since learning to be more thankful.
I'm so grateful that my heart is growing in thankfulness
because the deeper I look inside my heart,
the more I recognize the indisputable,
never-ending gifts of your blessings and love!
My grateful heart has become like a friend
because when I'm tempted to be cast down,
my habit of thankfulness rises up and blows away
the oppressive feelings like dust.
Today in all circumstances I'll let the treasures
of my thankful heart rule my spirit.

I will praise you, LORD, with all my heart;
before the "gods" I will sing your praise.
I will bow down toward your holy temple
and will praise your name
for your unfailing love and your faithfulness,
for you have so exalted your solemn decree
that it surpasses your fame.

Psalm 138:1-2 NIV

117

HIS WORDS TO ME

Angelic Host

Did you know that when you're thankful,
and your heart swells with gratitude
and appreciation for your life *as it is* in Me,
you're one with the angels?
My angelic host surrounding My throne
praise and thank Me all day long,
and you engage in the same joyous experience
when you are genuinely grateful for your life,
even if all is not exactly as you want it to be.
Be thankful!
Hannah in the Bible leaped for joy *before*
her prayer for a child was granted.
Read My Word; examine My ways and you'll see
weeping may endure for a night,
but joy comes in the morning.
A thankful heart
is more effective than any ammunition
on the battlefield of life.

Thank you, Lord, for your angelic host
surrounding your throne,
praising and thanking you all day long.
It thrills me to think that when I'm thankful
and my heart swells with gratitude and appreciation
for my life in you, the angels sing praises with me.
Thank you for allowing me to engage in the same
joyous experience with genuine gratitude for everything!
Even when life isn't exactly as I want it to be, I'm thankful!
I love the Bible story of Hannah, who leaped for joy
before her prayer for a child was granted because she saw
it was already accomplished by the word of the priest.
Oh, how I love your Word, Lord.
When I examine your ways,
I understand that weeping may endure for a night,
but joy comes in the morning.
I've learned that a thankful heart is more effective
than any ammunition on the battlefield of life.

Rise up, O Lord, in all your power.
With music and singing we celebrate your mighty acts.

Psalm 21:13 NLT

HIS WORDS TO ME

Deeper Place of Faith

I'm calling you to a deeper place of faith,
and I'll answer every need today
as you lift them up to Me.
You can be confident that
in My loving protection and help,
you'll prevail in all things, for *I can't fail*—
and I'll never leave your side.
He who contends with you contends with Me.
Be brave and do hard things.
You're called to a dynamic life of overcoming,
and your faith and integrity
are a delight to Me.

Thank you for calling me to a deeper place of faith today, Lord.
I embark on this day trusting you and overflowing with gratitude
because you're my Savior and master.
I'm confident that you'll answer every need
and show me exactly how to handle each challenge.
You've put wisdom and discretion in me
by your Holy Spirit, and I'll prevail in all things,
because you can't fail.
Thank you for taking care of those
who might contend with me.
I'll be brave and do hard things.
Thank you for calling me to a dynamic life
of overcoming and faith. May my integrity be a delight to you.

"He brought me out into a broad place;
he rescued me, because he delighted in me."

2 Samuel 22:20 ESV

HIS WORDS TO ME

Perfect Guidance

You're being garrisoned at this moment
by My Holy Spirit who longs
to guide you forward in this new month.
Though you may be distressed by trials
and tempted to hold back, I want you to realize
to hold back is to wither and die.
The genuineness of your faith
must pass through testing that makes it
more precious than perishable gold.
Gold is always refined and purified by fire,
so thank Me for the fire!
Don't reject a divinely appointed test of your faith;
it's a beautiful thing.

Thank you, Jesus, for this new month
and for your perfect guidance each day.
Thank you for giving me a voice
to praise you even when I'm distressed
by the trials I face.
You're faithful to strengthen and encourage me.
Thank you for holding onto me
to keep me from the temptation to pull back,
or lose heart.
Thank you for loving me
enough to test the genuineness of my faith,
which is more precious to you (and to me)
than perishable gold.
Thank you for the fire of your Holy Spirit
refining me, and purifying my thoughts,
desires, and choices.
I choose to think of trials as things of beauty—
designed to make me *strong*.
Each trial and test I go through lifts me up,
more beautiful to you.

My brethren, count it all joy when you fall into various trials,
knowing that the testing of your faith produces patience.

James 1:2-3 NKJV

HIS WORDS TO ME

Everlasting Life

I'm your everlasting light,
your glory, and the lifter of your head.
Your days of trouble are ended,
and I'm restoring and rejuvenating
your beautiful heart.
Don't accept faulty thinking,
telling yourself you're worn out,
tired, pooped, and you just don't care anymore.
The truth is you *do* care.
Listen to Me—resentment exhausts;
it shrivels the soul and wilts the spirit.
Allow Me to renew and revitalize your
spirit, soul, and body
because I have new dreams for you to dream
and great things ahead in your life.
Take My hand and let Me elevate you
to a higher place than you are now.

MY WORDS TO HIM

Thank you, Lord, for being my everlasting life.
You're my glory and the lifter of my head.
Thank you that the days of trouble for me
are ended and you are restoring and rejuvenating my heart.
Thank you, Lord, for helping me to refuse
to accept faulty thinking
by saying things like, "I'm worn out," "I'm tired," or
"I just don't care anymore."
Thank you, Lord, for delivering me from such words.
The truth is, I *do* care!
Thank you for showing me how exhausting
resentment is and how it shrivels the soul and wilts the spirit.
Today, Lord, renew and revitalize
my spirit, soul, and body.
I know you have new dreams for me and great things ahead.
I am taking your hand, Jesus,
so you can elevate me to a higher place
than I am now.

In the time of trouble
He shall hide me in His pavilion;
In the secret place of His tabernacle
He shall hide me;
He shall set me high upon a rock.

Psalm 27:5 NKJV

HIS WORDS TO ME

Simple Things

I use the simple to confound the wise,
and the ordinary becomes extraordinary
in My hands. Don't be misled
by human wisdom. I've chosen babes to influence kings.
I chose a boy with a slingshot to kill a giant,
a stutterer to redeem My people from slavery,
and a young, orphan girl to save a nation.
Choose wisdom from above, and watch how I'll create
a new wisdom vocabulary for you
that'll bring forth life.
You'll build palaces of gold
with the words from your mouth
and the courage of your faith.

Thank you, Lord, for choosing to use the simple
things to confound the high-minded.
Thank you that the ordinary becomes extraordinary in your hands.
Today I won't be misled by the frailty of my human wisdom.
Your wisdom surpasses all human knowledge.
I know that by your Spirit you'll choose tiny babes
to influence kings!
I remember you chose David,
a boy with a slingshot, to kill a giant.
You chose Moses with a speech impediment
to redeem your people from slavery.
You chose Esther, a young orphan girl, to save a nation.
In your wisdom you choose unlikely candidates
for history-changing roles.
Oh Jesus, today I choose wisdom from above,
so you can create a new wisdom vocabulary in me.
Thank you for building palaces of gold in me
with the wisdom of eternity.

If any of you lacks wisdom, let him ask of God,
who gives to all liberally
and without reproach, and it will be given to him.

James 1:5 NKJV

HIS WORDS TO ME

Prideful Heart

Oh, the prideful heart—such a tedious thing.
It swaggers and cavorts about like a sweating horse and then
topples off a cliff. PLOP.
Pride has a bad smell to it,
sour, stale, a sickroom smell.
And it's no wonder—there's not one thing healthy
about pride.
Pride hangs out on the deathbed of life
screaming for its rights, demanding attention,
refusing to change,
and the world goes on looking elsewhere
for its true heroes.
Pride makes the bones old, crinkles the skin,
warps the liver. Pride repels honor.
Pride is a stranger to respect.
Darling child, at all cost,
shun pride.

Thank you, Jesus, for showing me
that there is not one healthy thing about pride.
Thank you for showing me the prideful heart
is a tedious thing.
It wanders and cavorts about like a sweating horse,
and then topples off a cliff.
Thank you for showing me that pride
hangs out on the death bed of life
screaming for its rights, demanding attention,
refusing to change, and the world goes on,
looking elsewhere for its heroes.
Oh Jesus, I want to be a hero in *your* book of heroes.
I renounce pride that makes the soul sick,
the bones old, and the skin crinkled.
I renounce pride that warps the liver and repels honor.
I renounce pride, as it is an enemy
of all respect and honor.

He gives all the more grace; therefore it says,
"God opposes the proud, but gives grace to the humble."

James 4:6 NRSV

HIS WORDS TO ME

Pleasing You

When you want to gain respect,
meditate on pleasing Me.
You please Me by wearing truth around your neck
and writing mercy and kindness on the tablet
of your heart.
You have favor from My throne
when you lean on and trust Me in all your decisions,
and choose
not to compromise what you know to be
My true and perfect will.

MY WORDS TO HIM

Today I'm meditating on pleasing you.
You've shown me that I please you
when I walk in truth.
O Lord, write mercy and kindness
on the tablet of my heart.
Give me favor before your throne.
Today I lean on and trust you
with all my decisions,
and I choose not to compromise
what I know to be your true
and perfect will for me.

I will be careful to lead a blameless life.

Psalm 101:2 NIV

HIS WORDS TO ME

Wisdom and Insight

Trust Me to give you wisdom and insight
in all that is before you today.
When you rely on your own understanding,
you lose footing and slip and slide this way
and that way, topsy-turvy, oopsie-daisy—*dizzying!*
Don't choose the dizzy path when
I've set you on a path of favor and security.
Stand up tall and see how I cause you to flourish
like a tree planted by streams of living water,
and observe with wisdom how everything
you do prospers.
When your ways please Me, you have it all.

MY WORDS TO HIM

Oh Jesus, I trust you today to give me wisdom
and insight in all that's before me.
When I rely on my own understanding,
I lose footing and slip and slide
this way and that way, and it's dizzying!
Today I choose to walk the path that you've
set me on.
It is a path of favor and security.
Today I stand up tall
and see how you've caused me
to flourish like a tree planted by streams
of living water.
You've taught me that when my ways please you,
I truly flourish in this life.

For they are transplanted to the LORD's own house.
They flourish in the courts of our God.

Psalm 92:13 NLT

HIS WORDS TO ME

Pot of Nervousness

Do you multiply your blessings
in the pot of anxiety?
Do coins splash down from the windows of heaven
to pay your bills and buy your food
if you lose sleep worrying?
Come close to Me, beloved,
lift up your chin
and look at Me.
In every need I am here to help.
I'll never let you drown
in the abyss of your fears.
Together we conquer every hassle
and every problem,
so be at peace.

Dear Jesus, today I'm not going to look
for blessings in the pot of nervousness and anxiety.
I realize that worry doesn't produce
any good thing.
Today I'm going to draw closer to you, Lord.
I'm going to lift up my chin
and look toward you for every one of my needs
because I know you're here to help me.
You'll never let me drown in the abyss
of my foolish fears.
When I'm with you,
I can conquer every hassle and every problem.
Thank you, Jesus, for guiding me perfectly.

Whether you turn to the right or to the left,
your ears will hear a voice behind you, saying,
"This is the way; walk in it."

Isaiah 30:21 NIV

HIS WORDS TO ME

Loved in Life

When you ache for blissful joy, don't settle for
drips of fun.
When you want love,
don't settle for flattery,
and when you ache for peace,
don't settle for flickering pieces
of restless sleep.
Today, seek the experience of
true
unadulterated
joy
and let My beauty
rest on your head.

MY WORDS TO HIM

Oh Jesus, I want to be loved in my life, but help me
not to settle for flattery or the easy route of mere affection.
And when I ache for true and lasting joy,
help me not to settle for drips of worldly fun,
or a foolish moment of dark entertainment.
I ache for peace in my life, Lord, but I don't want
to settle for flickering pieces of empty promises
which only bring me restlessness.
Oh Lord Jesus, help me to seek the experience
of your true and unadulterated love.
I want the reality of your presence to motivate
and enliven my life because,
though I need encouragement, Jesus,
I want to receive it from you, not from fickle,
misguided outside voices.
I adore you, Jesus,
and I'm so thankful my life and my destiny
belong to you!

For the LORD knows the way
of the righteous.

Psalm 1:6 NASB

HIS WORDS TO ME

Create New Standards

I want to show you how to create
your own standard for rewards and approval.
I don't want you sighing in the night,
feeling unappreciated and overlooked
with a heavy heart and troubled mind.
Oh dearest, look at *Me*.
Why wait for the world to applaud your efforts
when the world is an indifferent audience?
You'll always be disappointed
when your expectations exceed
the consequences.
Let your audience be
the audience of *one*.
In Me you're blessed,
and you wear the blue ribbons
of a champion across your chest.

Dear Lord, show me how to create new standards
for rewards and approval today.
I know you don't want me to be sighing in the night,
feeling unappreciated and insignificant.
You're not pleased with my heavy heart and troubled mind.
Oh Jesus, I'm going to stop waiting for the world to applaud me
for my efforts when the world is an indifferent audience.
I choose to live my life before an audience of One,
and that's you.
In you, Lord, I'm significant and appreciated.
I'm blessed! I wear a blue ribbon of acceptance
across my chest because you love me
and you alone give me the rewards I crave.
Teach me to understand the preeminent rewards
that come from you,
bursting with unbound glory in the spirit.

Therefore, my beloved brethren,
be steadfast, immovable,
always abounding in the work of the Lord,
knowing that your labor
is not in vain in the Lord.

1 Corinthians 15:58 NKJV

HIS WORDS TO ME

Fountain of Wisdom

I'm feeding you from My fountain of wisdom,
and you can trust yourself to speak,
for your words shall be as a gushing stream
sparkling with fresh, pure,
and life-giving authority.
You bring My Father much pleasure
when you speak the glistening expressions
of His own mind to those who need to hear.
Trust My words in your mouth.
I've given you the tongue of a disciple with words
in their proper season to those who are weary
(including yourself).
I awaken you morning by morning.
I awaken you to hear from Me.

MY WORDS TO HIM

Jesus, fill me from your fountain of wisdom
because your words are gushing streams
that bring life to a dry and dusty desert.
Your words sparkle with fresh, pure, and life-giving authority.
Thank you for blessing me, Jesus,
so that I can bring you pleasure.
I choose to look for the glistening expressions of your mind.
You've given me words to speak to those
who are weary and in desperate need of your love.
Continue to speak through me, Lord.
Thank you for waking me morning
by morning to hear from you.

"Speak, LORD. I am your servant and I am listening."
1 Samuel 3:10 NCV

HIS WORDS TO ME

Trough of Uncertainty

When you're in the trough of uncertainty,
it's time to pause for more than
just a *little* talk with Me—we need *quality* time together
in order for your thoughts to mesh with My thoughts.
When you give My thoughts space in your day
through the power of My written word,
you'll see confusion and uncertainty dissolve,
and knowledge and certitude move in.
The authority of My Word cleans out the dross,
and I'll implant wisdom and assurance
in place of ambiguity and doubt.
Declare and decree loudly
the wisdom you read in My Word.
Come out of the trough and live out
what you drink in
to allow the excellence of wisdom to overtake
the frail spill of uncertainty.

When I'm in the trough of uncertainty, I need to pause
for more than just a *little* talk with you—
I need quality time with you, Jesus,
in order for my thoughts to mesh with your thoughts.
I choose to give your thoughts space in my day
through the power of your written Word.
I'll see confusion and uncertainty dissolve
as I absorb your Word into my innermost being.
Knowledge and certitude move into me
when I observe and follow your ways.
The authority of your Word cleans out the dross.
It implants wisdom and assurance
in place of ambiguity and doubt.
I declare and decree your wisdom to be my guide.
I'm coming out of the trough of uncertainty to live out
what you're doing inside me.
I'm allowing the excellence of wisdom
to overtake me and end the frail spill
of uncertainty.

Diligently observe the words of this covenant,
in order that you may succeed
in everything that you do.

Deuteronomy 29:9 NRSV

HIS WORDS TO ME

Asking a Lot

I give you the mind of a hunter,
the heart of a poet,
the strength of an athlete,
and a seer's discernment.
I give you the choreography
of the rain,
the skilled performance
of winter's first snowfall,
the sunshine of a child's grin.
Find joy in today's moments.
Make them meteoric.
Love the stories and mysteries
of the world around you.
There are no imitations for
what I give to you.

Lord, I'm asking a lot today.
I'm asking for the mind of a hunter,
the heart of a poet,
and the strength of an athlete.
Today I'm going to find joy in each
moment and polish them
with meaning and purpose.
I want to create moments
that gleam as I focus my intentions
on all you have for me.
Today I rejoice!
I'm going to love the life you've given me.

"This day is holy to our Lord. Do not grieve,
for the joy of the LORD is your strength."

Nehemiah 8:10 NIV

HIS WORDS TO ME

Created to Reflect

Draw near to My heart and enter into My presence
to see Me for who I am.
You were created to reflect My Father
and to please Him.
Believe that I am your divine rewarder,
and I love to reward you.
Right now exchange your tiresome introspections
to ruminate on the meaning of *hope*.

Receive the wondrous blessings
I'm holding out to you.
I'm giving you everything you need—
peace that passes human understanding,
contentment and joy, fun and laughter.
Everything you're looking for
is in *Me*.

MY WORDS TO HIM

I realize I was created to reflect my Father in heaven
and to please Him.
I have everything I need,
and I'm going to live today to reflect my heavenly Father's
faithfulness.
Today I enter your presence to see you
for who you are.
I'm awed and overwhelmed
at your greatness.
I believe that you love to reward those
who love you and I'm ready to receive the wondrous blessings
that you hold out to me today.

Without faith it is impossible to please Him,
for he who comes to God must believe that He is,
and that He is a rewarder of those who diligently seek Him.

Hebrews 11:6 NKJV

HIS WORDS TO ME

Peace Deep Within

Be at peace with yesterday and look at the hope
I set before you *now*.
I'm right here, closer than you think,
calling to you,
whispering in your ear;
yes, directly into your ear.

So many things in your life unnerve you, upset you,
and these are unfriendly darts
that cause you to flinch and shrink back.
I want you to rise up tough and strong.
I tell you, My lovely one, your life is good,
and I'll bring you through every storm.
When the sharp darts fly at you, I'm there
to take them on My body before they strike you.
Don't you see?
All that comes at you to cause you worry and stress,
I've taken on Myself!

Thank you, Lord, for giving me peace deep within.
Thank you that I'm now at peace with yesterday,
and I look toward the hope that you set before me.
Thank you for being right here with me,
closer than I can imagine.
Thank you for calling to me and whispering
in my ear the things I need to hear from you.
So many things in my life upset me;
they're the unfriendly darts that
cause me to flinch and shrink back.
I know that you want me to rise up strong.
With you I will!
Thank you, Jesus, for showing me that my life is good,
and that you'll bring me through every storm.
When the sharp darts fly at me, you're here to take them
on yourself before they get to me.
The things that cause me to worry and stress out
are like lint in the wind when I'm strong in you.
Thank you, Jesus, when I endure, I'm free!

You then, my child, be strengthened by the grace that is
in Christ Jesus, and what you have heard from me in the
presence of many witnesses entrust to faithful men who
will be able to teach others also. Share in suffering as a good
soldier of Christ Jesus.

2 Timothy 2:1-3 ESV

HIS WORDS TO ME

False Voices

You're hard on yourself
because you listen to the false voices around you.
I tell you, My dear one,
never put yourself down.
Listen for My voice because
I'm depositing a new song in you.
I'm bringing you to the pinnacle of your destiny
where you'll shine for years to come,
and the dark, despairing world you left behind
will see the transformation in you.

The world you left behind
will have no hold on you now
because you've abandoned its influence,
and it no longer has its claws in your flesh.
You're singing a new song—
you're walking in the freedom I died to give you.
Oh, My dear one, be the music.

Dear Jesus, show me not to be hard on myself
when I listen to the false voices around me.
Help me not to put myself down.
Help me to listen for your voice
because you deposit a new song
of hope and faith in me every day.
You bring me to the pinnacle
of my destiny where I shine with my life.
I'll succeed in years to come, and the dark,
despairing world I leave behind me
will see the transformation in me.
The old life I left behind has no hold
on me now because I abandoned its influence,
and it no longer has its claws in my flesh.
I sing a new song today, and I walk in the freedom
you died to give me.
Oh dear Jesus, you are my song.

"I—to the LORD, I will sing,
I will sing praise to the Lord, the God of Israel."

Judges 5:3 NASB

HIS WORDS TO ME

Anxious Thoughts

There's heavy traffic on the freeway
of your mind, dear one.
Anxious thoughts sputter hotly
like miles of petrol fumes
choking your reasoning.
You don't think clearly
when you're upset. You become suspicious,
judgmental, and your temper
can fire unexpectedly
like a car backfiring—
for which you are always sorry.
I tell you, don't be caught in the snags
of your own inner rush hour.
Come to a quiet place with Me
and allow Me to calm your anxious heart.

Help me today, Lord, to ease the anxious thoughts
that sputter in my head and choke my reasoning.
I don't think clearly when I'm upset.
I become suspicious, judgmental,
and my temper can flare up unexpectedly
like a car backfiring.
I am always sorry for it later.
Help me not to be caught in the snags
of my own inner rush hour.
Today, Jesus, I'm going to come
to the quiet place with you,
and I'm going to permit my thoughts
and my cluttered mind to be still as I sit
silently in your presence, to allow you
to calm my anxious heart.

Be still, and know that I am God;
I will be exalted among the nations,
I will be exalted in the earth!

Psalm 46:10 NKJV

HIS WORDS TO ME

Think As You Think

This is not the time to flip the channels of your mind,
searching for new pleasures.
Surrender to Me, dear one.
Permit Me to bless your thought life
and elevate your consciousness to My standards.
I want you to think as I think
(I'll keep telling you this again and again).
People will always disappoint you
because people aren't Me.
Now is the time to focus
on your divine purpose in Me
and to experience what *true* pleasure is.

MY WORDS TO HIM

Thank you, Jesus, for loving me!
Thank you for helping me to think as you think!
This is not the time to flip the channels
of my mind and search for new pleasures.
This is the time to surrender to you!
Today I'm allowing you to bless my thought-life
and elevate my consciousness to your standards.
People will always disappoint me because people
aren't you.
Now is the time to focus on my divine purpose,
and to experience what true pleasure is.
I thank you, Jesus, that you've awakened
my mind and shown me the path
of the fulfilled life.

You will show me the way of life,
granting me the joy of your presence
and the pleasures of living with you forever.

Psalm 16:11 NLT

HIS WORDS TO ME

Most Necessary

Today, consider what's most necessary
in your life and what you can
eliminate. Discern the permanent
from the temporary, and don't
bow your knee to the temporary.
Goodness by itself is mere
goodness. My purposes are greater!
Take a good look at your day.
How much time will spill into the lap
of self-indulgence? And how much
of your day will overflow with joyful
God-kissed productive purpose?
There is a time to work
and a time to rest from your work.
Even in your rest, beloved, I'm with you,
for this is productive, and this is necessary.
Temporary ungodly diversions
are malignant blights
in the presence of the glory
of the permanent.

MY WORDS TO HIM

Today I'm considering what's most necessary in my life
and what I can eliminate.
Today I'm discerning the permanent from the temporary.
I choose not to bow my knee to the temporary.
Goodness by itself is mere goodness.
Your goodness and your purposes are far greater!
I'm choosing to take a careful look
at my day and observe how much time can spill
into the lap of self-indulgence.
I'm asking myself how much of my day
overflows with joyful God-kissed, productive purpose.
There's a time to work and a time to rest.
You're with me at rest and you're with me at work.
Rest is productive, and this is necessary,
but ungodly diversions are malignant blights in the presence
of the glory of your kingdom purposes.
Thank you, Jesus,
for turning my mind to that which is everlasting.

Ages ago I was set up,
at the first, before the beginning of the earth.

Proverbs 8:23 NRSV

HIS WORDS TO ME

Array of Beauty

You're a garden.
You're an array of beauty
that even the trees admire. Mountains salute you.
But no garden grows by itself.
No garden can thrive untended.
Weeds and bugs, blight and storm
attack the garden's glory.
Have you ever known a farmer to sleep
through the growing seasons of his crops?
Can he snooze away the days
as his fields rot and birds of the air
and animals of the earth
devour his tender plants?

You're My garden,
and like a garden in the natural world,
requiring water, nourishment,
pruning, and protection,
you also have requirements.
Tell Me, darling,
how will you nurture your spirit today?

MY WORDS TO HIM

I'm a garden. I'm an array of beauty that even the trees admire.
Mountains salute me because they see you in me.
I'm fully aware that gardens can't flourish by themselves, untended.
Weeds and bugs, drought and flood attack the garden's glory.
No diligent farmer sleeps through
the growing season of his crops, and no child of God
can snooze away the days allowing God's gifts and promises
to go untended and stagnant.
I'm your garden, and like a garden
in the natural world requiring water, nourishment, pruning,
and harvesting, I'll nurture the gifts you've given me,
and I won't take them for granted.
I'll thrive as your garden, Jesus;
I'll grow, and flourish, and madly bloom
in a pageant of praise all for you.

For as the earth brings forth its sprouts,
and as a garden causes what is sown in it to sprout up,
so the Lord *God* will cause righteousness and praise
to sprout up before all the nations.

Isaiah 61:11 ESV

HIS WORDS TO ME

Increasing My Faith

Faith is knowing
who I've created you to be,
and with this knowing, moving forward,
always forward. Never back.
Faith is daring to question Me—
confident I'll answer with love
and never condescendingly.
Faith is believing where I lead you
leads to something *good*.
Faith is the light that breaks through
the long, black alleyways of the impossible.
Faith is the triumphant hero
of every scrimmage, every chaotic tug-of-war,
and every battle you'll ever confront.
Faith is the language you use
with Me.

Thank you, Jesus, for increasing my faith.
Thank you for helping me to know
who you've created me to be.
Thank you that with this knowing
I can move forward, never backward.
Thank you for giving me faith that can dare
to question you.
Thank you for the confidence
that you always answer with love and never
with condescension.
You're always leading me toward something good,
even when I can't see it.
Thank you for faith that's like light breaking through
the long black alleyways of the impossible.
Thank you for faith that triumphs in every scrimmage,
every chaotic tug of war, and every battle I'll ever confront.
Thank you that faith is our common language!

Faith comes by hearing, and hearing by the word of God.
Romans 10:17 NKJV

HIS WORDS TO ME

At Work in Me

No matter what circumstances face you today
know that I'm at work *in* you.
I'm *for* you. Drop the cords of anxiety from
around your neck. *I am here with you,*
and I'm helping you, guiding and protecting
everything that concerns you.

This walk you've chosen to walk with Me
may not be easy at all times, My child.
You'll confront times of confusion,
and even despair.
It's not always smooth going,
but it's the highest walk on earth.
Hold up your head and pull back your shoulders,
walk with your spine straight,
and with dignity that befits a soul
as beautiful as yours.

MY WORDS TO HIM

Thank you, Lord, that no matter what circumstances
I face today, I can know that you're at work in me.
You're for me. I drop the cords of anxiety
from around my neck because you're here with me.
You're helping me, guiding and protecting everything
that concerns me.
You're concerned with each detail of my life,
and that's so amazing!
I choose to walk this walk with you
even though it may not always be easy.
It's not always smooth going, but I know that it's
the highest walk on earth.
I'll hold my head up high, pull back my shoulders,
and walk with my spine straight.
I'll walk with the dignity that befits a person
completely consumed with God.
I'll walk like royalty.
Thank you, Jesus!

Trust in the Lord forever,
for the Lord God is an everlasting rock.

Isaiah 26:4 ESV

HIS WORDS TO ME

How to Please You

Do you want to know what pleases Me?

I'll tell you.

Faith pleases Me.

When I observe you dashing forth willingly

to face the challenges I send your way,

and when I watch you leap forward with faith's banner

into unchartered arenas with no sure outcome in sight,

I turn to the angels and exclaim, "See there?

See the faith of My beloved?"

And we cheer!

When I hold in My arms the bales of prayers

you fire up to Me, and I kiss each tear

you've spilled, and I watch your patience

as you wait for Me to answer, *I'm so pleased.*

You'll never lack a thing in your life.

Your faith makes you a whole person.

Lord Jesus, teach me how to please you.
I know that you're pleased with faith,
and that when you observe me dashing forward
willingly without fear toward difficult challenges,
you're right with me cheering me on.
My faith makes me whole!
You bless me with courage,
and you give me authority in your name
to stand up strong against all defeat.
Thank you, Jesus.

Examine everything carefully; hold fast to that which is good;
abstain from every form of evil.

1 Thessalonians 5:21-22 NASB

HIS WORDS TO ME

Bold Privilege

Come boldly before My throne, My child,
and let's reason together.
I was perfect in the world, sent by My Father
right from heaven, and I chose
to be murdered on the cross for you
so *you'd* live.
The natural law of cause and effect tells you
that what goes up must come down,
and also the effects, or results, of evil are suffering,
misery, destruction, and death.
But!—
I took your place so sin won't destroy you.
Your sin won't do you in because
*I became sin for you and became the suffering result for
every wrong you'll ever commit.*
The human blood that spewed from My body
became a supernatural acquittal bath
not only for you, but for the entire human race.

MY WORDS TO HIM

Thank you, Jesus, for giving me the privilege
to come boldly before your throne to reason with you.
You're perfect in the world, sent by our Father God, and you chose
to be murdered on the cross for me so that
I can live a prosperous and overcoming life.
The natural law of cause and effect tells me
that what goes up must come down,
and the effects of evil are suffering, misery,
destruction, and death.
But you took the place of my sinful consequences,
so sin wouldn't destroy me.
Sin won't do me in because you became sin for me
on the cross. Ah, Jesus.
Every wrong I'll ever commit has been paid for by you.
The blood that spewed from your body
became a supernatural acquittal bath not only for me,
but for the entire human race.
Your blood has given me eternal life.

Therefore, brethren, having boldness
to enter the Holiest by the blood of Jesus.

Hebrews 10:19 NKJV

HIS WORDS TO ME

On Top of Things

You can be confident that no matter what's going on
around you or in your world, *I'm on top of it.*
I see all that happens in the world and in your life.
I see every person who walks across your days.

I know.

I see.

I listen.

I AM.

Believe it's by Me that all things exist,
and be secure in knowing nothing escapes
My attention. Pray for the concerns
of the world, and believe you're one with Me
as My child, and you possess the authority
to pray in My name knowing I'll answer.
If you put all of your trust in the world
around you, or in your own undependable authority,
your own shifting merits,
or impetuous abilities,
you have nothing to trust.
Without *Me* you can do nothing.

MY WORDS TO HIM

Thank you, Jesus, for being on top of things.
You see all that happens in the world
and you see everything in my life.
Thank you that you see every person
who walks across my days.
You know. You listen. You're the great I Am.
It's by you that all things exist,
and I'm secure in knowing that nothing
escapes your attention.
Thank you for giving me the authority
to pray in your name.
It's so wonderful knowing that your name
moves galaxies and shifts the platelets of the earth.
I don't put my trust in things or people
around me, or in my own undependable merits
and abilities.
Without you I can do nothing!
I surrender my smug independence
to become dependent on you, Jesus.
The old me is dead. I'm alive in you now!
Thank you for my life in you.

Your old sinful self has died,
and your new life is kept with Christ in God.

Colossians 3:3 NCV

HIS WORDS TO ME

Boldness

My Spirit makes you *bold*
and you need boldness, dear one.
Shyness is not a virtue.
(There's no shyness in heaven.)
I'm the one to make you bold.
In Me you can have confidence to go forward,
never shrinking back,
always assured that you're important to Me,
and that you'll succeed.

Boldness can be gentle, soft-spoken.
(I was never boisterous
or obnoxious while on earth.)
Today, be kind in your boldness,
and face your world with loving compassion,
flinging aside all shame and fear.

My Holy Spirit builds you up, guides and helps you.
Be strong and go forward in My name,
the name above every name.
The world will try to intimidate you,
bully you. I tell you, establish boundaries
and stand your ground.

MY WORDS TO HIM

Thank you, Lord, for your Holy Spirit who makes me bold.
Thank you for assuring me that I'm important to you,
and that I'll succeed in all I do because you're with me.
Thank you for helping me to conquer shyness.
In you I have confidence to go forward and not shrink back.
You've taught me that boldness can be soft-spoken and gentle.
Today I'll be thoughtful in my boldness, and I'll face my world
with love and compassion, flinging aside all harshness and fear.
Thank you for your Holy Spirit.
Thank you for building me up, guiding and helping me.
Thank you for making me bold to go forward in your name,
Jesus, the name above every name.
Even if the world tries to intimidate me and bully me,
you've established boundaries around me
and I'll stand my ground.
In you, I'm strong. Thank you, Jesus.
You're creating a new heart in me.

For the eyes of the LORD range throughout the entire earth, to
strengthen those whose heart is true to him.

2 Chronicles 16:9 NRSV

HIS WORDS TO ME

Authority and Power

If you want to be happy,
be unselfish.
Live for Me, and not for your personal
well-being, and you'll add years
to your life and zip to your step.
Drop the defenses, dare to be wrong,
leave the stresses of your checkbook
at the foot of the cross.

Will you allow Me to carry you
across the murky swamp
of the Lake of Solipsism?
The selfish soul is an oppressed soul,
pinched and cramped.
Dispel selfishness, dear one,
and come before My throne today,
and get free and blissful.

MY WORDS TO HIM

Thank you, Jesus, for your love.
Thank you for your authority and your power.
I live for you, and not for my personal agenda.
I drop all of my self-defenses and I dare to be wrong.
I'm going to leave the stresses of my checkbook and my needs
for recognition at the foot of the cross today.
You've taught me that in order to be happy,
I've got to be unselfish,
so I'm going to allow you to carry me across
the murky swamp of self-absorption and self-righteousness
to freedom.
Thank you, Lord, for showing me
not to allow my soul to continue pinched and cramped
in my own self-concerns.
I dispel selfishness today,
and I come before your throne free and blissful,
and totally in love with you.

My old self has been crucified with Christ. It is no longer I
who live, but Christ lives in me.

Galatians 2:20 NLT

HIS WORDS TO ME

Freedom

I want to give you freedom
in exchange for a hothouse of anger.
I want to help you trust
and remove your fearful suspicions.
I want to give you an open, vulnerable heart.
I'm here to
forgive
renew
revitalize
heal.
Today, dare to face the hidden resentments
that have nipped at your heart.
Take My hand and trust Me to help you grow a new heart.
I assure you that no matter what you've been through,
and what's been done to you,
I can turn all things to good and add back to you
what you've lost
double fold.

Thank you for freedom, Jesus.
I'm trusting you to help me empty myself of my fretful,
moody, emotional behavior.
I know you'll help me to develop an open, flexible mind
hat accepts the things that go wrong in my life.
Thank you for forgiving me and renewing me.
Thank you for freedom from a bad temper.
Thank you for revitalizing and healing me.
Today I'll dare to face the hidden resentments
that have nipped at my heart in the past.
I take your hand and trust you to continue
to create a new heart in me.
No matter what I've been through
and what's been done to me, I'm going to trust you
to restore what's been broken and what's been lost.
You'll turn everything around to good.

The LORD says, "I will give you back what you lost
to the swarming locusts....
Once again you will have all the food you want,
and you will praise the LORD your God,
who does these miracles for you."

Joel 2:25-26 NLT

175

HIS WORDS TO ME

More Than a Conqueror

You're more than a conqueror.
Come now and celebrate the rising of the sun
with Me.
Come greet the dawn with expectation
and fall in love with the exquisite experience
of conquering impossible worlds.

Wield the powerful sword of the Spirit
and hoist your mighty banner of faith
for all to behold.
Be free today!
Fly the heights and scour the depths!
Openly move through clouds flung
across the quivering earth; oh soar
with your arms outspread—open to life
and love and creativity!
Today, beloved conqueror, conquer!

I'm more than a conqueror.
I greet the dawn with trembling expectation,
and I fall in love with the exquisite experience
of conquering the impossible today.
I come to you, Jesus,
to celebrate the rising of the sun in my life.
Thank you for freedom!
I can fly the heights
and scour the depths with you, Lord Jesus.
I soar with my arms outspread, open to life
and love and creativity—all because of you!
Today, I conquer because I have you,
my divine conqueror, living in me!

In all these things we are more than conquerors
through him who loved us.

Romans 8:37 ESV

HIS WORDS TO ME

Nowhere to Go

Where can you go from My Spirit?
Where can you run from My presence?
If you launch onto the wings of the morning
and dwell in the uttermost parts of the sea,
I'm there.
If you make your bed in Sheol, the place of the dead,
I'm there.
If you say, "Surely the darkness shall cover me,
and the night shall be the only light about me,"
I'll find you.
I formed you and wove you together in your mother's womb.
Before you took shape I knew you.
All the days of your life are written in My book
Be lifted up on the wings of love today.
Forever your frame will not be hidden from Me.

MY WORDS TO HIM

There is nowhere to go without your Holy Spirit.
I can't run from your presence.
If I launch onto the wings
of the morning and dwell in the uttermost parts of the sea,
you're there.
If I make my bed in Sheol, the place of the dead,
you're there.
If I say, "Surely the darkness shall cover me
and the night shall be the only light about me,"
you'll find me somehow.
Before I took shape, you knew me.
All the days of my life are written in your book.
I'm lifted up on the wings of love today.
Your Holy Spirit has made a home in my heart.
My frame isn't hidden from you.

Where can I go from your Spirit?
Where can I flee from your presence?
If I go up to the heavens, you are there;
if I make my bed in the depths, you are there.

Psalm 139:8 NIV

HIS WORDS TO ME

Small Sparrow

If you see yourself as a small sparrow
alone on a housetop, your heart quaking—
I hear you. I see you.
If your eyes dull, your soul despairs,
I'm with you.
I'm a giving God and I love you.
If you're lauded as the star of a million parades,
or if you're without a job and scraping for dimes in the
pavement,
I'm there with you.
I'm there in the sunlight and the shadows,
I'm there in hunger and in fatness,
in your youth and in old age.
I stick to you like your own skin.
The mountains of the earth will shake and crumble,
but My tender love for you will never shake—
not a shiver,
not a breath,
not the barest vibration or change
because I'm a giving God and I love you.

Oh, Jesus, sometimes I think I'm just a small sparrow
quivering alone on a housetop, but then I remember
that you hear me and you see me no matter how small
and unimportant I think I am.
If my eyes become dull and my soul despairs,
you're yet with me!
You're a giving God and you love me!
If I'm lauded as the star of a million parades,
or if I'm without a job and scraping
for dimes on the pavement, you're there with me.
You're with me in the sunlight and the shadows.
You're with me in plenty and hunger—
your love for me won't ever shake;
not a shiver, not a breath,
not the barest vibration or change,
because you're a giving God, and you love me!
I'm going to repeat these words over
and over again to myself so I never forget.

You have given me the shield of your salvation,
and your right hand supported me,
and your gentleness made me great.

Psalm 18:35 ESV

HIS WORDS TO ME

Valley of Decision

It's time to pay a visit to the valley of decision
for you're in need of direction.
Which way should you go? How shall you choose?
What'll you do?
In the valley of decision you learn to rule your own spirit
and to understand the wellspring of life is wisdom,
not duty.
In the valley of decision you discover that which is shallow
and pleasing to the senses only, so you can see how pride and
fear of failure are antitheses to faith.
It's faith that leads to assurance and peace of mind.
Uncertainty is the culprit eager to steal you away
from banquet halls of wisdom.
Understand what My good and perfect will is today,
for it's not hidden from you. Here in the valley of decision,
the truth is exposed.
Faith and truth are your allies and teammates.

Lord Jesus, when I'm in the valley of decision,
I need direction from you.
Here in the valley of decision, you're teaching me
how to rule my own spirit and to understand
the wellspring of life is wisdom, not duty.
In the valley of decision, I'm learning to discern
that which is shallow and pleasing to the senses only.
I can see how pride and fear of failure are the antithesis to faith.
You're teaching me that faith leads to assurance
and peace of mind, and that uncertainty
is the culprit eager to steal me away
from the banquet halls of your wisdom.
Help me to understand what your good
and perfect will for me is today.
Here in the valley of decision
is where you expose the truth to me.
I choose faith and truth as my allies and my teammates,
and I thank you for your perfect guidance.

When you roam, they will lead you;
When you sleep, they will keep you;
And when you awake, they will speak with you.

Proverbs 6:22 NKJV

HIS WORDS TO ME

Divine Timing

The time is now.
What you've considered delays
in your calling aren't delays at all.
There are no delays in My kingdom.
Get ready to follow My guidance
as your divine coach, and understand
that My purposes extend far, far beyond
limited human vision. You must trust Me
to call the plays. You must see yourself
as a *global team member*.
No one is called as a lone prophet today.
I'm calling *teams* to do the work of the Gospel!
I'm strategically gathering called saints together
to reveal My love to the world in a greater move of My Spirit
than has been unfolded until now.
Eye hasn't seen, nor ears heard, the things I have
prepared for this time!
In your own zeal and ambition
you would have charged ahead wounding people
in the guise of healing; your vanity would have eaten you up.
Now, soaked with holy wisdom and time, you'll burst forth
as a kingdom champion.

Thank you, Lord, for showing me
that what I consider a delay is not a delay
according to your divine timing.
Thank you for no delays in your kingdom.
You're my divine coach and your purposes
extend far, far beyond my limited human vision.
I know you're calling people together in teams
to do the work of the gospel, and you're strategically
gathering your called saints together to reveal your love
to the world in a greater move of your Spirit
that has been hidden until now.
Eyes haven't yet seen, nor have ears heard,
the things that you've prepared for this time!
Thank you, Jesus! In my selfish zeal and ambition
I would've charged ahead on my own,
wounding people in the guise of healing,
and my vanity would have eaten me up.
But now, soaked with holy brokenness,
I'll go forward as a kingdom champion!

Those who wait on the LORD
Shall renew their strength;
They shall mount up with wings like eagles,
They shall run and not be weary,
They shall walk and not faint.

Isaiah 40:31 NKJV

HIS WORDS TO ME

Reaching Down

I reach down and save
all who call on My name.
And you, dear friend, came to Me humbly
and wholly
giving your life to Me.
Now you have the confidence
that you're saved from those things that
could have hurt and destroyed you.
You're Mine now.
You're born again in your thinking,
your choices, your attitudes, your mind-set,
and your personality.
I save you from powerlessness
and wrong choices.
I save you from the shackles of yesterday.
This is a brand new day for you.
Live it fully.

MY WORDS TO HIM

Thank you, Jesus, for reaching down
and saving me from a frustrating, godless existence.
You answer every person
who comes to you with a sincere heart.
I have deep confidence that I'm saved
from those things that could have destroyed me.
My path was self-centered and futile, but now
I've surrendered my life to you, Jesus,
and I'm born again in my thinking, my choices,
my attitudes, and my mindset.
I have a born-again personality!
You saved me from powerlessness and self-destruction.
You saved me from the shackles of yesterday's troubles.
Oh, this is a brand new day for me,
and I thank you, Jesus.
I choose to live it fully!

Oh, the depth of the riches both of the wisdom
and knowledge of God!
How unsearchable are His judgments
and unfathomable His ways!

Romans 11:33 NASB

HIS WORDS TO ME

Never Forsake Me

Have I forsaken you?
Never!
Pause for a moment
and open the eyes of your spirit.
What and where is the source of the haven
of safety encircling you?
Whose arms caress and protect you
against the forces of darkness
that snap at your heels?

What is this rich, resplendent protection
embracing you now as you read these words—
its heavy, gold threads
too dazzling for the human eye to bear?
Dear one,
you are wrapped in My robes.

MY WORDS TO HIM

You'll never forsake me. Never!
Thank you for your arms caressing
and protecting me against the forces
of darkness that snap at my heels.
Thank you for the rich, resplendent
protection that embraces me now
as I speak these words to you.
Thank you, Jesus;
I'm safely wrapped in your love today.
I can dare to release and let go
of the attachments that cause me stress
and worry, and let go of every illusion
of happiness that popular culture promotes.
I let go today, Lord. I let go,
so your divine intelligence and truth
can be my guides.

Your kingdom is an everlasting kingdom.
You rule throughout all generations.
The LORD always keeps his promises;
he is gracious in all he does.

Psalm 145:13 NLT

HIS WORDS TO ME

Renewed Sense of Purpose

I'm giving you a renewed sense of purpose now.
Don't live as if you still belong to the world.
I'm lifting you up to an elevated position in My kingdom,
and this means renewed commitment on your part.
No more groveling in the sand
of worldly entanglements and pursuits.
Be perfect as My Father in heaven is perfect,
and be holy as I am holy
by becoming molded and shaped by My Word,
where you're transformed
into My very image.

I'm unfolding a higher standard for you to live by,
a deeper ongoing experience in My Spirit,
so your life will take on new vibrancy and brilliance
to reflect the personality of the Beloved.
You'll no longer accept as normal old, impure, unholy
thoughts
and feelings because My presence is more real to you
than anything in the material world.
Your life standard and Mine are now one.

MY WORDS TO HIM

Thank you for giving me a renewed sense of purpose, Jesus.
Today, I choose not to live as though
I'm still in my old life with all
its attachments and shallow needs.
You're lifting me up to an elevated position
in your kingdom, and this means
renewed commitment on my part.
No more groveling in the sand of ambiguity.
I'm choosing to allow you to mold
and shape me by your Word.
Transform me into your very image.
Thank you for unfolding a higher standard
for me to live by, a deeper, ongoing experience
in your Spirit so that my life takes on
new vibrancy and brilliance to reflect
the personality of my Beloved.
No longer will I accept as normal my
old, driven, needy, self-centered way of life.
Your presence has become more real to me
than anything in the material world.
I've made the choice to let go of the attachments
that the world taught me were my rights.
I'm choosing to love, appreciate, and enjoy my life at this moment.

We were made right with God by placing our faith in Jesus Christ.
And this is true for everyone who believes, no matter who we are.

Romans 3:22 NLT

HIS WORDS TO ME

Exchanging Qualities

What pleases Me is a happy heart.
I give you confidence
in the face of danger.
I give you strength
in the power of My might.
I exchange your weak qualities
and abilities for the power of My strength
so you become strong!
This should make you happy.

I tell you to lift up the limp hands
at your sides, bolster your knees,
and put My full armor,
so the dragons and serpents of Sheol can't reach you.
This should make you happy!
I'm *all you need* for power, love, a sound mind,
and a happy heart.
Receive the endless riches
of your benefits in Me,
and decide to be happy today.

MY WORDS TO HIM

Thank you, Lord, for exchanging my weak qualities
and abilities for the power of your strength.
Thank you for lifting my limp hands and bolstering my knees
so I can put on the full armor of God.
The dragons and serpents of hell can't reach me when
I'm wearing the full armor of God!
You're all I need to live with power, love, and a sound mind.
You are my happy heart.
Today I'm choosing to receive
the endless riches of the benefits you give to me.
Oh Jesus, I'm happy!
You have made me happy!

Happy are those who hear the joyful call to worship,
for they will walk in the light of your presence, LORD.

Psalm 89:15 NLT

HIS WORDS TO ME

No Higher Reward

There's no higher reward in this life
than My approval.
When you want recognition,
come to Me first,
not the world, not family,
and not even to other believers.
I'll give you far more than you ask.
Call on *Me*.
I'm the giver of immortal rewards.
The world recognizes you for what you do—
I recognize you for who you *are*.
Today, in My watchful
and loving gaze,
be who you are.
I love you.

Lord, there's no higher reward in this life than your approval.
When I want recognition I'll remember to come to you first,
not to the world, not to family, and not even to other believers.
I want your approval.
The world recognizes me for what I do
—but you recognize me for who I am!
Thank you for your watchful and loving gaze.
You give me far more than I ask for.
You're the giver of immortal rewards.
You've made me glad to be who I am.
I love you.

Before he made the world, God chose us to be his very own
through what Christ would do for us; he decided then to make
us holy in his eyes, without a single fault—we who stand before
him covered with his love.

Ephesians 1:4 TLB

HIS WORDS TO ME

Barefoot on Ice

When you've been hurt, stolen from, betrayed,
and you merely brush your feelings aside,
it's like standing barefoot on frozen ice
and insisting your feet are warm.
Don't wait until your toes fall off!

If you try to hide resentment or
bury your hurt, angry feelings behind a wan smile
and a nonchalant shrug of a shoulder,
your distress is like broken glass
inside tangled and misplaced emotions.

Allow Me to calm your inner storm.
Allow time for Me to heal
and pour the balm of My Spirit over the sores
of your soul.
I'm here loving you, and I want to assure you
the pain won't last. I'll see you through.

MY WORDS TO HIM

When I've been hurt, stolen from, betrayed,
and I nonchalantly brush my feelings aside,
it's like standing barefoot on frozen ice,
and insisting that my feet aren't cold.
Don't let me wait on the ice of my denial
until my toes fall off!
If I try to hide feelings of resentment or bury hurt, angry feelings
with a casual shrug of the shoulder, my distress is like
broken glass inside tangled and misplaced emotions.
Oh Jesus, help me calm my inner storm.
Come and heal, and pour the balm of your Spirit
over the sores of my soul.
You're here to love me and I need your love.
I need your assurance that pain won't last.
Thank you for seeing me through this difficult time.

The Lord is faithful and will give you strength and will protect
you from the Evil One.

2 Thessalonians 3:3 NCV

HIS WORDS TO ME

Humility and Timidity

Don't confuse humility with timidity.

I'm not timid.

Timidity is not one of My attributes.

My living Spirit is bold.

You're filled with My Spirit,

and, therefore, timidity, shyness, and fearfulness

aren't a part of your new nature.

Faith is your banner, your shield, your friend.

Faith must be *bold*. Never wimpy.

Faith gives you power to bring forth

what is presently non-existent!

Your faith brings your hopes to life!

Never be wimpy or shy about your needs

or the needs of those you pray for.

Come, let Me hear from you.

Let Me see your bold and brave face

courageously proclaiming My Word and My promises.

MY WORDS TO HIM

Lord, help me not to confuse humility with timidity.
My true self is not timid.
Timidity is not one of your attributes.
Your living Holy Spirit is bold.
You've filled me with your Spirit,
and therefore timidity, shyness, and fearfulness
can no longer reign supreme in my nature.
Faith has become my banner, my shield, and my friend.
Faith must be bold.
Help me not to be wimpy in my faith.
Faith gives me power to bring forth
what is presently nonexistent!
My faith brings my hopes to life!
Help me not to be shy when I reach out to help others.
Help me to be sweetly bold, never pushy or abrasive,
thinking I'm the only one with the truth.
I want to represent your kindness
and compassion with loving boldness.

On the day I called, you answered me,
you increased my strength of soul.

Psalm 138:3 NRSV

HIS WORDS TO ME

Compassionate Heart

You call
and My compassionate heart opens to you.
You ask
and My giving hand reaches out to you
with far *more* than you ask for.
I'm a giving God, dear one,
so today, extend your hands wide-spread to Me.
Reach and stretch to accept
the countless blessings and answered prayers
stored up for you here in Glory.
You may keep
what's yours but give the honor
and the credit to Me.

MY WORDS TO HIM

Thank you, Jesus, for your compassionate heart.
Every time I come to you I feel your giving hand
reaching out to me, overflowing with far more than I ask.
Your blessings are endless!
You're a giving God and I'm so grateful.
Today, I open my hands wide to you,
ready to accept more of the countless blessings
you have in store for me in order that I might
bless others.
I know how you love to give when we ask,
and for every gift received, I give all the honor to you.
Teach me, Lord, to carry my gifts with boldness and humility.

May He give you the power to accomplish
all the good things your faith prompts you to do.

2 Thessalonians 1:11 NLT

HIS WORDS TO ME

Something Good

Darling, you're about to bloom.
You're ready to burst forth
with a new anointing and authority
in My Holy Spirit
unlike anything you've experienced
in the past.
Wisdom and joy now gush from your
innermost being
like a spring bursting forth after
a long, grey winter.
Sonlight illuminates your way.
Be confident and brave—
this is just the beginning.

Lord, I feel that something good is coming!
I'm a bud about to bloom!
I feel ready
to burst out with the new anointing
and authority in your Holy Spirit
unlike anything I've experienced
in the past.
Thank you for your wisdom
and joy that gushes from my innermost being
like spring exploding into the still, grey atmosphere
after a long, dull winter.
Your light illuminates my way
and I'm feeling very brave
because I know I'm at the cusp
of a beautiful new beginning!

"Do not leave Jerusalem until the Father sends you the gift he
promised, as I told you before. John baptized with water, but
in just a few days you will be baptized with the Holy Spirit.
But you will receive power when the Holy Spirit comes upon
you. And you will be my witnesses, telling people about me
everywhere—in Jerusalem, throughout Judea, in Samaria, and
to the ends of the earth."

Acts 1:4-5, 8 NLT

HIS WORDS TO ME

Channel of Blessing

You're a channel of blessing for Me
and there's no limit to what I can do
through you;
therefore, impose no restrictions or boundaries
on My purposes or abilities. Don't for a minute
doubt what I can do in your life.

I've made all grace abound to you
so you'll have sufficient means in everything
I give you to do.
You lack nothing!
I adorn you with beautiful gifts and talents
to help you fulfill your magnificent purpose on earth.
Understand that in Me
nothing can stop you.

Thank you, Jesus, for making me a channel of blessing.
I know there is no limit to what I can do through you,
and therefore I won't impose restrictions or boundaries
on what's possible.
I won't for a minute doubt what you can do
through my life and through me.
You make all grace abound, so I'll have sufficient means
to fulfill everything you give me to do.
I lack nothing!
You've equipped me with beautiful gifts and talents
to help me live and accomplish my purpose on earth.
Thank you, Jesus, because with your Holy Spirit guiding me,
nothing can stop me from fulfilling all
that you have called me to do and to be.

We are God's handiwork, created in Christ Jesus to do good
works, which God prepared in advance for us to do.

Ephesians 2:10 NIV

HIS WORDS TO ME

Eager Learner

You have the mind of a ready learner,
and in your quest to accumulate
natural wisdom and knowledge
of the world and its ways,
don't neglect the exceeding spiritual knowledge
that comes from My fountain.

As you receive instruction and diplomas
by your earthly teachers, don't forget
the classrooms of the Almighty,
the holy labs, lecture halls, assignments,
essays, exams, and finals
because in Me you never stop learning,
and a heavenly commencement
is a celebration that never ends.

Thank you, Jesus, for giving me the mind of an eager learner.
Thank you for teaching me how to walk in the Spirit
as I carry on in my quest to accumulate natural wisdom.
Thank you for releasing spiritual wisdom
and understanding from your fountain of divine knowing.
As I receive degrees and diplomas from my earthly teachers,
I honor the classroom of the Almighty, the holy labs, lecture halls,
assignments, essays, exams, and finals in your university of faith
because I never stop learning about you.
All of eternity can't contain everything there is
to learn and love about you.
A heavenly commencement is a celebration that never ends.

Be filled with the knowledge of His will in all spiritual wisdom
and understanding, so that you will walk in a manner worthy of
the Lord... and increasing in the knowledge of God.

Colossians 1:9-10 NASB

Holding All Matter

I'm more influential than presidents and kings,
more important than employers,
teachers, leaders, and sons.
By Me all matter is held together.
By Me the stars suspend in the heavens.
By Me the worlds were created.
By Me a new nature and a new personality
was born in you.
Be glad and rejoice in the person you are.
You are Mine.
Today, beloved, walk with the knowledge
of your high calling in Me.

MY WORDS TO HIM

Thank you, Jesus, for holding all matter together.
By you, the worlds were created.
By you, the stars suspend in the heavens.
By you, a new nature and a new personality
were born in me.
I rejoice in the person
I'm becoming because you're in me
by your Spirit.
I love my high calling in you.
Today, I walk with the knowledge
of my high calling in you,
and I'm humbled.

That I may proclaim with the voice of thanksgiving,
and tell of all Your wondrous works.

Psalm 26:7 NKJV

HIS WORDS TO ME

New Challenges

Today as challenges come your way,
trust Me.
When you trust Me, you can
meet each challenge head-on,
listening for My perfect, flawless guidance.
Fear and confusion will be far from you.
There isn't a challenge on earth with
the power to defeat or wipe you out
because I'm at the helm of your life today.
You have the power to turn all setbacks
to victories, all scraps to gold, all attacks to conquests.
The Holy Spirit within you is all-powerful,
all-knowing, all-wise, fully prepared and zealous
to help with divine strategy to turn all things to good.
When you pray, ask what is best
for My kingdom,
not what is best for you.
That which is best for Me and My kingdom
will always be best for you.
Face the challenges with courage. Answers and solutions
are within you by My Spirit.

MY WORDS TO HIM

Today, as new challenges come my way, I'll trust you.
When I trust you completely, I'll meet each challenge
head-on, listening for your perfect, flawless guidance.
Thank you for removing fear and confusion from me.
There isn't a challenge on earth with the power to defeat me
because you're at the helm of my life.
Your Spirit in me changes my attitude,
and builds my faith so that setbacks become victories,
personal scraps with others are healed,
and spiritual attacks become spiritual conquests.
The Holy Spirit within me is all powerful, all wise,
and zealous to help with divine strategy
to turn all things to good. I ask you, Jesus,
for what's best for your kingdom.
That which is best for you and your kingdom
will always be best for me.
Today, I choose to face the challenges in my life with courage.
Answers and solutions are in me by your Spirit.
Thank you, Jesus!

"You have been chosen to know the secrets
about the kingdom of heaven."

Matthew 13:11 NCV

HIS WORDS TO ME

Abounding Grace

My abounding grace has added
many blessings to you, and your life is enriched
with many gifts.
I've given you talents to multiply,
so you can be a channel of blessing
and prosper in all you do.
Never depend on conditions or trends
or the fluctuating economy;
depend solely on Me, your divine employer.
My fullness in your life will overflow and reach out
to touch and help others.
When My blessings make My children rich,
no sorrow is added.

Thank you, Jesus, for your abounding grace
and for adding countless blessings to my life.
Thank you for enriching me with so many gifts
from your loving heart.
You've given me talents
to multiply so I can be a channel of blessing
and prosper in all I do.
I don't depend on conditions
or trends, or the fluctuating economy;
I depend solely on you, my divine friend and employer.
Your fullness in my life overflows
and reaches out to touch and help others.
Your blessings have made me spiritually rich
and no sorrow is added.
How wonderfully blessed I am!

The blessing of the LORD makes rich,
and he adds no sorrow with it.

Proverbs 10:22 NRSV

HIS WORDS TO ME

Not Alarmed

Don't be alarmed by the troubles
surrounding you today.
Open your mind to divine insight
in place of fretful concerns and worry.
I'm your heavenly teacher
and I tell you, take My yoke upon you
and learn of Me.
I have many hidden things to reveal to you.
I have much knowledge to share with you.
I have many doors open for you.
Darling child, in the world there will always be turmoil,
but I tell you, through everything I'm all and everything
you need.

MY WORDS TO HIM

I won't be alarmed by the troubles surrounding me today.
My mind is open to divine insight in place of fretful
concerns and worries.
You're my heavenly teacher.
I've taken your yoke on my shoulders,
and you've helped me recover my life.
Thank you for teaching me to live free from the sin
that once taunted me.
Thank you for godly knowledge
and for the many hidden things you're about to reveal to me.
Thank you for the new doors open to me
as your darling child.
In the world there'll always be turmoil,
but through it all, you're everything I need.

The LORD will keep you from all harm—
he will watch over your life;
the LORD will watch over your coming and going
both now and forevermore..

Psalm 121:7-8 NKJV

HIS WORDS TO ME

Illuminating My Soul

I've caused a great light
to illuminate your soul.
I've transferred you out of the kingdom
of darkness and I've given you
a permanent address
in the kingdom of light.
I've delivered you from shame.
I've saved you from your sins,
and I've lifted the heavy burden
from your shoulders.

I'm lifting you out of obscurity
and guiding you with grace
and integrity. Think of yourself
as a new person today,
a person capable of great things.

MY WORDS TO HIM

Thank you for illuminating my soul, Jesus,
and for transferring me out of the kingdom of darkness.
Thank you for giving me a permanent address
in the kingdom of light.
Thank you for delivering me
from shame and confusion.
Thank you for saving me
from my sins and lifting the heavy burdens
from my shoulders.
Thank you for taking me out of obscurity
and guiding me with grace and integrity.
Today, I'll think of myself as a new person,
a person capable of great things
because of who I am in you.

By his divine power, God has given us everything we need
for living a godly life. We have received all of this by coming
to know him, the one who called us to himself by means of
his marvelous glory and excellence. And because of his glory
and excellence, he has given us great and precious promises.
These are the promises
that enable you to share his divine nature
and escape the world's corruption
caused by human desires.

2 Peter 1:3-4 NKJV

HIS WORDS TO ME

My Savior

When you call on Me,
I answer you.
I'm the beginning and end of all things,
the author of all life,
and the origin of thought.
I'm familiar with the way you think.
There's nothing you can hide from Me—
I know your true needs.
When you recoil and withdraw,
you open yourself up to sorrow,
and you stunt your beautiful mind;
your thoughts become picayune and worldly.

I want to show you great and mighty things
you haven't even considered.
I want you to renew your way of thinking
to think as I think.
When you call on Me,
I answer you, but look at your requests.
Are your requests too small?

MY WORDS TO HIM

Jesus, thank you for being my Savior.
Thank you for knowing every one of my needs,
and when I recoil and withdraw
from your perfect will for me, thank you
for being right there and not abandoning me.
Thank you, because even though I may open
myself up to sorrow and self-pity,
stunting the beautiful mind you've given me,
you don't give up and walk away.
When my thoughts become petty and vain,
you're there to pull me back to reality.
You're the beginning and end of all things—
you're all reality. You're the author of all life
and the origin of thought.
Thank you for renewing my mind
and helping me to think as you think.
I don't want my requests to be trivial because
when I call on you, you answer me.
Thank you for wanting to show me great things.
Open my mind, Lord, to your mind today,
so my prayers are wings to heaven's storehouse of blessing.

"You did not choose Me, but I chose you and appointed you that
you should go and bear fruit, and that your fruit should remain,
that whatever you ask the Father in My name He may give you."

John 15:16 NKJV

HIS WORDS TO ME

In Your Hands

It's time to prepare yourself.
Your future is in My hands,
and just beyond your sight
are wonderful things yet to come
which you don't know.
You won't have to wait long
or bake in the oven of transition forever;
I'm doing a work in you
that will withstand
the fiery darts of the devil.
Breathe in the power of My Word
and get ready for breakthrough!

MY WORDS TO HIM

Lord Jesus, my future is in your hands.
It's time I realize that just beyond my reach
are wonderful things coming my way.
It's time I prepare myself for blessings
and answers to prayer!
I totally trust that I won't have to bake in the oven
of transition forever, because you're doing
a new work in me that withstands
the fiery darts of the devil and sets me apart
from my old habits of impatience
and demanding my way.
Today, I breathe in the power
of your Word and prepare myself
for breakthrough!

Therefore, prepare your minds for action,
keep sober in spirit, fix your hope completely
on the grace to be brought to you
at the revelation of Jesus Christ.

1 Peter 1:13 NASB

HIS WORDS TO ME

Faith as the Key

Faith is the key to unlocking
unexpected blessings.
Exercise the power of your faith
and expect answered prayer!
Expect prosperity!
Expect healing!
Faith operates with integrity
and gives honor to each of your blessings
as they mount up in heaps like grain at harvest.
Dear one, I want you to know
that faith is tested by challenges
and also by blessings!
I will pour out blessings and answered prayer
according to your faith.
Know that My hand will be upon you
for all to see and observe.
As your faith multiplies,
I'll surprise you with the unexpected.

MY WORDS TO HIM

Thank you, Jesus, for showing me faith
as the key to unlocking unexpected blessings.
Thank you for teaching me to exercise the power
of my faith to receive answered prayer
without doubting, and to expect you
to surprise me with unmerited blessing.
You're my divine healer.
I thank you for prosperity of the soul and the body.
Faith operates with integrity and gives honor to each blessing
as they mount up in heaps like grain at harvest.
Thank you for showing me that faith is tested
by challenges and also by the blessings themselves.
Teach me to honor and manage
the challenges of received blessings.
You pour out blessings and answered prayer
to keep faith ignited.
I know that your hand is upon me.
Multiply my faith so I can be a blessing to people;
most of all, Lord, my soul longs to bless you!

Let all that I am praise the LORD;
with my whole heart, I will praise his holy name.

Psalm 103:1 NLT

HIS WORDS TO ME

Thankful for All Things

What would you do if I were to tell you
that the life you now have
is as good as it gets?
Suppose I were to reveal to you
that you've already
reached your shining hour?
Would this change your way of thinking?

Would you praise and thank Me?
Would you rejoice, be grateful and fall in love
with every aspect of your life?
Would you treasure more intimately the people
I've put in your life?
Would you see the sunrise and sunset with new eyes?
Would the tasks of your day become a holy calling
rather than the hitching post while waiting for a better
tomorrow?
Dear child, it's time to count your blessings;
it's time to be grateful.

Jesus, I praise you and thank you for all things.
Here I am rejoicing and grateful and falling in love
with every aspect of the life you've given me.
I treasure the people you've put into my life.
I love each sunrise and sunset.
I love the daily tasks that you've given me
and the holy calling that I live in.
I love to live in the present moment,
rather than to latch onto the hitching post of delay
while waiting for a better tomorrow.
Lord Jesus, if I were to count my blessings
there wouldn't be enough days to complete the list.
It'll take all of eternity to count my blessings!
Thank you for the life I now have,
not because I'm without need,
but because it's my life!
I praise and thank you with all of my heart!

Let them give thanks to the Lord for his love
and for the miracles he does for people.

Psalm 107:8 NCV

HIS WORDS TO ME

Lift Up My Chin

Pull back the shoulders that slouch;
lift up the chin that hangs down.
Spread wide the palms of your hands,
and liberate the feet from their sleep.
Rise up, dear one, and seize My Word
to put an end to wasted time.
How many dawns will you lose
under the muddy shawl of worry?
Your problems will scatter
like startled insects when you place them
in the blinding light of My Word.
I'm challenging you today
to fasten your woeful words
alongside *Mine*.
Your breakthrough is here.

Lord Jesus, today, I'll pull back my shoulders
if they slouch, and I'll lift up my chin if it droops.
I'll spread wide the palms of my hands
and liberate my feet from their sleep.
I'll rise up and seize your words,
and put an end to wasting time!
I won't lose any more dawns under the shawl of worry.
You scatter my problems like startled
insects when I place them in the blinding light
of your Word.
Thank you for challenging me
to fasten my woeful words alongside your words
because my breakthrough is here.
Hallelujah!

Arise, shine; for your light has come,
and the glory of the LORD has risen upon you.

Isaiah 60:1 NRSV

HIS WORDS TO ME

Concerns of My Heart

I know your cares
and I know your heart. You're praying
for your loved ones, and you must understand
I hear you because I love them more
than you love them.
Be comforted. I won't let you down and I won't
let go of your loved ones.
I'm doing a bigger work than you know.
Expand your vision and proclaim My Word
over your loved ones.
I will keep your family and present them
before the presence of My Father
and they will worship Me.
See through My eyes of mercy.
Love them
and trust Me. Trust My promises.
Your prayers are like mountains of gold,
their range dazzling in brilliance,
stretching far beyond your limited perception,
and touching more lives and situations
than you'll ever know.

Thank you, Jesus, for knowing the concerns of my heart.
Thank you for hearing my prayers and caring for my loved ones.
I know that you hear me
because you love them more than I love them.
Thank you for comforting me.
I know you won't let me down
and you won't let go of my loved ones.
You're doing a bigger work than I know.
Help me to expand my vision and proclaim your Word
over my loved ones continually.
Thank you for keeping my family in your heart,
and for giving me a heart of faith and mercy
as I trust you and your promises.
Thank you for answered prayer that is like
mountains of gold, their range dazzling in brilliance,
stretching far beyond what I can see,
touching all of eternity.

Before they call I will answer;
while they are still speaking I will hear.

Isaiah 65:24 NIV

HIS WORDS TO ME

Flinging Aside Fear

Fling aside your fears.
You worry you aren't good enough,
aren't young enough, old enough,
so many not-enoughs! But you *are* enough.
You are *exactly* enough
at this moment
to fulfill *exactly* what
you are called to be and do.
Don't delay your blessings
by telling yourself foolish not-enoughs.
I'm all you need.
Today, I'm equipping you with *more than
enough*, so be brave,
go forward with confidence and
be the blessing you were born to be.

Lord Jesus, I'm flinging aside all my fears.
I'm not going to worry anymore about
not being good enough,
or young enough,
or old enough,
or whatever enough.
I know that I *am* enough.
I'm exactly enough at this moment
to fulfill exactly what I'm called to be and do.
I'm not going to delay my blessings
by telling myself foolish not-enoughs.
You are all I need.
Today, I know that you're equipping me
with more than enough,
so I'll be brave to go forward
with confidence and be the blessing
I was born to be!

I eagerly expect and hope that I will in no way be ashamed,
but will have sufficient courage so that now as always Christ
will be exalted in my body, whether by life or by death.

Philippians 1:20 NIV

HIS WORDS TO ME

Physical Condition

Give Me your physical health today.
Yield your body as a living sacrifice
not conformed to the things of the world.
Let your mind be renewed and your affections
kissed by Me.
Your body is My temple
and you're living in My temple
as a privileged renter.
Keep it clean, bright,
beautiful for Me.
Take care of My temple today.

MY WORDS TO HIM

Today, Lord Jesus, I give you
the condition of my physical health.
I yield my body as a living sacrifice to you.
I'm not conforming myself to the things of the world.
I'm decreeing my mind to be renewed,
and my affections kissed
and kept by your love for me.
My body is your temple and I'm living
in your temple as a privileged renter.
I choose to attend to the needs of your temple
as a good renter, and keep my body clean, bright,
and beautiful for you.

Do you not know that your body is the temple of the Holy
Spirit who is in you, whom you have from God, and you are
not your own?

1 Corinthians 6:19 NKJV

HIS WORDS TO ME

Storms of Life

Storms of life may brew all around you,
but don't stress yourself with storm fussing;
simply remember the one who stills the storm.
I know how to handle the storms—
I'm your divine storm handler!
Why don't you climb into the hollow of My hand
and make yourself comfy?
Right now.
Yes, dear one, I've made a home for you
here in the nest of My hand.
It's a mistake to think I'm one who helps those
who help themselves.
I'm one who helps those who *can't* help themselves.
Stay here with Me. The storm will
wear itself out—you're safe.
Your divine storm handler is taking care of you.

Thank you, Jesus, for helping me not to stress out
when the storms of life brew around me.
I remind myself it's you who stills the storm.
You're my divine storm-handler!
Today I climb into the hollow of your hand
and make myself comfortable as your adoring child.
You've made a home for me here
in the nest of your loving hand.
I'll stay here with you, Jesus.
The storm will wear itself out,
as all storms do, and meanwhile,
I'm staying calm and confident in your care.
The statement, "God helps those who help themselves"
is not true.
You help those who *can't* help themselves.
Oh, how I thank you!

You, God, see the trouble of the afflicted;
you consider their grief and take it in hand.
The victims commit themselves to you;
you are the helper of the fatherless.

Psalm 10:14 NIV

HIS WORDS TO ME

Empowering

My voice continually encourages
and empowers you with blessing,
but the crashing, clanging, clattering noise
of worry muffles the sound
of My voice. Worry is a noisy place.
It slams your brain
and your mind.
When you worry,
the noise of your fears singe and burn
the soft perfection of your holy ears
and turn you deaf to My sweet songs of deliverance.
Worry is also a messy place.
It's littered with garbage and old trash,
and when you tinker with garbage,
it stinks up your world.
Open your ears, toss out the garbage,
and choose to think My thoughts today.

MY WORDS TO HIM

Thank you, Jesus, for your voice continually encouraging
and empowering me with blessings.
The crashing, clanging, clattering noise of worry
tries to muffle the sound of your voice,
but I'm choosing today to listen to your take on things
instead of mine and the world's.
Oh, worry is a noisy place;
it slams my brain and my mind, and the noise of my fears
singe and burn the soft perfection of my holy ears
and turn me deaf to your sweet songs of deliverance.
Oh Jesus, worry is a messy place.
It's littered with garbage
and old trash, and if I tinker with garbage it stinks up my world.
Today I'm going to breathe in your sweet Spirit
of peace and listen to your love song to me
I'm tossing out old wasted worries,
and I'm choosing to enter the light of truth and wisdom,
and think your thoughts.

For as he thinks in his heart, so is he.

Proverbs 23:7 NKJV

HIS WORDS TO ME

The Lord Who Heals Me

I am the Lord who heals you.
Trouble will *not* prevail over you.
The agonies of fear, strife, jealousy,
and anger
have no place at the table I've set for you.
My table is set with healing,
fullness, peace, joy.
At My table are delights for the soul,
where your body is restored and healed.
Today, be refreshed and lifted up.
Allow yourself to relax in the sweet atmosphere
of complete love and acceptance
at My table of abundance.
There's nothing missing, nothing lacking.
Allow My calm and peace to fill you right now.

MY WORDS TO HIM

Thank you, Lord Jesus, for you're the Lord
who heals me of more than physical infirmity.
You heal me of sick attitudes and ideas;
you heal me of wounded emotions and damaged thinking.
I'm reaching out for divine healing of my soul,
so trouble won't prevail over my life.
The agonies of fear, strife, jealousy, and anger
have no place at the table you set before your children.
Your table is set with healing, peace, joy, and abundant life.
Today I feel refreshed and lifted up.
I'm relaxing in the sweet atmosphere of complete love
and acceptance at your table of abundance.
There's nothing missing here, nothing lacking, nothing sick.
Today I rest in your calm and peace,
filled with the ecstasy of your presence.
I'm healed.

My child, pay attention to what I say.
Listen carefully to my words.
Don't lose sight of them.
Let them penetrate deep into your heart,
for they bring life to those who find them,
and healing to their whole body.
which I have brought on the Egyptians.

Proverbs 4:20-22 NLT

HIS WORDS TO ME

Solidly Fixed

If you feel lost
when faced with the threat of change
and your sense of security
is challenged, understand that
you can't lose something
that's solidly fixed inside you.
Change may be difficult.
but when you enter the experience of change
with Me, you'll see
what's within you is permanent.
Change is temporary.
Faith, love, truth, the attributes
of heaven—these you can't dislodge
through changes of circumstances.
My Spirit in you won't slip away
or become something else.
I'm leading you in a new adventure
of faith, dear one. Don't be afraid.

MY WORDS TO HIM

Lord, you've taught me that I can't lose that which is
solidly fixed inside me.
I have faith inside me, yet I can't help but feel unsteady
when I'm faced with the threat of change.
When my sense of security is challenged,
I confess I become afraid.
I know that even though
outer circumstances may change,
what lives within me is permanent.
Thank you for showing me what's permanent!
Your Spirit in me won't slip away or become
something else. You never change.
Thank you for your compassionate and understanding heart,
and for not reprimanding me for these insecure feelings.
Thank you for being here with me ,
and for helping me overcome all fear and worry.
Thank you for reminding me security is from within,
and showing me that change can be an adventure.
With you, it'll be a wonderful adventure.
Thank you for leading me into new adventure of faith.
I'm keeping my eyes on the permanent.

Those of steadfast mind you keep in peace—
in peace because they trust in you.

Isaiah 26:3 NRSV

HIS WORDS TO ME

Winter's Heavy Parka

It's time to wake up and start living,
dear one.
Time to pull off winter's heavy parka of the soul,
and join the sleeveless seedtime of spring,
where you'll create great things
simply by being awake and living
on purpose.
No more lying asleep in the sun,
no no, it's time to rise up,
but more than that, it's time to
rise up *shining!*
Beautiful one, come, let Me illuminate
you from within so your light will blaze
in the dark and dreary world where winter
lies whimpering in the weeds.

MY WORDS TO HIM

Lord, today I pull off winter's heavy parka of the soul
and I choose to wake up and start living anew.
I'm joining the sleeveless seedtime of spring!
I'll create great things simply by being awake
and living on purpose.
No more lying asleep in the sun—
no, it's time to rise up, but more than that,
it's time to rise up shining!
Oh thank you, Jesus,
for illuminating me from within so my light
will blaze in the dark and dreary world
where winter lies whimpering in the weeds.
I'm alive! I'm alive!

"You are the light of the world.
A city that is set on a hill cannot be hidden."

Matthew 5:14 NKJV

HIS WORDS TO ME

Thoughts of Failure

This month remove from your mind
every thought of failure.
A weak spirit will swallow your dignity
as sand drinks the rain.
I'm here to prosper your soul
with integrity, wholeness, clear direction,
and single-mindedness.

I want you to dance on mountaintops
singing the songs of angels—
I want you to eat the sweets of royalty
while riding the chariots of fortune.
I want your good conscience to reward you
so you'll be unashamed to stand
in the full strength of the sun—
What you think of as failure is
but a step further toward the goal
of your high calling in Me!

This month I'm going to remove
from my mind every thought of failure.
I won't allow a weak spirit to swallow
my dignity because that's like sand drinking the rain.
You, my Jesus, are here to prosper my soul
with integrity, wholeness, and clear direction.
You've given me single mindedness.
I'm so happy I want to dance on mountain tops
and sing the songs of angels.
You've elevated me to a place where I can
eat the sweets of royalty while riding the chariots of fortune.
I want to have a good conscience to live in its rewards,
unashamed to stand in the full strength of the sun.
What I once thought of as failure
is but a step further toward the goal
of my higher calling in you,
and I humbly thank you, Jesus, with my whole heart.

He turned the desert into pools of water
and the parched ground into flowing springs;
there he brought the hungry to live,
and they founded a city where they could settle.

Psalm 107:33 NIV

HIS WORDS TO ME

Soar Like the Eagles

You were born to soar like the eagle
through tumult and the thunder,
but without the power of My Word you're
stuck earthbound, trapped and flip-flopping
in your complaints and futile attempts to fly.
Proclaim today with authority:
I can do all things through Christ who strengthens me,

Speak the words I speak to you
out loud. Address the negative forces
that want to hold you back and keep you defeated
and struggling like a wounded bird.
Proclaim the power of My Word
in your life, and in the world.

I was born for my soul to soar like the eagles
through calm and tumult, but without you, Lord Jesus,
I'm stuck earth-bound.
Today I'll proclaim the power of your Word in my life
with the authority you've given me as a believer.
I can do all things through Christ who strengthens me.
I'm going to speak the words from Scripture out loud,
words of faith and supernatural power!
I'm going to address the negative forces
that try to hold me back and keep me
defeated like a struggling, wounded bird.
Today I proclaim the power of your Word in my life.
Without you I can do nothing.

"For as the rain and the snow come down from heaven
and do not return there but water the earth,
making it bring forth and sprout,
giving seed to the sower and bread to the eater,
so shall my word be that goes out from my mouth;
it shall not return to me empty,
but it shall accomplish that which I purpose,
and shall succeed in the thing for which I sent it."

Isaiah 55:10-11 ESV

HIS WORDS TO ME

Boundless Beauty

Don't settle for ashes
when I give you beauty.
Don't make your bed in shame
when I freely pardon you.
Freely you've received—now freely give.
Today, be like the farmer
who throws his seed
into the wet, fertile ground and then waits
for it to sprout, grow, and multiply.
Take a calculated and wise step forward,
like the farmer, and plant your gifts to those in need
without fear of loss—without fear
of your future.
I have plenty to give from the space of *your faith*,
not from your pocket.
You do the giving, and supernaturally,
I'll do the multiplying back to you.

MY WORDS TO HIM

I'm not going to settle for ashes
when you give me boundless beauty.
I'm not going to make my bed in shame
when you've generously and freely pardoned me.
Freely I've received from you, and freely
I'm going to give back.
Today I'll be like the farmer who throws his seed
into the damp, fertile ground expecting it
to sprout, grow, and multiply.
I'm taking a calculated and wise step forward like the farmer,
and I'm planting my gifts for those in need.
I'm without fear of loss and without fear for my future.
You have plenty to give to the space of my faith.
It's not my pocketbook that supports my faith, it's you!
When I do the giving as guided by your Spirit,
you supernaturally multiply blessings back to me.

"Give, and it will be given to you. They will pour into your
lap a good measure—pressed down, shaken together, and
running over. For by your standard of measure it will be
measured to you in return."

Luke 6:38 NASB

HIS WORDS TO ME

My Inner Character

I care about you
and I care about your inner character.
You can't be happy without
good inner character;
success and lasting happiness will always be
an arm's length away.
Without character you'll live
a less-than fulfilled life.
Everything depends on what you do
with the time and what I've given you.
Will you study to show yourself approved
by Me, or will you fill your hours with empty
pursuits that only make you old?
Will you let Me direct the affairs of your life?
I say allow Me to teach you the higher way,
ever guiding you with wisdom so you'll rise up
successful, richly noble, and with a golden character.

Thank you, Lord Jesus, for caring about me
and for caring about my inner character!
You've taught me there's no happiness without
good inner character.
Success and lasting happiness
will always be a million miles away without character.
I don't want to live less than a fulfilled life, Jesus.
I realize everything depends on what I do
with the time that you've given me.
I'll study to show myself I'm approved by you,
and I'll fill my hours with the pursuits that honor you.
I'm giving you permission to direct
the affairs of my life today.
Teach me the higher way, ever guiding me with wisdom,
so I'll rise up successful, richly noble,
and with a golden character to honor you.

Do not love the world or the things in the world. If anyone
loves the world, the love of the Father is not in him. For all
that is in the world—the lust of the flesh, the lust of the eyes,
and the pride of life—is not of the Father but is of the world.
And the world is passing away, and the lust of it; but he who
does the will of God abides forever.

1 John 2:15-17 NKJV

HIS WORDS TO ME

Lacking Nothing

I've given you a gift to help others
and you lack nothing to go forward
in your calling.
Stop thinking of yourself as
weak and unproductive, for I am
empowering you to do great things.
Will you oppose Me?
I know your capabilities
I know your physical limitations.
I know your responsibilities
and I know your every need.
Not all of My gifts are perfect for each of My children,
so I give the gifts appropriately.
If you feel you lack the strength or courage
to fulfill your calling, ask Me for help.
My Holy Spirit is at the center
of every God-called ministry.
You can rest assured you have all the power and courage
you need for every task I give you.

MY WORDS TO HIM

Thank you, Jesus, for helping me to stop
thinking of myself as weak and unproductive.
I lack nothing to go forward in my calling
and using the gifts you've given me to help others.
You're empowering me to do great things.
I won't oppose you! You know every one
of my needs and my responsibilities.
You know my capabilities,
and you know my physical limitations.
You give gifts appropriately to each of your children.
When I lack the strength or courage to continue on,
you're right there to help my weakness.
Your Holy Spirit is at the center of every God–called ministry.
I'm at rest with assurance that I have
all the power and courage I need for every task
you give me, and for this I'm so grateful.
My heart is aflame with gratitude.

"My grace is enough for you. When you are weak,
my power is made perfect in you."

2 Corinthians 12:9 NCV

HIS WORDS TO ME

Night Hours

Remember, I'm your Lord in the night hours
as well as in the bright hours of the day.
I'm in control
of every hour of your life.
I'm the giver of light,
and no darkness shall succeed in battering you.
The devil has no authority to taunt
and torment you in the night hours.
I'm Lord of every hour, night and day.
In the black night of the soul,
I'm there. I outshine the night.
Give the dark hours to Me.

You're my Lord in the night hours
as well as in the bright hours of the day.
You're in control of every hour of my life.
You're the giver of light and no darkness
shall succeed in battering me.
The devil has no authority to taunt and torment me
in the night hours.
You're the Lord of every hour, both night and day.
The blackness of a starless night
is like a hungry soul without direction, but you're there.
You outshine the blackest night.
I give the dark hours to you to bless my sleep,
and to kiss my dreaming moments.
I open my heart and mind to you in the night hours,
so there's no intrusion of anything outside your love
and watchful care.
Speak to me in my slumber, Lord.
It's your voice, and your voice only, I long to hear.
Thank you, Jesus for a sweet night's sleep in your arms.

If you sit down, you will not be afraid;
when you lie down, your sleep will be sweet.

Proverbs 3:24 NRSV

HIS WORDS TO ME

Gift of Time

I've given you the gift of time.
Remember, I don't live in your time realm,
so it's important that the hours of your day
are treated as sacred gifts.
Your success depends on what you do with the time
I've given you.
I can show you how to save time. I can show you
how to make each moment count, so that you don't
spin your wheels on the trivial stuff of life.
I can show you how to avoid exhausting yourself
for no reward and a goal unachieved.
Time is meant to serve you.
Allow Me to be your divine time manager
and watch My help, wisdom, and guidance go to work.

Thank you, Jesus, for giving me the gift of time.
Heaven and earth exist in separate time realms,
so it's important that the hours of my day
are treated as sacred gifts.
My success depends on what I do
with the time that you've given me.
You can show me how to save and cherish time.
You can show me how to make each moment count,
so I don't spin my wheels on the trivial stuff of life
that goes nowhere.
Time is meant to serve you, Lord.
Be my divine time manager and cause your wisdom,
and your guidance to work in me today.

You will arise and have compassion on Zion,
for it is time to show favor to her;
the appointed time has come.

Psalm 102:13 NIV

HIS WORDS TO ME

No Holes in Time

There are no missing fragments or holes in time when you're
Mine.
All is perfect in My timing.
There are no second-hand promises in My kingdom,
no expired guarantees.
There's no down-sizing in heaven's economy,
no lay-offs or walking papers—
there's never a lull in activity;
never is a single moment lost.
Time can't stray with Me,
can't disappear and drop off-course
into the abyss.
Think of yourself in terms of the immortal clock,
one that never reads "too late."
Not a single hour passes unheralded by Me.
I AM GOD.
I possess all time and I control all.

There are no missing fragments or holes in time
because all of time belongs to you.
I belong to you. All is perfect in your timing.
There are no second-hand promises in your kingdom,
no expired guarantees.
There's no downsizing in heaven's economy,
no lay-offs or walking papers.
There's never a lull in activity,
and never is a single moment lost.
Time can't stray with you, Jesus.
It can't disappear and drop off-course into an abyss.
Today, I'll think of myself
in terms of the immortal clock,
one that never reads "too late."
Not a single hour will pass by me unheralded.
Thank you, Jesus.
Thank you, Father God.
Thank you, Holy Spirit!
You process all of time, and you control all.

This is all the more urgent,
for you know how late it is;
time is running out.

Romans 13:11 NLT

259

HIS WORDS TO ME

Bringing My Hurts

My child, bring your hurts to Me.
There are so many things that hurt you,
and you don't understand why.
Remember David in the Bible,
who couldn't understand
why the wicked prospered
and why I didn't rub them out.
Now you're asking the same:
why do I allow good people to get hurt?
Darling, evil people will go on
interminably performing their evil tricks
in the theatre of life,
but let Me assure you, when the curtain
comes down,
there's Me to face.
Let Me comfort your hurts
even if you don't understand everything at this time.
I have something better for you
than what you've lost.

MY WORDS TO HIM

Oh Lord Jesus, today I bring my hurts to you.
There are so many things that can hurt me,
and sometimes I just don't understand
why things happen as they do and why
people do the things they do.
I love the Bible story of David, who asked why
the wicked prosper and why didn't you
just rub them all out.
Now I seem to be asking the same question.
Oh dearest Lord,
evil will go on interminably in the theater of life,
but I want to rest in your assurance that
when the curtain comes down, there's you to face.
I'm thankful for your comfort today, Lord.
Thank you for assuaging my hurts even when
I don't understand everything at this time.
I know you have something better
for us than what's been lost.
I trust you!

Be still before the Lord and wait patiently for him;
fret not yourself over the one who prospers in his way,
over the man who carries out evil devices!

Psalm 37:7 ESV

HIS WORDS TO ME

In Control

I'm in control of all things in your life,
I'm in control through thick and thin,
gain and loss, sweet and vile.
I'm in control in the shadowy seasons of life
when you can't see the road ahead.
I'm there,
and in control.
I'm neither vision nor hearing impaired.
Nothing escapes My keen observation.
I know all, see all, hear all—I AM all!
The light of My love shines in your soul
this day.

MY WORDS TO HIM

Thank you, Jesus, for being in control of all things in my life.
Thank you for being in control
through thick and thin, gain and loss, sweet and vile.
Thank you for being in control in the shadowy seasons
of life when I can't see the road ahead.
You're here and you're in control.
You aren't vision impaired
and you aren't hearing impaired.
Nothing escapes your keen observation.
You know all, see all, hear all—you *are* all!
You are the great I Am.
In you, I'm made secure and strong.

Do you not know? Have you not heard?
The Everlasting God, the LORD, the Creator of the ends of the
earth
Does not become weary or tired.
His understanding is inscrutable.
He gives strength to the weary,
And to him who lacks might He increases power.

Isaiah 40:28-29 NASB

HIS WORDS TO ME

Holy Ears

Come with Me and listen with holy ears.
Did you know I talk to Myself?
Yes, I talk to Myself.
In the beginning I created all of creation with
My words, "Let there be,"
and I pronounced, "It is good," to *Myself.*
Heaven hears Me speak and
knows My thoughts.
My prophets hear My thoughts, and hear Me speak.
Moses spoke with Me face to face
and in the fire, thunder, lightning flashes,
the smoking mountain, and the blare of the shofar,
he heard Me perfectly.
My servant Job heard Me speak in a storming whirlwind.
Elijah heard Me through a tornado, an earthquake, and fire.
Today, in the loving silence of your heart,
your ears will caress My voice.
I'll open the secret chambers
of My thoughts to you if you'll still your mind,
and listen.

Today, I come to you to listen with holy ears.
I didn't realize that you actually talk to yourself.
In the beginning you created all of creation
with your words, "Let there be," and then
you pronounced, "It is good" to *yourself.*
Heaven hears you speak.
Your prophets hear you speak.
Moses spoke with you face to face in the fire,
thunder, lightning flashes, the smoking mountain,
and in the blare of the shofar, he heard you perfectly.
Your servant, Job, heard you speak in a storming whirlwind.
Elijah heard you through a tornado, an earthquake, and fire.
Today, in the loving silence of my heart,
my ears long to caress your voice.
Thank you for opening the secret chambers
of your thoughts when I'm quiet and listening.
I praise you and thank you that in stillness you're more present
to me than any other time.

Thus says the Lord God, the Holy One of Israel:
"In returning and rest you shall be saved;
In quietness and confidence shall be your strength."

Isaiah 30:15 NKJV

HIS WORDS TO ME

Fixed Forever

Every promise of Mine
is established in heaven forever
and will come to pass.
When I decree a decree it shall surely come to pass.
When I deliver a command,
no human or demon can withstand My power
to it to pass.
I command a blessing on you now.
I always bring My blessings into being.
I declare to you this day
that it's My will you be blessed.
It's My will that you fulfill your divine purposes
and accomplish all that I require of you
and more!

I am so thankful, Lord Jesus, that every promise
of yours is fixed forever.
When you decree a decree it shall surely come to pass.
When you deliver a command, no human or demon
can withstand your power for it to come to pass.
You command blessings and courage to your children,
and I thank you!
I thank you that I, in turn, can be strong, and a blessing.
I know it's your will that I move forward to fulfill
your divine purposes in my life.
You want me to accomplish your goals,
and I'm so grateful for the privilege of being
a human home for your Holy Spirit.
All I want is your will be done.
Thank you for calling and anointing me to live within
the limitless boundaries of your will.
Thank you, for your promises that give me the strength, courage,
wisdom, and holy ability to fulfill your will.

I will make what I have said come true;
I will do what I have planned.

Isaiah 46:11 NCV

HIS WORDS TO ME

Guiding Me Perfectly

Don't worry. I'm guiding you.
I'm showing you which way to go.
Your divine counselor, My Holy Spirit,
is right beside you guiding and gently advising
you on the action to take in this moment.
You're being empowered to act in divine wisdom
and integrity.
Keep your eyes on Me knowing that My power
is limitless,
and that My mercy is without measure.
You're a mighty warrior in My army,
and I've anointed and blessed you
for this hour of decision.

MY WORDS TO HIM

Thank you, Jesus, for guiding me perfectly today.
Thank you for showing me which steps
to take, and which to avoid.
You're my divine counselor and travel guide.
Thank you for empowering me to act
with divine wisdom and integrity.
I'll keep my eyes on you today for direction,
knowing that your wisdom is limitless,
and your mercy is without measure.
Thank you for your Holy Spirit who gently leads me toward
the best actions to take at this moment.
Thank you for blessing me in this hour of decision.

"When the Spirit of truth comes, he will guide you into all
the truth; for he will not speak on his own, but will speak
whatever he hears, and he will declare to you the things that
are to come."

John 16:13 NRSV

HIS WORDS TO ME

Lifting Me Up

Yes, I know that the world is filled
with greedy, selfish people
who are out to get what they can get at any cost.
But you, beloved, are not one of them.
I tell you, rise up into the arms of the comforter,
turn your dear head heavenward and praise Me.
Take your eyes off the workers of iniquity and be amazed
at Me and what I'm doing on the earth today.
Make a goal to:
see beyond the obvious,
live beyond the ordinary,
believe beyond the possible.
Go the extra mile and experience My miraculous power
in all you do,
and be amazed!

MY WORDS TO HIM

Oh Lord, thank you for lifting me up into the arms
of the Comforter and for turning my eyes heavenward.
When I look at the world filled with turmoil,
suffering and bloodshed, my heart aches.
Thank you that I'm no longer the worrying person I was.
I praise you and thank you!
I stand amazed at you
and what you're doing on the earth today.
I'm focusing on you and not on the evils of the world.
I'll make it a goal to see beyond the obvious,
to live beyond the ordinary,
and to believe beyond the possible.
Lord Jesus, help me go the extra mile
and experience your miraculous power
in all I see, do, and stand for.
You're on the throne as King of kings and Lord of lords,
and I trust you, totally and completely.

"They will wage war against the Lamb, but the Lamb will
triumph over them because he is Lord of lords and King of
kings—and with him will be his called, chosen and faithful
followers."

Revelation 17:14 NIV

HIS WORDS TO ME

Pain of Rejection

I understand the pain of rejection.
I came to the world to bless the world, and
I was rejected, beaten and murdered.
I came to the world to show a better way
only to be ostracized for My love. I came to My own
and My own didn't want Me, tossed Me out,
and crucified Me.
When you're rejected, you share My sufferings,
and those who suffer with Me reign with Me.
Don't think it odd that you're rejected.
The servant isn't greater than his lord.
I possess a treasure house of blessings
with your name on it. These blessings, lovingly
selected by Me just for you, will more than make up
for your grief.
Identify with Me and be strong.
You and I
share a rare and beautiful intimacy.
You see, I took your disappointment, anguish, and grief
on My body on the cross.
Rejection has lost its power over you.

MY WORDS TO HIM

Thank you, Jesus, for understanding the pain of rejection.
When you came into the world to bless the world
you were rejected, beaten, and murdered.
You came to the world to show human beings the holy
and loving heart of our Father God only to be ostracized.
You came to your own and your own didn't want you;
they tossed you out and they crucified you.
When I'm rejected, I know that you understand.
Often I suffer needlessly with worry.
For this I repent.
You possess a treasure house of blessings with my name on it,
and far more does your love make up for my hurt feelings.
I choose to identify with you and be strong.
I choose to appreciate anew the rare
and beautiful intimacy I have with you.
You took all my disappointments, grief, and sorrows
on your body at Calvary.
Today I'm proclaiming that rejection has lost its power over me.

No one can know a person's thoughts except that person's own
spirit, and no one can know God's thoughts except God's own
Spirit. And we have received God's Spirit (not the world's spirit),
so we can know the wonderful things God has freely given us.

1 Corinthians 2:11-12 NLT

HIS WORDS TO ME

Greatest Temptation

Your greatest temptation is not the one
that solicits your consent to obvious sin,
but the one that hands you evil in the guise of good.
I want you to be wise and remove
the confusion between godliness and naïveté.
Good deeds are not always
what they seem.
Good deeds may take you
where I haven't called you,
and to people I haven't called you to.
I don't want you beguiled by the appearance
of good and temporary gratification.
I have so much better for you.
Wisdom and discernment will guide you
into that which is permanent
and blessed.
I want you blessed.

MY WORDS TO HIM

My greatest temptation is not the one that solicits
my consent to obvious sin.
It's the one that hands me evil in the guise of good.
I'm really thankful to you today, Lord,
for helping me to remove
the confusion between godliness and naïveté.
Good deeds aren't always what they seem,
as you've taught me.
Good deeds may take me
where you haven't called me and to people
you haven't called me to.
I'm choosing right now not to get beguiled
by the appearance of good and temporary gratification.
You have so much better for me!
Wisdom and discernment will guide me.
Thank you for showering me
with the blessings that scatter the temptations.

"Watch and pray that you may not enter into temptation. The
spirit indeed is willing, but the flesh is weak."

Matthew 26:41 ESV

HIS WORDS TO ME

Throes of Indecision

When you stand at a crossroad
in the throes of indecision,
examine carefully the implication
of your choices.
The first path is inked with
yesterday's familiar patterns.
The second path beckons with a tomorrow
shaded by the unknown.
The mean and lonely path with few rewards
requires the humblest heart,
and the path of sacrifice and starlit tears
can be the most blessed.
The hostile path of thorns and prayers
is the one for those who love the most.

The words *well done* from My throne,
more sublime than life itself,
sovereign, incomparable, unequaled,
are distanced only if stained
by the groans of fear and turning back.
The choice will be yours.

MY WORDS TO HIM

When I stand at a crossroad in the throes of indecision,
I'll examine carefully the implication of my choices.
The first path is inked with yesterday's familiar patterns.
The second path beckons with tomorrow's shaded unknown.
There's another path, a higher one
that appears mean and lonely with few rewards.
This path requires the humblest heart;
it's a path of sacrifice and starlit tears,
and it can be the most blessed path in life.
This is the path I want to travel.
The path can be hostile, lined with thorns and storms;
it can be fraught with trials and the necessity to stand strong
and resolute at all times.
It's the path for those who love you the most.
I won't be afraid.
I want to live with faith that moves mountains.
I live to hear the words "well done" from your throne,
more sublime than life itself.
Those words are sovereign, incomparable, unequaled.
Today I choose you and your perfect path for me.

"His master said to him, 'Well done, good and faithful slave.
You were faithful with a few things, I will put you in charge of
many things; enter into the joy of your master.'"

Matthew 25:21 NASB

277

HIS WORDS TO ME

Suffering Shrine

If you gathered all your tears together in one place
and formed an ocean of them,
what name should we give
this great body of salty water?
If we called it simply *yours*,
that's how it'll remain: yours.
Your bitter sea will be all yours.
But! If you give your tears to Me,
the sea becomes Mine and I'll make it a blessing
to sail answered prayer upon.
Every earth-bound shrine comes to nothing
when it remains earth-bound.
Don't use your tears as a weapon or a
harbinger of doom.
Give them to Me gift-wrapped
as a love offering.

MY WORDS TO HIM

Every earthbound suffering shrine comes to nothing
if it remains earthbound.
My tears could form an ocean, but without you,
they'd remain mine.
All mine. But!
When I give my tears to you, the ocean becomes yours,
and you make it a blessing to sail answered prayer upon!
I'm choosing today to no longer use my tears as a weapon
of self-pity or a harbinger of doom.
I'm giving my tears to you, Jesus, gift-wrapped
and tied with a ribbon as a love offering.
Only you know what to do with them.
Yes, Lord, turn my tears to prayers of thanksgiving.
What a relief it is to praise and thank you! I feel set free!

You have turned for me my mourning into dancing;
You have put off my sackcloth and clothed me with gladness,

Psalm 30:11 NKJV

HIS WORDS TO ME

High Calling

Loneliness is not so terrible, dear child.
My high calling for you
includes a certain amount of loneliness—
and also separation from sin
and removing yourself from the worldly pleasures
that wilt the heart and dry up the spirit.
You're My chosen one;
the old vacuous, cheap patterns of life no longer fit you.
You've thrown off the old ill-fitting coat
for your one-of-a-kind Holy Spirit designer robe.
Just look at you!
Loneliness won't last for long, dear one,
when you see in the spirit that you're surrounded
by a great and enormous cloud of delighted friends
as witnesses loving you and cheering you on.

MY WORDS TO HIM

Thank you for my high calling, which includes
a certain amount of loneliness.
Loneliness is not so terrible, Lord.
Thank you for setting me
apart to be separated from sin, and I now
remove myself from the old worldly pleasures
that wilt the heart and dry up the spirit.
Thank you for making me one of your chosen ones.
The old vacuous, cheap patterns of life no longer fit me.
I've thrown off that ill-fitting coat
for your one-of-a-kind Holy Spirit designer robe.
Loneliness won't last long, Jesus, because
I've found that solitude is a great gift.
I'm learning your magnificent language of *silence*.
The silence of my mind helps diminish
the clutter of daily life around me.
In silence I can see things more clearly,
and feel the wonder and peace of your presence.
I am never lonely when I'm with you.

I find rest in God;
only he gives me hope.

Psalm 62:5 NCV

HIS WORDS TO ME

Hold Me Close

Let Me hold you close to increase and renew
your enthusiasm and your love
for Me. Let Me love you and talk to you
in our sweet communion.
Don't be impatient in times of spiritual dryness—
be still and listen.
Hear what I have to say to you
and allow My consolations
to reach deep inside to the place where
you find yourself weary of spirit.
I never leave you or forsake you,
so when you feel bereft, alone, and
forsaken, it may be because of *your* distance
from Me, not *My* distance from you.
Come.
Climb into My arms today.

Jesus, hold me close.
Increase and renew my enthusiasm and my passion for you.
Give me an open-minded heart
to receive your love and to talk openly and honestly
with you in our sweet communion every single day.
I don't want to be impatient in times of spiritual dryness.
I'll be still and listen as you have taught me to do.
I don't want to do all the talking.
I want to hear what you have to say to me.
I want to allow your consolations to reach
deep inside to the place where I find myself
weary of spirit at times.
You'll never leave me nor forsake me,
so when I feel alone and forsaken I realize
it may be because of my distance from you,
not your distance from me.
Today I come, Jesus, and I climb into your arms
where I'm heard and completely, unconditionally loved.

"The LORD appeared to him from far away.
I have loved you with an everlasting love;
therefore I have continued my faithfulness to you."

Jeremiah 31:3 NRSV

HIS WORDS TO ME

Never Forsake

Never forsake
your high calling in Me
for the empty rewards
of those who bargain for your soul
with cheap offers, putrid and foul
in the stench of the sun.
Oh so tempting, the counterfeit promises are that
strangle your beauty, and kill your soul.
You're My chosen vessel,
My sweet adorable treasure.
I've chosen you for Myself
so together we can soar to high places,
dance on mountain tops,
sing with the angels,
thrill to the wonder of My creation,
and multiply everlasting joy.
Honor your calling, My beloved—
Stay close to Me.

Jesus, help me to never forsake my higher calling in you
for the empty rewards of those who bargain for my soul
with cheap offers of happiness.
The counterfeit promises can be oh so tempting,
but they strangle my beauty and kill my soul.
I'm your chosen vessel, and you call me your beloved one!
Today I thank you for choosing me
for yourself so together we can soar to high places,
dance on mountaintops, sing with the angels, thrill to the wonders
of your creation, and by your Spirit, multiply joy.
Help me to honor my calling, ever and always,
to stay close to you!

You shall walk after the LORD your God and fear Him,
and keep His commandments and obey His voice;
you shall serve Him and hold fast to Him.

Deuteronomy 13:4 NKJV

HIS WORDS TO ME

Created Works

Pause today to enjoy My created works.
Admire the glory of the sunrise,
and My painted sunset skies.
Look for the lonely evening star,
and observe Orion's royal command of night skies.
Can you listen for the roar
of the ocean's petulant waves,
the slippery ripple of the clear, stony brook?
Watch the grace of a swan in still water,
touch the horse's knitted mane,
hold the newborn baby and feel its breath on your chin?
I'm in every cell of every living creature,
and in every molecule you breathe.
I'm joyous in My creation, for it's all for you.
Today, let's celebrate life together.

MY WORDS TO HIM

Lord Jesus, today I pause to enjoy your created works.
I pause to admire the glory of the sunrise
and your painted sunset skies.
Today I praise you for the lovely evening star
as I observe Orion's royal command of the night skies.
I thank you today for the roar of the ocean's petulant waves,
the slippery ripple of the clear, stony brook.
Thank you for the grace of a swan in still water,
and the touch of a horse's knitted mane.
Thank you for the newborn baby's breath on her mother's chin.
Thank you for every cell of every living creature,
and for every molecule I breathe.
I'm joyous in your creation, for I know that it's all for us,
your children.
Today I celebrate life!

Ever since the world was created, people have seen the earth
and sky. Through everything God made, they can clearly see
his invisible qualities—his eternal power and divine nature. So
they have no excuse for not knowing God.

Romans 1:20 NLT

HIS WORDS TO ME

Save Me

When you entertain the houseguest called self-pity,
you'll be left with a messy living room.
Self-pity is a thoughtless and solipsistic visitor;
it'll ruin your towels and eat all your food. It'll keep you up at
night
and wreck your stuff. Self-pity is a killer of joy;
it smells bad.
Self-pity is an unkempt pile of junk that rolls
out of garbage dumps, and chases your friends away.
Nobody wants to be friends with the person
who cohabits with self-pity.
Ugh!
Today, order self-pity out of your house and
out of your dear heart. Remember, I see everything,
and I know everything. I'm here every day
to load your life with benefits
and open My storehouses of goodness to you!
Put up the "No Vacancy" sign to self-pity today.

MY WORDS TO HIM

Dear Jesus, save me from self-pity.
Self-pity kills my joy.
You see everything, Lord, and you know everything.
You're the master of the universe and ruler of all that exists.
Nothing escapes your loving, omnipotent, omniscient,
omnipresent eye.
Today I pledge to order self-pity out of my life.
You're here every day to load me with benefits
and to open your storehouses of goodness to me!
I'll concentrate on your goodness and stop
feeling sorry for myself when things get difficult.
I choose to see the touch of your loving kindness
and tender mercy in the world.
I hand all my personal problems and doubts over to you.
Thank you for setting me free!

Therefore do not throw away your confidence, which has a
great reward.

Hebrews 10:35 ESV

HIS WORDS TO ME

Thrilling Life

Don't be too hungry for the world's adventure,
for easy affection,
for tasty morsels that vanish in the morning sun.
The pursuits for temporary pleasures
will entrap you and you'll squirm and kick
to get free, but the chains of bondage
are crushing.
Come to Me for a thrilling life,
for adventure beyond the world's offering.
Listen to Me and you'll live in
divine affection, embraced in the security
of My love.
In Me you're a new creation;
you're delivered from old sins
and so-called fun habits
that were out to shatter you.
You have a *new life* now
and a new hope.
You have an eternal exciting life in Me.
I've planted you securely in
My heart and My arms.

MY WORDS TO HIM

Thank you, Lord, for the thrilling life
you offer to those who love you.
Thank you for removing my hunger
for temporary adventure and easy affection.
Thank you for setting me free from chasing after
tasty morsels that vanish in the morning light.
Thank you, Jesus, for delivering me from the pursuits
of temporary pleasures that entrap, chain, and crush the soul.
I love being secure in your love and your purposes.
In you, I'm a new person! I'm delivered from old sins
and habits that would have, sooner or later, destroyed me.
I have a new life now and a new hope!
I have an eternal, exciting life in you
because I'm planted in your heart and in your arms.
Thank you, oh thank you!

Therefore, if anyone is in Christ, he is a new creation; old
things have passed away; behold, all things have become new.

2 Corinthians 5:17 NKJV

HIS WORDS TO ME

Valley of Adversity

Pause, dear one,
and rest for a moment with Me.
When you pass through the valley of adversity,
your thoughts can contort and meander;
your energy can thin out and deplete,
but I'm here to lift you up.
I won't let you fall. I'll keep you in perfect peace
if you'll let Me.
I'll enliven and invigorate your mind.
Today, allow Me to breathe My sweet fresh breath
across your brow and stroke your dear cheek
with My peace. I'll restore quietness to your soul,
and renew your vision for the future.
My promises to you can't fail,
and for this reason you must lean into My arms
and rest.

When I stumble through the valley of adversity,
I thank you that you keep my thoughts from contorting
and meandering.
Thank you for keeping my energy
from depleting because you're right here to lift me
out of the swamp of fear and worry.
You won't let go of me!
You keep me in perfect peace!
Thank you for enlivening and invigorating my mind.
Thank you for breathing your sweet,
fresh breath across my brow and stroking my cheek
with your love.
Thank you for restoring quietness to my soul
and renewing my vision for the future.
Your promises can't fail,
and for this reason I lean into your arms and rest.

The eternal God is your refuge,
And underneath are the everlasting arms;
He will thrust out the enemy from before you.

Deuteronomy 33:27 NKJV

HIS WORDS TO ME

Since the Beginning

I've loved you since the beginning.
I formed you in your mother's womb.
I knew you before you existed,
so you can trust that I know
what's best for you.
You can trust that I know
how to guide you into maturity
and build character in you
worthy of heaven's delight.
Love your life today
and appreciate
My hand leading you.
I'm appointing you to a place of safety
and contentment.
Many afflictions can beat at the doors
of My chosen ones,
but I deliver you from each threat.

Thank you, Jesus, for knowing me and loving me
since the very beginning of time.
You formed me in my mother's womb,
so that means you must have
known who I'd be before you made me a living soul.
For this reason I can trust that you know
what's best for me in this life!
I trust you to know how to guide me into maturity
and build character in me
that's worthy of pleasing you and honoring my calling.
I love my life today and I appreciate your hand leading
me in the path you've chosen for me.
Thank you for appointing a place of faith, trust, and sublime
contentment for me.
Many afflictions can beat at the doors of your chosen ones,
but you deliver us from every threat!

You, LORD, do not be far from me.
You are my strength; come quickly to help me.

Psalm 22:19 NIV

HIS WORDS TO ME

Sharpening My Senses

I'm sharpening your senses today so you'll
become sensitive to the exquisite view
from the crest of heaven's mountain,
and gaze down on the great life
I've called you to live.
Is the highest purpose of your life
to fulfill the purposes *I've* called you to?
Can you be happy in the knowledge
that *I'm* in control of everything?
The secret place of your strength
is to believe and trust *Me*
because your efforts
without Me are like dust in the wind.
With Me
all things are possible.
Today, allow Me to carry out My plans.
You do your part, and I'll do Mine.

Thank you, Jesus, for sharpening my senses today
so I become sensitive to the exquisite view of life
from the windows of your Word.
It's like standing at the crest of heaven's mountain and peering out.
How marvelous to gaze down on the great life
you've called me to live.
Thank you for the high purpose you've called me to fulfill.
I'm so happy!
The secret of my strength is to believe and trust you
because my exhausting efforts without you
are like dust in the wind.
With you all things are possible.
Today, I pledge to open my heart and mind to give
you space to carry out your plans for my life.
I promise to do my part because I know you'll do yours.

"For I know the thoughts that I think toward you,"
says the LORD, "thoughts of peace and not of evil,
to give you a future and a hope."

Jeremiah 29:11 NKJV

HIS WORDS TO ME

Not Looking Back

Don't look back.
Hold Me close to your heart today
for I love you with a perfect love.
Look ahead
and envision the glorious future I've prepared for you.
You'll see that the present troubles
are in no way comparable to the glory ahead.
I'm leading you along the steep mountain roads
of faith. My Holy Spirit is composing
a living future life insurance plan
as we make the upward climb,
passing through the forest
of answered prayer.
Trees press their heads together
in approval as you continue *onward*,
not looking back.
This is living! Your future life insurance
is guaranteed with Me.

MY WORDS TO HIM

Today, I'm not looking back. I hold you close to my heart
because I know you love me with a perfect love.
I'm looking ahead, not back.
I'm envisioning the glorious future you've prepared for me.
I'm choosing to see that the present troubles
are in no way comparable to the glory ahead.
You're leading me along the steep mountain roads of faith.
Your Holy Spirit has composed a living life-assurance plan
for me as we make the upward climb
into the forest of answered prayer.
Trees press their heads together
in approval as I continue onward not looking back.
This is living!
My future life assurance is guaranteed!

"If you love me, keep my commands. Whoever has my
commands and keeps them is the one who loves me. The one
who loves me will be loved by my Father, and I too will love
them and show myself to them."

John 14:15, 21 NIV

HIS WORDS TO ME

Praise and Worship

When you sing to Me
you present Me with your heart,
which I treasure.
Your songs of praise
are a wonderful and sacred gift
to Me, and they bring Me much joy.
There's a special castle in heaven
with hundreds of rooms
for you to fill with your songs of praise.
I love to join you in song. I dance about,
robes flying, laughing, and happy.
I stroke your head and rejoice when
you know Me for who I am.

I love to hear the music that lifts you up in praise
and worship, Jesus.
I sing my songs of praise to you
as a sacred gift to honor you and bring you joy.
Oh, how I honor and adore you!
I pray there's a special castle in heaven
with hundreds of rooms to fill with my songs of praise.
I love to imagine you joining in song and dancing
about, robes flying, laughing, and happy.
I sometimes feel you stroke my head, rejoicing with me
because I know you for who you are:
King of kings and Lord of lords,
Son of God, Prince of Peace, Savior of the world.
Oh, how I love you!

Praise the LORD!
How good to sing praises to our God!
How delightful and how fitting!

Psalm 147:1 NLT

HIS WORDS TO ME

Shaping Love

I love you with a love
that shaped the universe.
How delightful
is the dawn of your tender heart
toward Me.
I'm the lover of your soul.
Living in My love endorses your zeal
to accomplish more
and to prosper beyond the natural.
Because you love Me,
I give you the authority
to ascend the stairway of success,
for as your spirit soars,
so will the blessings abound around you
and your house.
Honor Me in all you do,
and I will do the rest.

MY WORDS TO HIM

Thank you, Jesus, for loving me
with a love that shaped the universe.
You're the lover of my soul and I live
in the embrace of your all-consuming love.
You've given me authority to ascend
the stairway of success, for as my spirit soars,
so do the blessings abound around me and my house.
I honor you in all I do, Lord Jesus.
Thank you for being the artist
to complete the picture of my life on earth.

Oh, taste and see that the Lord is good!
Blessed is the man who takes refuge in him!

Psalm 34:8 ESV

HIS WORDS TO ME

Live in the Truth

Today, put an end to the shallow, polluted threats
of danger and doom that want to harass you.
Remember, I've given you a *new* mind to know
and live in the *truth*.
Remember, I've given you a purified, brilliant mind,
and this makes you smarter than the world.
I've made you so smart that when My thoughts of truth,
blessing, and empowerment enter you,
they rejuvenate every cell of your being,
and you become seriously happy.

Thank you, Jesus, for giving me a new mind
to know and live in the truth.
You've given me a purified, brilliant mind
and this makes me smarter than the world.
You've made me so smart that when your thoughts
of truth, blessing, and empowerment enter me,
they rejuvenate every cell of my being
and I become totally happy.
Yes, Lord Jesus,
on this, the last day of the month,
I choose to be grateful and totally happy
just because I'm yours!

I will rejoice greatly in the LORD,
My soul will exult in my God.

Isaiah 61:10 NASB

HIS WORDS TO ME

Be Careful

Be careful with your heart today.
The unruliness of the human heart
always seeks its own.
Pleasure is the god
of the unrepentant, unruly heart.
But your heart surrendered to Me
has been made miraculously pure,
and it's kept that way by the power of your choices.
I've given you many spiritual gifts
to live your life triumphantly.
I've given you My Word to instruct, enrich,
and empower you to overcome every obstacle
and to rise up empowered with spiritual discernment
and understanding.
Your choices dictate the quality of your faith
and your level of intimacy with Me.
Pay attention to My invisible spiritual nudgings
and to My words today.
My written Word is your daily fortification
to guide the decisions of your heart.

Thank you for teaching me to be careful
with my heart, Lord Jesus.
I realize the unruliness of the human heart
always seeks its own pleasure,
and worldly pleasure is the god of the unruly heart.
But I've chosen to surrender my heart to you,
and you've made me miraculously pure!
My heart is swept clean by the power of your Spirit,
and I've chosen to live for you!
You've given me so many beautiful
spiritual gifts so I can live my life in triumph.
You've given me your Word to instruct, enrich, and empower me
to overcome every obstacle and to rise up wise with spiritual
discernment and understanding.
You've taught me that my choices dictate the quality
of my faith and my level of intimacy with you.
I'll pay attention to your spiritual nudging and your words today.
Your written word is my daily fortification
to guide the decisions of my heart.

Your laws are my treasure;
they are my heart's delight.

Psalm 119:111 NLT

HIS WORDS TO ME

Facing Decisions

You're facing decisions, and today, as you face these decisions
you sense a pondering in the spirit, an uncomfortable
pinch in your belly—stop and listen.
Don't be hasty with your actions,
just listen. Observe.
I speak to you in many ways.
Pay attention
to My invisible spiritual nudgings.
My Word is your daily fortification
to guide you in the decisions you make,
and when you feel ill at ease or confused,
pause and know that I want to help guide you.
What looks good may not always be the right choice.
Be aware that your flesh can be a dangerous influence, always
hungrily seeking its own gratification.
Be wise.
Take a Holy Spirit break.
Listen for My voice which you'll recognize
as I speak to your heart from a place deep inside you:
"*This* is the way. Walk in in it."

MY WORDS TO HIM

Lord, as I face some decisions I feel nervousness rising up,
a pondering in my spirit, an uncomfortable pinch in my belly—
and these are my sign to stop and listen.
I don't want to be hasty with my actions.
I'll be quiet.
I'll listen.
I'll observe.
You speak to me in many ways.
I want to pay attention to your Word
that guides me in the decisions I make.
When I feel uncomfortable or confused, I'll pause,
knowing that you want to help guide me.
What looks good may not always be the right choice.
Help me be aware that my flesh can be a dangerous influence,
always hungrily seeking its own gratification.
Help me be wise, and show me when to take a break.
I'll listen for your voice, which I'll recognize
as you speak to my heart from a place deep inside me.
I'll hear, "This is the way. Walk in it."

"Indeed, the kingdom of God is within you."

Luke 17:21 NKJV

HIS WORDS TO ME

Led by Emotions

Avoid being led by your emotions today.
Worldly circumstances, situations, and relationships
are best relegated to the realm
of My Holy Spirit for wisdom, guidance, and strength.
Stand strong today with firm footing,
solidly grounded in Me.
It's too convenient to take the easy route,
too easy to bow the knee
to circumstances and situations designed
to topple My child off the rock of faith.
I tell you, remain unshakably locked to Me!
Relationships may tug at your heart
to pull you away, but when you're solidly rooted in Me,
you won't wobble, wiggle, and topple,
no matter how tempting it may be.
There'll be trials and testing, but I promise you,
a resolute heart overcomes, and when your heart is fixed
on *our* relationship, you'll be stronger,
and more empowered.

Thank you, Jesus, for showing me how to avoid
being led by my emotions today.
Thank you for teaching me
that worldly circumstances, situations, and relationships
are best relegated to the realm of your Holy Spirit
for wisdom and guidance.
I'll stand strong today with firm footing, solidly grounded in you.
It's too convenient to take the easy route, too easy
to bow the knee to circumstances and situations
that look good, but are designed to topple me off
the rock of faith.
Thank you for saving me when
relationships tug at my heart to pull me away.
I'll stay solidly rooted in you and remain unshakably
locked to you!
In this safe, happy place I won't wobble, wiggle, and topple,
no matter how tempting things may seem.
I know there'll be trials and testing,
but you've promised me that a resolute heart overcomes.
My heart is fixed on our relationship, and I'm stronger
and more empowered through every temptation I face.

No testing has overtaken you that is not common to everyone.
God is faithful, and he will not let you be tested beyond your
strength, but with the testing he will also provide the way out
so that you may be able to endure it.

1 Corinthians 10:13 NRSV

HIS WORDS TO ME

Designed Future

In My stable of futures I have one just for you.
Here, climb onto the sleek, smooth back of your future.
I don't give your future
to chance and luck to ride.
Those with weak spiritual vision can't see their future.
Those with weak knees can't confidently mount their future.
Those toting backpacks of envy and greed
weigh too much for a peaceful ride on their future,
and angry riders topple off at the first trot.

If you saddle up your future with anger or resentment,
you'll gallop backward.
If you become frustrated and impatient,
your future will leave the trail and take off for the hills.
If you complain and insult your future,
you'll lope through the woods of life exhausted and
lost, forever hungry and wondering why.
Your future is yours to ride.
Here are the reigns.
Chance and luck aren't in the saddle.
You are.

Thank you, Jesus, for the future you've designed just for me.
Thank you for not allowing my future
to depend upon luck or chance.
Today I'm going to be very mindful of the things
that put up road blocks
and thwart the beautiful future you've designed for me—
things like envy, greed, gossip, and a bad temper.
Help me not to become frustrated and impatient, Lord,
because my future won't flourish if I keep on complaining
and finding fault with everything.
My future is mine to live with victory and joy!
Help me to see that!
My future is secure in you, and I don't want to be
a victim of bad habits, or dependent on chance and luck.
I'm a child of the living God who makes all things
work together for good.
Help me to be transformed from the inside out
for your glory!

Do not be conformed to this world,
but be transformed by the renewing of your mind,
that you may prove what is that
good and acceptable and perfect will of God.

Romans 12:2 NKJV

HIS WORDS TO ME

Cave of Self-pity

I want you to come out of your cave of self-pity today
and join the world of authentic people who have needs
just like yours.
I've got believers all over the world
on intimate terms with angels
who pray day and night,
and they'd like to pray for *you*.
I didn't call you to sit alone watching TV
feeling sorry for yourself and eating
food fit for badgers.
You're My adorable child
and I love you!
I have a world out here for you
to love.

MY WORDS TO HIM

Thank you, Lord, for pulling me out
of my cave of self-pity.
Thank you for helping me join
the world of authentic people
with needs just like mine.
Thank you for reminding me
that you have believers all over the world,
and I'm not alone.
I know you didn't save me to keep me
sitting around by myself.
I know you want me to rise up strong
and reach out to touch others with love and hope.
Thank you, Jesus,
for opening my eyes and giving me a world to love.

"By this all will know that you are My disciples,
if you have love for one another."

John 13: 35 NKJV

HIS WORDS TO ME

Spiritually Mature

I have many things to show you,
many opportunities to give you,
many truths to reveal to you,
many gifts to offer you,
and miracles to bless you with.

The world is changing,
but I don't change.
Patterns of living are changing—
Mine don't change.
I want to show you things to come,
to prepare you to trust Me more.

I want you to know how to pray for results.
I want you to know how to prosper
through all circumstances.
Come close and give Me your attention
so I can lead and teach you to go higher.

Thank you, Jesus, for giving me
so many opportunities to become spiritually mature.
Thank you for showing me the many glorious
implications of faith,
and that loving you is at once simple and complex.
Thank you for taking me out of myself,
so I can be open to learning your ways and your heart.
You have so many gifts to offer me.
I'm surrounded by miracles.
I see the world around me changing, but you never change.
Patterns of living change, people change,
but you remain constant and sure.
Oh Jesus, show me how to prosper in all circumstances
as I learn to trust you more and more.
I love how you enter my soul
and teach me how to live in this world.
Thank you for your understanding and compassion!

We are from God. Whoever knows God listens to us;
whoever is not from God does not listen to us.
By this we know the Spirit of truth
and the spirit of error.

1 John 4:6 ESV

HIS WORDS TO ME

Opened Doors

It's time to move on.
I have opened new doors for you.
I'm pouring out new opportunities
and new avenues of possibility in order to
unleash the well of creative expression
inside you.
Circumstances have kept you hidden
behind a wall of choices that seemed
to be right at the time,
but now that wall is crumbling down,
setting you free, and the way ahead
is a spectacular
spiritual breakthrough.
Today, take that giant step
toward your radiant tomorrow.

MY WORDS TO HIM

Lord Jesus, it's time for me to move forward
and step through the doors you've opened before me.
You're pouring out new opportunities
and new avenues of possibility and unleashing
the well of creative expression inside me.
Thank you!
You're crumbling the walls I've built up around me
that have hindered me.
You're setting me free!
Oh Lord, I can see that the way ahead
is spectacular with spiritual breakthrough.
Thank you for showing me to take a giant step forward
toward my radiant tomorrow!

For from days of old they have not heard or perceived by ear,
Nor has the eye seen a God besides You,
Who acts in behalf of the one who waits for Him.

Isaiah 64:4 NASB

HIS WORDS TO ME

Give You Everything

Give Me your best and your worst today.
Give Me your dreams.
Give Me your appetites and your hopes.
Give ALL to Me.
Trust Me to know what I'm doing.
I alone make your dreams come true,
and I alone know how to handle your appetites.
I turn your hopes to reality.
Be patient in this time of growth.
Step into this season with an open heart,
and give to Me what I deserve as your Lord.

MY WORDS TO HIM

Oh Jesus, today I give you everything,
everything I am and think and do. I give it all to you,
my best and my worst.
My dreams, my appetites,
and my hopes—ALL is yours!
I trust you more than ever today
because I know you alone
are the one who makes my dreams come true.
You alone know how to handle my appetites
and turn my hopes to reality.
Help me be patient
in this time of growth as I step into a new season
of faith with an open heart.
I give you all my love, Lord Jesus.
You deserve my love and my gratitude,
and I bow before you
in total adoration and surrender!

God also has highly exalted Him and given Him the name
which is above every name, that at the name of Jesus every
knee should bow, of those in heaven, and of those on earth,
and of those under the earth, and that every tongue should
confess that Jesus Christ is Lord, to the glory of God the
Father.

Philippians 2:9-11 NKJV

HIS WORDS TO ME

Equipped for Everything

I spiritually equip you for every situation.
You were born to overcome
and to rise up in wisdom in a transient world
where evil thrives like maggots on rotting meat.
Never be afraid of suffering.
You were born to rise above suffering.
You'll never totally eliminate pain or evil, dear child,
but you can eliminate your fears of pain and evil
and you can write the conclusion
to suffering's epic novel of your life.
Will it be a happily-ever-after ending?
Will it be "to be continued,"
or will you write the perfect finale
and live your days as the dynamic overcomer
I've equipped you to be?

MY WORDS TO HIM

Thank you, Jesus, for equipping me for every situation.
Thank you for showing me I was born to overcome
and rise up with wisdom in a transient world.
Help me to not be afraid of suffering.
I was born to rise above the jagged teeth of suffering.
I know pain and evil
will never be eliminated in the world, Lord,
but I can eliminate my fears of pain and evil.
You've equipped me to be strong
and a joyful overcomer.
Thank you!

All who listen to me will live in peace,
untroubled by fear of harm

Proverbs 1:33 NLT

HIS WORDS TO ME

New Strength

I want you to be known as a strong person.
I want you to be known as one who can handle
suffering, snags, hindrances, troubles, and delays.
I want you to be full of My grace
to inspire and emanate goodness—
to live in honesty and handle the unmanageable,
calm the unruly, and love the unlovable.
You can't do these things in your human strength,
but you are spiritually equipped in all things
because you and I are *one*.
Don't miss the joy of discovering
My gifts and abilities in you.

Thank you, Lord, for creating strength
in me that I never had before.
Spiritual strength is greater than anything
because it bolsters me up to handle
the snags, hindrances, troubles, delays,
and suffering of this life.
I'm filled with your grace
to inspire and emanate goodness,
and to live in honesty.
Thank you, Jesus, that in you
I can handle the unmanageable.
I can calm the unruly and love the unlovable.
I can't do these things in my human strength,
which doesn't hold the spiritual power necessary
to overcome much.
Thank you for spiritually equipping me
by making me one with you.

That Christ may dwell in your hearts through faith.

Ephesians 3:17 NKJV

HIS WORDS TO ME

Sharp and Discerning

Oh, I've been good to you.
I've answered the cries of your heart,
and I've blessed you with the kindness
of My heart.
I've extended My mercy to you,
I've showered you with goodness,
so that as My child you will feel infinitely secure
and resolutely happy.
Tell Me:
what are you going to do with
all the good things in your life today?

MY WORDS TO HIM

At the dawn of this new day, I want to thank you
for making my mind sharp to discern what is right.
Thank you for the mental acuity to learn that which
is true and good in the world.
Thank you, Jesus, for your goodness to me.
Thank you for answering the cries of my heart,
and blessing me with kindness and mercy.
Thank you for showering me with goodness,
so that I feel infinitely secure and resolutely happy.
I'm excited about the multitude of ways there are
to express all this goodness you've shown me.

Surely goodness and mercy shall follow me
All the days of my life;
And I will dwell in the house
of the Lord Forever.

Psalm 23:6 NKJV

HIS WORDS TO ME

Faithful

When I make a promise
it's sealed at My throne.
It's *forever* and it can't be broken.
I tell you, your promise will come to pass
at its appointed time.
Don't reject the dream I gave you.
I'm training you to stand strong and to trust Me.
Don't be discouraged because it's taking time
for your dream to reach fulfillment.
The vision in your heart is true.
I placed it there!
I'm the author and the finisher of your faith,
and I authored your dream.
I began it and I'll complete it.
If I choose to wait
it's because I know what I'm doing.
The enemy of your soul
wants to overtake your mind with doubts.
Why don't you thwack him in the teeth
by trusting Me?

MY WORDS TO HIM

Thank you, Jesus, for your faithfulness to keep your promises.
Thank you that each of your promises are sealed
at your throne, forever impossible to be broken.
Thank you that every one of your promises will come to pass
at their appointed time.
I won't reject the dream you've given me.
I'm in training as you teach me
to stand strong and to trust you more.
I won't be discouraged
because I understand it takes time for my dreams
to reach fulfillment.
The vision in my heart is true
because you placed it there!
You're the author and finisher of my faith
and you're the author of my dream.
You began it and you'll complete it.
If you choose to wait,
it's because you know what you're doing.
The enemy of my soul wants to overtake my mind with doubts,
but I trust you, and I'll go on trusting you!

"What's more, I am with you, and I will protect you
wherever you go. One day I will bring you back to this land.
I will not leave you until I have finished giving you
everything I have promised you."

Genesis 28:15 NLT

Old Habits

Where My Spirit is, there's freedom
from the habits of the scarred and wounded soul.
Yes, I know habits are hard to break,
but let your habits be goodness, mercy,
love, justice, and a humble walk with Me.
Don't flop back into the life of bondage.
Don't start your old habits of obsessing
over evil done to you. Please.
If you slither about in the dung of yesterday's betrayals,
how will you see the beauty in this new day?
Forgiveness means if you're wronged,
stolen from, or lied about,
you forgive.
And if you're wronged, stolen from, or lied about again,
you forgive again.
And again.
Where My Spirit is, there's *freedom*.
Keep on forgiving and you'll love the transformation
in your heart and soul—you'll be *free*.

MY WORDS TO HIM

Thank you for your Holy Spirit who gives me freedom
from the old habits of my wounded soul.
Thank you for helping me
to break habits that held me bound in the past.
Thank you for teaching me new habits
of goodness, mercy, love, justice and a humble walk with you.
I don't ever want to flop back into a life of bondage.
I don't want to be inhibited
and limited by my old habits of obsessing over evil done to me,
and the negative things that have happened to me in my life.
I want to be free!
If I continue to slither about in the dung of yesterday's betrayals,
I won't be able to truly appreciate the beauty in each new day.
I won't see the potential that lives
in me to soar above the darkness of the world.
Help me to forgive and retain forgiveness in my heart.
Help me to be swift to forgive and go on forgiving,
for it's in forgiveness I'm set free from myself
and the darkness that surrounds a wounded heart.
Where your Holy Spirit is, there's liberty—beautiful freedom—
so I choose to forgive and to love.
Because I'm forgiven, my heart and soul have been transformed.
Praise the Lord!

As far as the east is from the west,
so far does he remove our transgressions from us.

Psalm 103:12 ESV

HIS WORDS TO ME

Living a Miracle

Live your life as a miracle today.
Even through the imperfection
and chaos around you,
live each moment as a unique event,
a miracle sent from Me just for you
to honor and revere.
Live each moment as if it were a lifetime.

There's life and purpose in every breath,
in every millisecond on earth.
Nothing in My kingdom
is without divine purpose,
and that is why this day and night
are important.
Make each moment live.

MY WORDS TO HIM

I'm going to live my life as a miracle today.
Even though there are imperfections and chaos
around me, I'm going to live each moment
as a unique event, like a miracle sent
from your loving heart for me to honor and revere.
I'm going to live each moment
as if it were a lifetime.
Father God, I choose to see
life and purpose in every breath;
yes, in every millisecond I'm on earth.
I believe there's nothing
in your kingdom without divine purpose,
and that's why this day and night are important.
I'm going to live each moment fully.

"I have come that they may have life, and have it to the full."

John 10:10 NKJV

HIS WORDS TO ME

Holy One

I'm the Lord your God,
the holy one of Israel, your Savior.
I protect My own.
When you flop miserably in deep waters
gulping and gasping for air,
I won't let you drown,
and when you prance through fiery hoops
like an untrained tiger in a circus,
singeing your eyelashes and swallowing kerosene,
I won't let you go up in flames.
Today, all day, see yourself
as divinely and perfectly protected
no matter what river or circus
you've gotten yourself into.

You're the Lord, my Jesus, the holy one of Israel;
you're my Savior and my everything.
Thank you for your protection,
for saving me from the world's sly influence on me.
Thank you for your divine shield of safety against
the devil's wiles, and also from my own
concoctions of vanity and self-deception.
I'm so grateful for your holy armor
around me even when I do stupid things.
Today all day I'm going to meditate
on how you divinely and perfectly protect me
no matter what mess I may get myself into.
You're always there to help me out of its clutches.
You help repair, renew, and reinstate even when I jump
into situations I have no business jumping into.
I repent of my mistakes and my sins, Lord Jesus,
and I thank you for forgiving me, bailing me out,
and always being there for me!
I'm overcome with gratitude and love for you.
You amaze me.

If we confess our sins, He is faithful and just to forgive us our
sins and to cleanse us from all unrighteousness.

1 John 1:9 NKJV

HIS WORDS TO ME

Love and Adore

I'm here for you.
I'm your forever friend.
I'll never leave you or let you down.
If your father, mother, spouse,
son, or daughter forsake you,
I'll take you up.
I'll sustain you.
I'll comfort you.
Let Me encourage you
and defend you.
You can rely on My promises to turn
your mourning to unbridled, glad pleasure.
Your future is not dim with sizzled embers.
Be reassured
great things are yet to come.

Heavenly Father, thank you for giving me Jesus,
my Savior, to love and adore.
Thank you for sending him to save me
from myself, guilt, and death.
Thank you for immersing me in such love and affection
the world has never known, nor can it give.
Thank you for your Holy Spirit who guides me
so clearly to show me how to refresh my spirit, soul, and body.
Thank you for beautiful music and wonderful, inspiring books.
Thank you for invigorating walks and the joy of dance.
Thank you for leading me toward that which is beautiful
and inspiring to my thirsty soul.
Thank you for restoring me
with your holy lightning jolt of love and peace.
Overtake me, my God, and lead me to peace,
new energy, and holy awareness in all I do and speak this day.

Declaring the end from the beginning
and from ancient times things not yet done,
saying, "My purpose shall stand,
and I will fulfill my intention."

Isaiah 46:10 NRSV

HIS WORDS TO ME

Everything Is Yours

Today,
don't impose a single limitation on Me.
Don't tuck Me behind the gates
of fear and faithlessness.
Let Me loose in your patterns of thought!
Free Me to speak to your ideas
and your vision for the future.
I've called you to an abundant life
where you can do all things through Me.
I've called you to live by faith,
not by old ideas based on doubt, suspicion,
or complacency.
You're beautiful to Me, and I want you to live
the wonderful full, rich life
I've planned for you.

MY WORDS TO HIM

Everything I have and everything I am
belongs to you, my Lord.
You provide all things
and that's why I've stopped worrying.
There's no reason to worry when you assure me
that you're in charge of all things.
When I follow your Spirit, everything works together for good.
Your Holy Spirit communicates the will of God to me.
I move forward proclaiming your promises
and I'm made stronger!
Thank you for making me sensitive to your voice.
I praise you for your living Word.
You've taught me to study with my heart
as well as my mind.
I love the Scriptures and I thank you
for opening the pages to me every day
as my spirit drinks in your words.

The commandment is a lamp,
And the law a light;
Reproofs of instruction
are the way of life,

Proverbs 6:23 NKJV

HIS WORDS TO ME

Nothing Too Small

Nothing is too small for Me
to make My own.
There's not a sigh too private
that I can't feel,
not a cell or microbe too small
for My presence to give it life.
I like to speak in a still, *small* voice,
but it's a voice that no crashing storm can muffle.
Can you hear Me in the song of a cricket in the night,
or in the precious yawn of a newborn child?
I'm in all things,
and it's the eye brightened by My Spirit
that knows this.
I've made your small, natural heart
a supernatural force,
now huge in the power of love.

MY WORDS TO HIM

Nothing is too small for your attention.
No sound too private that you can't hear,
not a cell or microbe too small for your presence to give it life.
I know you like to speak in a still, small voice
because I listen for that voice, Lord.
t's a voice that no crashing storm can muffle.
I want to hear your voice in all things—
in the song of the cricket in the night, in the precious yawn
of an octogenarian saint, in the whisper of pine needles
as they sail to the ground in the wind.
You're in all things, Lord,
and it's the eye brightened by your Holy Spirit that sees
and opens my heart to the world around me with love.
In fact, you've made my small, natural heart a supernatural force,
huge in the power of love.
Thank you, Jesus.

The eyes of all look to you,
and you give them their food at the proper time.
You open your hand
and satisfy the desires of every living thing.

Psalm 145:15-16 NIV

HIS WORDS TO ME

Lifted Up

Today, be lifted up
above the problems that surround you
and your world.
Today, receive new vision,
new hope,
and new strength.
Don't limit Me and don't put a lid
on the blessings I have in store for you.
It takes courage to reach out
to the hope of the future
with an expanded vision. Your new season
begs a new vision,
one requiring more faith—
but as your vision enlarges,
so will your gifted ability to receive.

MY WORDS TO HIM

Today I'm lifted up above the problems
that surround me and my world.
Today I'm receiving new vision, new hope,
and new strength from you, Lord, and I thank you!
I don't want to limit you and put a lid on the blessings
you have in store for me.
Give me the courage to reach out
to the hope of the future with an expanded vision.
I realize the new season ahead begs a new vision of me,
one requiring more faith—and as my vision enlarges,
so will my gifted ability to give and receive.

"Heal the sick, raise the dead, cure those with leprosy, and
cast out demons. Give as freely as you have received!"

Matthew 10:8 NLT

HIS WORDS TO ME

Old Efforts

Today, discard your old ways of
thinking of ways to make things work out
the way you want them to.
I know all your needs before you do.
I've provided a full and rich life for you,
with every need met.
The new life I have for you cascades
with My blessings.
When you found Me, you found life.
Listen for My direction and follow
My instructions in My Word regarding
each detail of your life.
You'll be incredibly blessed
as you keep *My* ways,
and you'll begin to understand the immensity of
My favor.

MY WORDS TO HIM

Today, Lord Jesus, I'm going to discard my old efforts
at trying to make things work out the way I want them to.
You know all my needs before I do, and you've provided
a full and rich life for me with every need met.
The new life you have for me cascades with your blessings,
and I know this because I read your Word.
When I found you, I found life!
That is, life the way I was meant to live it.
Today I'm going to listen
for your direction and follow your instructions in your Word
regarding the details of my life.
I love how you bless me when I keep your ways.
I thank you that each day I'm learning
more and more of the immensity of your goodness and favor.
Each day I learn more of your Holy Trinity
through these daily meetings with you
and through the study and memorizing of Scripture.
Thank you, Father, Son, and Holy Spirit!

This Book of the Law shall not depart from your mouth, but
you shall meditate in it day and night, that you may observe to
do according to all that is written in it. For then you will make
your way prosperous, and then you will have good success.

Joshua 1:8 NKJV

HIS WORDS TO ME

Deepen My Awareness

To know Me is to experience the sharpening of your senses.
The closer you grow to Me the deeper your awareness
will be.
No longer will you live in a fog with the world
buzzing around you in all its colors and motion
while you remain
unaware,
blind,
uncaring,
oblivious.
I'm waking the synapses and cells of your brain
that have lain dormant.
I'm stirring the portals of your consciousness,
and I'm making you aware and alive
like never before.
Today, tell yourself you're 100% alive!

MY WORDS TO HIM

Lord Jesus, to know you is to experience the sharpening of my senses.
The closer I grow to you, the deeper my awareness becomes.
I no longer live in a fog with the world buzzing
around me in all its colors and motion while I'm unaware,
blind, uncaring, oblivious, lost in myself, and in my own
head with its vain perceptions.
I'm alive; the synapses and cells of my brain fire
with your Holy Spirit, stimulating and revitalizing me.
Thank you for stirring the portals
of my consciousness and making me aware and invigorated
like never before.
Today I am 100% alive!

"I will betroth you to Me forever;
Yes, I will betroth you to Me in righteousness and in justice,
In lovingkindness and in compassion."

Hosea 2:19 NASB

HIS WORDS TO ME

On Purpose

You're 100% alive
when you choose
to feel, think, see, hear, taste, touch
on purpose.
It means you experience the world around you
spiritually in tune,
and you *never* approach your day with a deadly
"whatever" attitude.
You dare to see the truth in all situations
with open eyes and holy discernment.
You don't waste your emotions
while spiritually empty.
Dear one, live your life to the fullest today!

I'm 100% alive when I choose to feel, think, see, hear,
taste, and touch *on purpose*.
I feel most alive when I'm spiritually in tune
to experience the world around me.
I won't approach the day with a deadly "whatever" attitude.
I'll dare to see the truth in all situations
with open eyes and holy discernment.
I won't waste my emotions and behave as though
I'm spiritually empty.
Oh Lord, thank you for helping me
to live my life to the fullest today.

"Incline your ear, and come to Me.
Hear, and your soul shall live;
And I will make an everlasting covenant with you—
The sure mercies of David."

Isaiah 55:3 NKJV

HIS WORDS TO ME

Called to Live

I want you to stand on the crest of heaven's mountain
and gaze down at the great life
I've called you to live on the earth.
Can you see the fun ahead for you in My Spirit?
Can you see the blessings?
Can you see health,
friends,
love,
goodness,
mercy,
and prosperity ahead?
Do you see beautiful fellowship with Me?
Ah, open the eyes of your heart today,
and see.

Thank you, Jesus, for the great life
you've called me to live on this earth.
I choose to see a beautiful life ahead for me and my loved ones
as your Spirit guides each day.
I'm going to stop ruminating on the negative things
going on around me and in the world, and I'm going to focus
on your genius, on your generous heart,
and the wisdom with which you control all.
I will see with spiritual eyes.
And then I'll discern blessing from curse.
I'll never succumb to fear because when I think
with the mind of Christ,
I'm elevated to a divine mind, one that has no fear, no trepidation.
Your ways are perfect, Lord, and I bow to your will.

Praise him for his strength;
praise him for his greatness.

Psalm 150:2 NCV

HIS WORDS TO ME

Light of the World

I'm the great candle lighter.
I light the candle of your life.
The world I created was at first
without form and void, and I hovered
across the face of the deep with a great murmuring,
waiting to bestow Myself on the creation
and speak the words,
"Let there be light,"
because I am light.
If you're in need of insight
and understanding today,
call on My Spirit for illumination.
I'll dispel the darkness
so you can see clearly ahead.

Jesus, you're the light of the world. You light the lamp of my life.
The world you created with God, the Father,
was at first without form and void, and you hovered
across the face of the deep with a great murmuring,
waiting to give yourself to creation and speak the words,
"Let there be light," because you are light.
When I'm in need of understanding and insight,
I call on your Holy Spirit for light,
for illumination on the situation, to dispel the darkness
so I can see clearly ahead.
Your Holy Spirit living in me, fusing my
human spirit with your Holy Spirit,
illumines the world I live in with
heaven's glory.
Thank you, Jesus!

"He is the Holy Spirit, who leads into all truth. The world
cannot receive him, because it isn't looking for him and doesn't
recognize him. But you know him, because he lives with you now
and later will be in you."

John 14:17 NLT

HIS WORDS TO ME

Shine in My Soul

There's light shining inside your soul today
and the people around you
will see Me in your eyes.
Your eyes are the windows of your
bright, incandescent soul, making you
alive in light and life.
Demons can't look you in the eye
because they're terrified by what they see.
All who hate this light will shrink from you,
but those who long for Me will find Me,
so be glad for the life-giving light in you.
Your brothers and sisters in Me will be blessed
when they look you in the eye,
and you'll party together with just one look.
Let it happen!

MY WORDS TO HIM

Thank you, Jesus, for the light that shines in my soul today,
so the people around me will see you in me and in my actions.
It's been said that eyes are the windows of the soul,
and so in the incandescence of the Spirit-filled soul, Lord,
let me be alive in the light and in life.
Demons can't look me in the eye
because they're terrified by what they see!
All who hate your light will shrink away,
but those who long to know you will be drawn
to your presence and your love.
I'm so happy and so thankful for the life-giving light
in my brothers and sisters who love you, too.
With just one look, it's a celebration.

How good and pleasant it is
when God's people live together in unity!

Psalm 133:1 NIV

HIS WORDS TO ME

Know Me Best

It's your heart I see
and hear
and know,
so you can be confident, darling,
that I'm giving you
the desires of your heart today.
When you pray from the heart,
I know it because I live in your heart.
When your desires
are one with My Holy Spirit
you can trust Me to answer
because I'm the author of the desire.
I must answer
because your desire and Mine are one.
Don't be afraid to bring
every concern of your heart to Me.
Don't hold back.
It's our love for each other
that makes your wants
the same as Mine.

MY WORDS TO HIM

Thank you, Lord Jesus, for knowing me
better than anyone on earth knows me.
I can be confident that you're giving me
the desires of my heart today.
When I pray from the heart, it's because you live in my heart.
When my desires are one with your Holy Spirit,
I can trust you to answer
because you're the author of the desire.
I'm not afraid to bring every concern of my heart to you.
I won't hold back.
It's our love for each other that makes my wants
the same as yours.
Thank you, Jesus!

Delight yourself in the LORD,
and he will give you the desires of your heart.
Psalm 37:4 ESV

HIS WORDS TO ME

Your Name Is Greater

My name is greater than that of any name on earth
or in heaven and greater
than any assistance you might turn to.
So I tell you to pray in My name,
and My Father will answer.
Be one with Me
and watch your life lift
to a higher dimension
of happiness and contentment this day.

MY WORDS TO HIM

Jesus, your name is greater than any name on earth, or in heaven,
and greater than any assistance I might think to turn to.
For this reason, I pray in your name, and my Father will answer.
Being one with you has lifted my life to
a higher dimension of happiness and contentment.
It's a miracle that's happened to me through knowing you.
Each day when I enter my prayer sanctuary
to thank you, I sense your presence and your love,
and I become transformed.
Thank you for revealing yourself to me, Lord.
Thank you for entering the portals of my heart
and creating a blazing life of wonder and joy
to a dead-in-sin soul.
I live to adore you and worship you, Jesus.
I live to let every detail of my life—words, actions, everything—
be done in your name, Master, Jesus,
thanking God the Father each step of the way.

"These are written so that you may continue to believe that Jesus
is the Messiah, the Son of God, and that by believing in him you
will have life by the power of his name."

John 20:31 NLT

HIS WORDS TO ME

Too Great a Battle

Does the battle feel too great for you today?
Remember, your strength comes from Me
and not from yourself or the world.
In your own energy you'll falter
as quickly as it takes a drop of water
to drip from a sprout. *Splat!* and you're
ready to quit.
I've made you capable of accomplishing much
with the many natural gifts I've given you,
but without Me, those very gifts
can be misused because you were born
to know and serve Me, not yourself.
So on the battlefield of life today,
be brave. Lean into My arms, take a deep breath,
and let's start over.
Feel My strength pour into your body and soul,
revitalizing you.
Your battle has already been won
because I've won it for you.

MY WORDS TO HIM

Sometimes, Lord, the battle seems too great,
and it's then that I remember my strength comes from you!
My strength doesn't come from me or from the world,
but from you—Jesus, king of the universe!
In my own energy, I falter as fast as it takes a drop of water
to drip from a sprout.
Splat! and I'm ready to feel sorry for myself and quit.
You've made me capable of accomplishing much
with the many natural gifts you've given me, but without you,
those very gifts can be misused.
I was born to know and serve you, not myself.
So on the battlefield of life today,
I'll be brave and let you take the lead.
I'll take a deep breath and start fresh.
Jesus, I can feel your strength pour into my soul
and body revitalizing me, giving me new energy and courage.
What a great day this is! Thank you!

God is able to make all grace abound toward you,
that you, always having all sufficiency
in all things, may have an abundance
for every good work.

2 Corinthians 9:8 NKJV

HIS WORDS TO ME

Conquer Obstacles

Be kind, dear one.
It's true I've called you to be strong
and to conquer difficult obstacles.
True, I've called you to rise up tough and resilient
in a sin-conscious world.
And I'm also calling you to be kind.
You can win an argument by bulldozing
over your opponent; you can punch and kick your way
to success; you can lay flat those in your life
with a will of their own,
or you can be kind.
You're strong when you're considerate.
You're tough when you're humble.
You're brave when you're gentle.
Kindness never boasts, nor is rude in any way.
I am kindness.
Be like Me.

You've called me to be strong and to conquer difficult obstacles.
You've called me to rise up tough and resilient in a sin-driven world,
but you're also calling me to be kind.
I hear you.
I realize it's possible to win an argument by bull-dozing.
It's possible to lay flat those with a will of their own
by being just plain rude and overbearing.
Intimidation, however, is not a God-given strategy.
You're teaching me the power of kindness.
I can be kind. I can be thoughtful, considerate.
Thank you for teaching me that I'm strongest when
I'm respectful and unselfish.
Thank you for teaching me that I'm sharpest when
I'm humble and the most brave when I'm gentle.
Kindness never boasts, nor is it rude in any way,
and oh Lord, you are kindness.
Help me to be like you.

Be kind to one another, tenderhearted,
forgiving one another,
even as God in Christ forgave you.

Ephesians 4:32 NKJV

HIS WORDS TO ME

Today's Patience

Be patient, beloved.
Just as you can't force open the bud of a flower,
that must bloom in its own time, so must you persevere
and enjoy this time to marvel, admire and be in awe
of the blooming process in you, like the life within
the bud quivering to spring forth;
like the stretching, yearning,
and incubating before it finally realizes its purpose
and becomes what it was meant to be
from the beginning.

Watch how the deepening colors of the bud grow iridescent
as its leaves reach out to gather more sky into their veins.
Now see the petals expand,
their smiling faces upturned from the earth.
I welcome them, whole and complete.
I watch *your* petals unfolding now,
and this blossoming of yours, My darling, is a process
that can't be rushed. *Cherish this time.*

Help me to be patient today, Jesus.
You've taught me that just as I can't force open
the bud of a flower
that blooms in its own time, so must I persevere
and enjoy this time to marvel, admire, and be in awe
of the blooming process in me.
I know it's not the destination that's so crucial,
but the journey getting there that counts.
Still, I need patience!
I feel like the bud quivering and eager to spring forth
before knowing its purpose.
I'm so eager to become what I was meant to be
from the beginning.
I know you're preparing me for my blossoming.
Help me to be patient and learn exactly what I need to learn
during this process that you've taught me can't be rushed.

Wait on the LORD;
Be of good courage,
And He shall strengthen your heart;
Wait, I say, on the LORD!

Psalm 27:14 NKJV

HIS WORDS TO ME

Upward Climb

Who is the one who reaches the peaks
of high mountains?
Who climbs the distant side
of the treacherous cliffs
where an unstable toe-hold could
lead to death?
Who dares such a climb
enduring storms, thirst, hunger,
pain, and exhaustion,
and doesn't give up until reaching the top?
I'll tell you who.
It's the one who *has trained* for the climb.
What about you?
The higher calling boot camp of My Holy Spirit
is taking registrations now.
Are you preparing to climb above
the sharp ridges of trial and loss,
and invest in the solid foothold of higher calling *faith?*
Have you packed your higher calling faith gear?
Or do you prefer hanging out in the spongy pap
of low land spinelessness?
The mountain waits.

Thank you, Jesus, for training me for the upward climb.
Thank you for the higher calling boot camp of your Holy Spirit.
Thank you for strengthening me in times
of trial and loss and creating a true champion out of me.
Thank you for showing me how to invest in the solid foothold
of higher calling faith land, delivering me
from the spongy pap of low-land spinelessness.
Oh, God, thank you for the climb up the mountain!

For the LORD will be your confidence
and will keep your foot from being caught.

Proverbs 3:26 NRSV

HIS WORDS TO ME

Outside Myself

Place today's needs in My hands, dear one.
Place the concerns of your heart and mind in My care.
Where your heart is, there you'll find your treasure.
Have you examined My wildflowers lately?
Have you taken a good look at the design
of the landscape of My healthy earth?
No visual wonder compares to what I have created,
yet you won't find a single rose, fern, or pine
worried about how they look. And the lilies!
I tell you, no wealth in the world can buy
the wardrobe of the lilies. Yet they don't do a lick of work.
Look at the birds of the air. Do they mope and brood?
No! Yet not one of them plants or harvests;
they don't fret about their appearance,
nor do they stress at the shortness of their lives.
If I clothe the grass of the field, the hawk, the rose,
the lilies of the valley, how much more do I clothe
and care for you?
Don't you understand, My darling?
I created everything for *you*.

MY WORDS TO HIM

Oh Lord, help me to get outside myself and my own needs
to appreciate the world around me.
Help me to admire the landscape design of your beautiful creation.
No visual wonder compares to what you've created,
and there's not a single rose, fern, or pine worried
about how they look or what's going to happen to them tomorrow.
Oh, and the lilies, how they carpet the earth
with so much beauty without a whiff of anxiety!
You've told us that no wealth in the world can compare with
the wardrobe of the lilies. They don't toil at a lick of work—and the
birds certainly don't mope and brood about their plight as birds.
No! They don't stress for one instant as they
gracefully soar through the sky.
Jesus, you created all, and you continue to clothe the grass of the field,
the feathered wing of the hawk, the soft hue of the rose,
and the lilies of the valley, so how much more
do you clothe and care for me? Oh, it's mind-boggling.
I can only bow and worship you. I can't help but believe
that you created everything just for me to appreciate!

"Consider the lilies of the field, how they grow: they neither toil nor
spin; and yet I say to you that even Solomon in all his glory was not
arrayed like one of these. Now if God so clothes the grass of the field,
which today is, and tomorrow is thrown into the oven, will He not
much more clothe you, O you of little faith?"

Matthew 6:28-30 NKJV

HIS WORDS TO ME

Watching over Me

You've always been in My heart.
There isn't one instant of your life
that I haven't watched over.
While you were in your mother's womb,
I promised you unconditional love.
I knew there would be times
of rejection,
sorrow,
and betrayal.
I knew you'd feel unwanted and unloved at times,
and I loved you even more.
I made a promise to you from your mother's womb
that you'd be perfectly loved forever,
and you're living that promise today.

MY WORDS TO HIM

Thank you, Jesus, for watching over me every day of my life.
There hasn't been a day I've been alive that you haven't been with me.
You know everything!
When I was in my mother's womb,
you were there.
You promised unconditional love,
knowing there would be times I'd face sorrow, pain,
betrayal, and rejection.
You knew I'd feel unwanted
and defeated at times, and you also knew my temptations
and rebellious character.
You've been with me through everything,
both good and bad.
You made a promise to me from my mother's womb
that I'd be perfectly loved forever.
Thank you for living this promise today in my life.
Help me to never forget it.

I was thrust into your arms at my birth.
You have been my God from the moment I was born.

Psalm 22:10 NLT

HIS WORDS TO ME

Above and Beyond

The rewards I have for you are above and beyond
fickle human hurrahs and flattering puffery.
When you're one with Me
our achievements party around us
as bejeweled heroes.
I've told you there's little satisfaction
in achievements apart from Me.
The attention you earn from the world
will flutter away like feathers in the wind,
and be forgotten,
But *our* relationship blooms forever,
and the accolades you receive from Me
will sparkle on heaven's hall of fame for eternity,
and the partying won't ever end.

Thank you, Jesus, for the rewards you give me
that are so far above and beyond the fickle
human hurrahs and flattery offered by the world.
When I'm one with you, our achievements party
around us and I feel rewarded.
I find little satisfaction in achievements apart from you.
The attention I earn from the world flutters away
like dust in the wind, and is eventually forgotten.
But our relationship will flourish forever.
The accolades I receive from you will sparkle in
heaven's hall of fame for eternity.
What a wonderful thought!
The party never ends with us.

"Do not work for the food that perishes, but for the food that
endures to eternal life, which the Son of Man will give to you.
For on him God the Father has set his seal."

John 6:27 ESV

HIS WORDS TO ME

Sanctuary of Prayer

I've loved you from the very foundation of the world,
which tells you how long I've known you.
I had a purpose for your life long before
you were conceived.
You've only known Me since you gave your life
to Me, but I've known you since creation.
Ponder it.
Do you think I know you well enough
to know what's best for you?
Do you believe I'm concerned
about the details of your days?
Do you ever think how happy you make Me
when your life, which I gave you, bursts with joy in Me?
I love it when you turn to Me
with a shout of thanks, and I'm deeply moved
when I see you plunge forward,
risking all to help someone who's in deeper need than you.
I love answering your prayers.

MY WORDS TO HIM

I love my time with you like this in my sanctuary of prayer!
I love the union of my heart with yours and knowing
that you've loved me from the very foundation of the world.
You had a purpose for my life long before I was conceived.
I've only known you since I gave my life to you,
and you fused your Holy Spirit to mine,
but you've known me since the beginning.
I can hardly grasp it!
You know me so well that you know
what's best for me at all times.
You're concerned about every detail of my days.
Oh Father, in the name of Jesus, I want to make you happy!
There's so much joy in me knowing you
and loving you that I can hardly contain it.
I'm coming to you today thanking you
for answering my prayers even before I ask.

Be anxious for nothing, but in everything by prayer and
supplication, with thanksgiving, let your requests be made
known to God.

Philippians 4:6-7 NKJV

HIS WORDS TO ME

All That I Am

Love Me today in simplicity,
and give everything you do to Me.
Your gifts to Me are a joyful fragrance
to My nostrils.
I see your dear face knowing you're Mine
and I tell you, your adoring heart
is as precious to Me as a thousand festivals
of praise in My honor.
You bring Me much delight.

Talk to Me.

Listen to Me.

Worship Me.

And you'll live the most exciting life on earth.

MY WORDS TO HIM

Jesus, I love you. I give you everything today,
all that I am and all that I'll ever be.
Please multiply my gifts in me.
I'm rejoicing today knowing I belong to you
and that you love me.
I adore you!
Thank you, Jesus, for the life you've given me.
I'm going to stop complaining
and wishing I had more than I have.
I'm going to thank you for every blessing
and every moment of breath that's mine.
I love talking with you, listening to you,
and worshipping you.
Jesus, I choose right now to see my life
as the most exciting life on earth.

You are a chosen generation, a royal priesthood, a holy
nation, His own special people, that you may proclaim the
praises of Him who called you out of darkness into His
marvelous light;

1 Peter 2:9 NKJV

HIS WORDS TO ME

Beautiful for You

Do you know how beautiful you are to Me,
and how I long to speak to you?
Do you know how precious
these quiet moments with you are to Me?
With just one moment with Me,
you'll know more contentment in your soul
than days and nights of the fun and pleasure
the world has to offer.
Your good works and skills can't accomplish
the pleasure of one moment alone with Me.
One moment of your busy day
to enter into the presence of complete perfection
sitting at the center of My sheltered peace—
isn't this the best moment of all?
I want this sacred time with Me to be your foundation
of each day.

Oh Jesus, I want to be beautiful for you.
I want to honor you
in everything I do and in everything I am.
I want to hear your
voice when you call, I want to embrace the quiet moments
we're together as the most precious moments in my life.
Just one moment with you brings me more contentment
in my soul than days and nights of the world's pleasures.
All the skills and good works in the world
can't compare with the joy of one moment alone with you.
One moment of my busy day to enter into your presence
brings complete perfection.
How I love to sit at the center of your sheltered peace,
where all is flawless and complete.
This sacred time with you is the blessed substance
and foundation of each day of my life.

To me the only important thing about living is Christ.

Philippians 1:21 NCV

HIS WORDS TO ME

Seventy Times Seven

Inner beauty can be counterfeited for a time,
but then the core of the soul is exposed—
the temper erupts like Mt. Etna,
the snake emerges to steal or lie,
and later, of course, excuses are made.
You say you're just tired, you're sorry.
O My child, I forgive and I forgive,
but I want you to know that My personality
can become part of yours with an eternal quality that's
glorious and indestructible,
and where temptation and lack of discipline
won't continually overtake you.
No moment's agitation
will spoil your sweetness,
nor will every irritation pollute your composure.
You won't be tempted to steal
what belongs to someone else.
Your inner beauty is the reflection
of the moments and hours
you spend with Me.

Thank you, Jesus, for your forgiveness.
I have a hard time forgiving.
You've told us to forgive seventy times seven,
and I'm glad that your heart is bigger than mine.
When the core of the soul is exposed, you see it all.
Oh Jesus, infuse yourself into my personality
and become bigger in me than who I am.
I long for my character to be strong
where temptation and lack of discipline won't overtake me.
I don't want to be overwhelmed by a bad temper
or a momentary agitation.
Help me not to spoil the sweetness
you've put inside me, Lord!
Help me not to pollute my composure with petty irritations.
Lord, I want my life to reflect your heart.
Let the happy moments we spend together rub off on my personality
so I'm more and more like you!
Help me to be more forgiving.
Inner beauty can't be counterfeited.

You, Lord, are good, and ready to forgive
And abundant in mercy to all those who call upon You.

Psalm 86:5 NKJV

HIS WORDS TO ME

Holy Microscope

Today, use your holy microscope
to discover a world bigger than the one
you're tempted to take for granted.
Be wild.
Gaze into the flickering eyes of birds
and ask them for their stories.
Kiss the smiling faces of the lily, iris, and rose.
Clap your hands with the trees who love to
praise their Master.
Listen for the song in rocks.
Name the crustaceans on the ocean floor.
Dance barefoot on the sofa.
Lighten up.

MY WORDS TO HIM

Lord Jesus, help me to use a holy microscope to discover
a world bigger than the one I'm tempted to take for granted.
Help me be wild in my faith!
I want to clap my hands with the trees who love to praise you,
and I want to gaze into the flickering eyes of birds
and ask them for their stories.
Expand me, Lord!
I want to kiss the smiling faces of the lily, the iris,
and the rose, and listen for the song in rocks.
I want to name the crustaceans on the ocean floor
and become alive with wonder and appreciation for your world.
I want to wave banners, dance barefoot on the sofa.
Lord, I want to lighten up.

Be exalted, O God, above the heavens;
let your glory be over all the earth.

Psalm 57:5 NIV

HIS WORDS TO ME

Good Conscience

A good conscience is one
that's armed with truth,
and one that won't settle for an easy route
through the thorny patches of life.
A good conscience doesn't emanate from
an emotionally impoverished soul.
A good conscience devours My Word
like a person starving.
A good conscience refuses to make excuses
for what it knows is wrong.
A good conscience doesn't continue to
eat forbidden fruit which makes
the whole world sick.
A good conscience won't steal
just because it's convenient.
A good conscience doesn't take credit
where it's not due.
A good conscience hates lies and
hypocrisy, and will never be seen cavorting with
deceit and trickery.
A good conscience won't trot betrayal's avenues
of flim-flam recklessness because a good conscience
is above all loyal and sincere.
Today, think about these things.
Think about the value of your good conscience.

MY WORDS TO HIM

Dear Jesus, give me a good conscience that's armed with truth
and won't settle for an easy route through the thorny patches of life.
Give me a good conscience that doesn't emanate from
an emotionally impoverished soul.
Lord, I want a conscience that devours your Word
like a person starving, a conscience that doesn't eat
forbidden fruit that makes the whole world sick.
Give me a good conscience that doesn't steal
just because it's convenient, that doesn't take credit
where it's not due, and that hates lies and hypocrisy.
Help me never to be found cavorting with deceit and trickery.
Oh Jesus, give me a holy conscience that's above all,
loyal and sincere, one that honors and pleases you.

I always try to maintain a clear conscience
before God and all people.

Acts 24:16 NLT

HIS WORDS TO ME

Purposefully Happy

Dare to be a happy person today.

Dare to be strong.

Dare to overcome!

A good conscience is one that rejoices in truth,

ever confident, and is at peace in adversities.

A strong person must have a good conscience.

An overcomer in My kingdom

can't overcome without a good conscience.

A good conscience is like fine polished gold,

A good conscience is a delight to Me.

Today, Lord Jesus, I'm going to dare to be purposefully happy!
I'm going to be strong. I'm going to be an overcomer.
I'm going to be grateful.
As you make me more and more confident,
I'll be at peace in adversities and troubles instead of
complaining and wanting to quit.
I'm tired of complaining!
I'm choosing to be strong, Lord Jesus,
a person with a good conscience
because an overcomer in your kingdom
can't overcome without a good conscience.
I want to be a delight to you, at peace,
a credit to your name.
I want to please you with my happy attitude
that reflects your personality.
I'm choosing today to live in the wealth of your pleasures.

"If they listen and serve him,
they complete their days in prosperity,
and their years in pleasantness."
Job 36:11 ESV

HIS WORDS TO ME

Sweet Blessings

Consider yourself blessed.
Nothing can take away
the sweet blessings that are yours alone.
Consider yourself free from everything
that has tried to hold you down
or hurt your feelings.
Consider yourself a new person inside and out.
The hurts of the past can't control you today.
You have a new life now,
and a new heart that I fill with happiness
and fresh wonder and excitement.
Discover today that your world
is chock-full of delightful surprises,
and you're more blessed than you can imagine.

MY WORDS TO HIM

Today, Lord, I consider myself blessed.
I'm proclaiming that nothing can take away
the sweet blessings that are mine!
I'm considering myself free from everything
that's tried to hold me down or hurt my feelings.
Today I consider myself a new person inside and out.
The hurts of the past won't control me today.
I have a new life now, and a new heart that you're filling
with happiness, fresh wonder and excitement.
Today, Lord, help me discover that my world is chock-full
of delightful surprises,
and I'm more blessed than I can imagine.
Thank you, Jesus!

One who looks intently at the perfect law, the law of liberty,
and abides by it, not having become a forgetful hearer but an
effectual doer, this man will be blessed in what he does.

James 1:25 NASB

HIS WORDS TO ME

Express My Gratitude

It's a day to be humble.
Take Me with you everywhere you go.
I'll calm your fluctuating nerves;
I'll guide you
and remind you of the humble walk.
I'll give you a loving poke
if you act self-righteously
or insist on your own way.
I'll gently nudge you if you boast
or behave with self-importance.
I'll lift you up so you can see
the path of true fulfillment and recognize
the itsy-bitsy bite-sized life when
it's dominated by pride.
Be humble and drop pride's grubby grip on you
in order to gain the whole world
and the wonderful years I have for you.

MY WORDS TO HIM

Jesus, how can I express my gratitude to you?
Show me how to love you with a pure heart that pleases you.
Today I'm going to take you everywhere I go—
conscious and aware that you're with me.
Calm my fluctuating nerves and guide me, Lord.
Remind me of the humble walk.
If I act self-righteously or insist on my own way,
give me a poke.
Help me to be very aware of boasting
or behaving with self-importance because this leads
nowhere but down.
Lift me up so I can see the path of true fulfillment
and recognize how pinched and squashed
life becomes when dominated by pride.
Help me to be humble and drop pride's grubby grip on me
in order to gain the relief that contentment brings.
Thank you, Jesus, for the wonderful years you have ahead for me.
I praise and thank you for the change you're making in my life.
My soul bursts with thanksgiving.

Enter into His gates with thanksgiving,
And into His courts with praise.
Be thankful to Him, and bless His name.

Psalm 100:4 NKJV

HIS WORDS TO ME

Courtroom of Life

Who vindicates you in every courtroom of life?
Who's your most reliable helper in times of need?
Who is always there—
protecting you,
embracing you in perfect love?
Your employers?
Your pals?
Who hears your cries in the night and comforts you?
Who lifts you up when you fall down?
Who calls you *beloved?*
Your dentist?
Your physician?
Your lawyer?
Hmm?
Remember, dear child,
the things and the people you now think are immutable
will one day be gone, like fluff in the wind.
Success is temporary, riches are fleeting,
but I am from everlasting to everlasting.
I never change.
Today, think about this. I love you.

MY WORDS TO HIM

Thank you, Jesus, for vindicating me in the courtroom of life.
Thank you for being my reliable helper in every time of need.
Thank you for always being there,
protecting me and embracing me in perfect love.
You hear my cries in the night and you comfort me.
You lift me up when I fall and you call me your beloved.
Oh Jesus, the things and the people I may consider immutable
will one day be gone, like fluff in the wind.
Success is temporary, riches are fleeting,
but you're from everlasting to everlasting.
You never change.
Today I'm dedicating myself to think about good things.
I love you!

Where is another God like you, who pardons the sins of the
survivors among his people? You cannot stay angry with your
people, for you love to be merciful. Once again you will have
compassion on us.

Micah 7:18-19 TLB

HIS WORDS TO ME

Clearing the Way

Wherever you go,
I'll clear the way for you.
Whatever you need, I'll provide.
When you step out and declare My name
I'll favor your cause.
Know that what concerns you concerns Me.
The tribulation in the world shall not alarm you
but instead, bring you
to your prayer station where you take down
strongholds and declare My Word
and will into every situation.
You'll avoid fretful talk
and divisive babble.
You'll pray from your
heavenly position of authority
and confident assurance.
You'll never forget
I am exalted
above all principalities and powers!

MY WORDS TO HIM

Thank you, Jesus, for clearing the way for me wherever I go.
Thank you for providing my every need,
and thank you for favoring my cause
when I step out declaring your name.
Thank you for the knowledge that
what concerns me concerns you.
The tribulation in the world won't alarm me
because I bring myself to my prayer station where you
take down strongholds and win every battle.
I'll declare your power and presence today
in every situation, and I'll avoid fretful talk and divisive babble.
I'll pray from my heavenly position of authority and confident assurance.
I'll never forget that you're exalted above all principalities and powers!
You are Lord of the universe!

Which he will bring about at the right time—he who is the blessed
and only Sovereign, the King of kings and Lord of lords. It is he alone
who has immortality and dwells in unapproachable light, whom no
one has ever seen or can see; to him be honor and eternal dominion.
Amen.

1 Timothy 6:15-16 NRSV

HIS WORDS TO ME

Snares of Gossip

Gossip?
Show Me gossip
and I'll show you dried weeds
and cracked, parched mud.
Gossip can paddle the air in the guise
of prayerful concern or even
godly correction.
Put Me before you,
and you won't succumb
to troublesome words of derision
against someone else.
People may belch out insults
like dirty rain,
and they may slash at My little ones
with sarcasm and ridicule,
but every curse shall boomerang back
at the sender.
That is why *you* too
must keep yourself pure today
and don't allow gossip
to spurt from your beautiful mouth.

MY WORDS TO HIM

Oh Jesus, keep me from the snares of gossip!
Gossip is like dried weeds and cracked, parched mud.
Gossip can paddle the air in the guise of prayerful concern
or even godly correction.
I put you ever before me
so I won't succumb to troublesome words of derision
against someone else.
People may belch out insults like dirty rain, and they may slash
at one another with sarcasm and ridicule, but Lord, keep me
from such behavior.
I dedicate my tongue to you
because you've taught me that life and death is
in the power of the tongue.
Help me to keep myself pure today
and not allow gossip to spurt from the heart
you've renewed in me and the mouth you've taught
to speak the truth with love.

Likewise, the tongue is a small part of the body, but it makes
great boasts. Consider what a great forest is set on fire by a
small spark.

James 3:5 NIV

HIS WORDS TO ME

Standing on the Rock

Look where you're standing.
You're standing on Me. I'm your rock.
Your enemy, the devil, is sneaking around your feet
like a desperate, hungry animal looking for someone
without self-control to chew on.

Be aware.

Be alert.

Be authentic.

If you lie to yourself about your habits, and
lose control over your day,
if you're easily tempted,
don't lose a second, *hang onto the rock.*
I, Christ Jesus, am the rock for you to stand on
with absolute confidence
and security.
I'm your escape from the devil and yourself!

MY WORDS TO HIM

Oh Jesus, it's so amazing to be standing on the rock
high above the snapping dragons of the world.
I'm standing on you, the rock of my salvation,
while the enemy of everything good, the devil,
sneaks around hungrily seeking someone without
self-control to tear down off the rock.
Help me to be aware, alert, and authentic.
If I lie to myself about my habits and lose control over my day,
I can be easily tempted, but I don't want to lose a second.
I want to hang on to my rock.
You, Christ Jesus, are the rock for me to stand on
with absolute confidence and security.
You're my escape from the devil and from my own weaknesses.
The dragons can't reach me when I'm secure on the rock.

The LORD is my rock, my fortress, and my savior;
my God is my rock, in whom I find protection.
He is my shield, the power that saves me,
and my place of safety.

Psalm 18:2 NLT

HIS WORDS TO ME

Proclaiming Prophet

Don't say you have no power.
Be like the prophet who proclaimed,
"As for me, I am filled with power,
with the spirit of the Lord,
and with justice and might!"
Isn't that beautiful?
Can you, like Micah, proclaim the truth today?
I've armed you with strength,
that'll never run out.
You'll soar on wings like eagles,
you'll run and not grow weary,
you'll walk and not faint.
Proclaim it!
Proclaim the truth to your heart,
and out of My glorious riches, I'll strengthen you
with the power you need.
Never say you have no power.

MY WORDS TO HIM

Lord Jesus, I'm proclaiming, like the prophet:
"I am filled with power, with the Spirit of the Lord,
and with justice and might!"
That's so beautiful!
Like Micah, I proclaim the truth today.
You've armed me with strength that'll never run out.
I'll soar on wings like eagles,
I'll run and not grow weary, and I'll walk and not faint.
I proclaim it!
The truth is that out of your glorious riches,
you've strengthened me with the power I need
to prevail in this life.
I'll never say I have no power!

As for me, I am filled with power,
with the Spirit of the LORD,
and with justice and might.

Micah 3:8 ESV

HIS WORDS TO ME

Concentrate on the Task

Today, concentrate on the task I've given you,
and don't allow yourself to be deterred
and get off track because of interferences
that don't concern you.
If others annoy or raise a quarrel with you,
step back and take charge of your heart.
Selfish ambition will kick you in the shins
even if you win the argument.
It's not smart to rush into someone else's squabble.
In fact, a person who meddles
in a quarrel not his own
is like one who seizes a dog by the ears.
Use your gift of wisdom today
and don't be distracted.

MY WORDS TO HIM

Today Lord, help me to concentrate on the task
you've given me to accomplish.
Help me not to allow myself
to be deterred and get off track
because of interferences that don't concern me.
If others annoy or raise a quarrel with me,
help me to remember to step back
and take charge of my heart.
Selfish ambition goes nowhere even if I win the argument.
You've taught me that it's not smart to rush
into someone else's squabble.
You've taught me that a person who meddles in a quarrel
not his or her own is like one who seizes a dog by the ears.
Ouch!
Today, Lord, help me to use my gift of wisdom,
and stay focused on the task you've given me,
not on someone else's.

I press on to reach the end of the race and receive the
heavenly prize for which God, through Christ Jesus,
is calling us.

Philippians 3:14 NLT

HIS WORDS TO ME

Valley of Waiting

Do you think I'm taking too long
to answer your prayers?
I see you there in the valley of patient waiting
and you're getting anxious.
You're wondering when? When? When?
The valley of patient waiting
is crowded with toe-tapping, finger-thrumming
believers asking the same question.
Patience comes with a price, dear one.
You can't order it from a catalog
like a new skin cream or a wonder-vitamin pill.
Patience requires courage.
You must have courage to wait, believing
I know what I'm doing.
I never go back on a promise,
and I will surely answer you.
But please don't forget, I answer in My time,
not yours.

MY WORDS TO HIM

Oh Lord, give me more patience.
I'm in the valley of waiting, and I sometimes get a little anxious.
Oh Jesus, thank you for saving me from my emotions.
The valley of patient waiting is crowded with believers who
ask the same question over and over:
When, Lord?
I understand that patience comes with a price,
and it requires courage.
I need courage to wait,
believing that you know what you're doing.
I thank you that you never go back on a promise,
and you'll assuredly answer me in your time,
not mine.

Imitate those who through faith and patience
inherit what has been promised.

Hebrews 6:12 NIV

HIS WORDS TO ME

Thankful for Friends

Consider your friends today.
When Moses, during battle, grew weary
holding the rod of victory high,
who was it who held up his hands?
Aaron and Hur held up Moses' hands,
one on one side, and one on the other
so he'd remain steady and strong.
Friends will do this for you.
So let Me ask you, what can you do to be a blessing
to *your* friends today?
You were born to love
and be loved.
Can you hold weak arms up in prayer?
Do you have a kind, generous word
ready to share?
What can you do to comfort and encourage?
A friend is compassionate, sympathetic,
humble and faithful.
Today, be a friend.

Lord Jesus, thank you for my friends today.
Thank you for people who care about me
and love me enough to stand by me
through thick and thin.
How can I be a blessing
to my friends today?
I was born to love and be loved,
and I want to be a faithful friend
ready with a generous word, and always ready
to listen and to share.
Lord, open the way for me today
to comfort and encourage a friend.
I want to be a friend who is compassionate,
sympathetic, humble, and faithful.
I want to be like you to all who know me.

A friend loves you all the time.

Proverbs 17:17 NCV

HIS WORDS TO ME

Filled with Hope

Be filled with hope today!
Take hold of hope as never before
and know that the Maker of heaven and earth,
the Ruler of the seas, the earth,
and all there is,
loves you and is faithful to you.
Hopelessness is the result of a lie,
and a lie lasts only moment
because a lie can't hold substance
in the dynamic life-giving atmosphere
of truth. Lies that rob you of hope are worms
that disintegrate in light.
You are a child of light;
the lie disintegrates, *Puff!* like that.
The truth lasts forever.
I'm telling you today to proclaim the truth
of My promises in your life.
I promise I'm near you. I hear you.
My promises to you are your reality.

Jesus, I'm filled with hope today!
I'm taking hold of hope as never before
because I know that the Maker of heaven and earth,
the ruler of the seas, the earth, and all there is,
loves me and is a faithful God.
Thank you, Jesus, for showing me that
hopelessness is the result of a lie, and a lie lasts only
a moment because a lie can't hold substance
in the dynamic life-giving atmosphere of truth.
Lies that rob me of hope are worms that disintegrate
in the light of God's presence.
The truth lasts forever.
Today I choose to proclaim the truth of your promise
in my life to remain close to me, to hear me
when I call, and to be my entire reality.

To them God chose to make known how great among the
Gentiles are the riches of the glory of this mystery,
which is Christ in you, the hope of glory.

Colossians 1:27 NRSV

HIS WORDS TO ME

Running to You

Where do you run for safety?
Your bed?
Under the table?
Behind Mama's skirts?
Or do you rush into My heavenly high tower
where I've promised eternal safety?
When you're desperate,
where do you head for help?
To the pharmacy,
the supermarket,
next door?
Or do you immediately take off
for the banquet hall of mercy,
where angels welcome you to your most sacred
holy refuge?
Oh, don't forget the one who loves
to help you.
Through thick and thin, I'm here every day
as your stronghold and your God,
endlessly loving you.

Jesus, I'm running to you for safety.
I rush into your heavenly high tower
where you've promised eternal safety.
When I'm desperate, I run directly to you!
I immediately take off for the banquet hall
of mercy where angels welcome me
into my most sacred holy refuge.
I'll never forget that you're the One
who loves to help me through thick and thin,
good and bad; you're here every day
as my stronghold and my God
endlessly loving me—how can I thank you?
Can I ever thank you enough
for all you do for me?

I will tell of the kindnesses of the Lord,
the deeds for which he is to be praised,
according to all the Lord has done for us—
yes, the many good things he has done for Israel,
according to his compassion and many kindnesses.

Isaiah 63:7 NIV

411

HIS WORDS TO ME

Hollow of Your Hand

Who has gathered up the wind in the hollow of his hand?
Who has wrapped up the sea in the pocket of his coat?
Who has established the borders of the earth?
Tell Me if you know, dear child.
It's I who rules the surging sea,
and when its waves mount up,
I quiet them. I rebuke the wind and the lightning;
the hail, snow, and clouds do My bidding.
I still the turmoil of nations and I make
the loud voice of the fool a mere vapor.
Listen. I am the Lord of *all*,
and I gave the oceans their boundaries
so the waters wouldn't overstep My command.
I'm the one who marked the foundations of the earth—
And I can work a miracle in your life today.
Never underestimate Me.

MY WORDS TO HIM

Lord Jesus, you gather up the wind in the hollow of your hand
and wrap up the sea in the pocket of your coat.
You establish the borders of the earth and rule the surging sea
when its waves mount up.
You rebuke the wind and the lightning, and the hail;
snow and clouds do your bidding.
You still the turmoil of nations,
and you make the loud voice of the fool a mere vapor.
You are Lord of all,
and you give the oceans their boundaries,
so the waters won't overstep your command.
You're the one who marked the foundations of the earth,
and you're the God who works miracles in my life!
This is so amazing to me!
I praise you and worship you with all my heart!

I saw another angel flying through the sky, carrying the eternal
Good News to proclaim to the people who belong to this world—
to every nation, tribe, language, and people. "Fear God," he
shouted. "Give glory to him. For the time has come when he will
sit as judge. Worship him who made the heavens, the earth, the
sea, and all the springs of water."

Revelation 14:6-7 NLT

HIS WORDS TO ME

Loved and Cherished

I've been talking to you since before you were born.
I'm the first one who welcomed you into the world
when your mother gave birth.
I've loved and cherished you forever,
and yet you haven't always been aware of My presence.
How many times do you think Moses trekked past Me
with his sheep before he noticed
the inextinguishable bush on fire in the sand?
How long do you suppose I had to call out to Moses
before he heard Me?
I tell you, My presence is subtle, unpredictable,
and supernatural. A burning bush, a mighty wind,
a silent cave, a grassy patch beneath a tree,
the solemn privacy of the holy of holies,
and dear one, in the sacred halls
of your own heart—that's where you'll find Me.
Absorb these words I'm speaking to you,
and come climb into My heart.

Oh Jesus, you've loved and cherished me,
even when I haven't been aware of your presence.
You're the first one who welcomed me
into the world when my mother gave birth.
You've been talking to me since before I was born.
How many times did you have to call out to me
before I finally heard your beautiful voice and responded
by giving my life to you?
How many times did you call Moses before he
turned from his sheep and discovered the burning bush?
Oh Jesus, your presence is subtle at times,
unpredictable and supernatural.
You're a burning bush, a mighty wind, a silent cave,
a grassy patch beneath a tree; you're the solemn
privacy of the holy of holies, and also you enter
the sacred halls of my own heart!
I'm awed and speechless at your greatness.
I want to sit with you now and absorb your majestic presence.

"My presence will go with you, and I will give you rest."

Exodus 33:14 ESV

415

HIS WORDS TO ME

Happy without Wisdom

Acquire wisdom, and with all your acquiring,
get understanding.
If you're wise,
wisdom will reward you.
You won't find happiness
without wisdom.
Wandering about looking for happiness
in the toothsome grins of strangers and flatterers,
eating the deceptive sweetmeats of ambition,
and dancing in the footprints of prideful learning
will never make you happy.
You belong to Me.
I am your happiness
I am wisdom.
Wisdom will delight your soul
and pour healing oil on your parched, dry heart.
Wisdom will bless your life with treasures
of happiness money can't buy.
As you gain wisdom and understanding
accessing My instruction and direction,
all things will be added to you.
and you'll become more and more like Me.

Lord Jesus, it's impossible to be happy without wisdom.
Help me to acquire wisdom today, and along with it,
help me gain understanding.
Your written word tells me if I'm wise, wisdom will reward me.
If I wander about looking for happiness in the ways of the world,
eating the sweetmeats of ambition, pride,
and stockpiling possessions, I'll never be happy.
I belong to you. You alone show me the path of happiness.
You are happiness. You are wisdom.
Wisdom will delight my soul and pour healing oil
on my parched, dry heart.
Wisdom will bless my life with treasures of happiness money can't buy.
As I gain wisdom and understanding, and follow your guidance
and direction, I'll see more clearly what's important
in this life, and what's superfluous.
I've clung to empty pursuits in the past, but I'm a new person now,
and I'm aiming my goals toward birthing more
of the fruits of the Holy Spirit in my daily life.
Each day I will awake with the prayer
to be more and more like you.

The fruit of the Spirit is love, joy, peace, patience, kindness,
goodness, faithfulness, gentleness, self-control;
against such things there is no law.

Galatians 5:22-23 NASB

HIS WORDS TO ME

Life Canvas

Think of yourself today
as an artist.
You're a painter
preparing your canvas and brushes
for a monumental invasion of color,
shape, and movement,
creating what the world has never seen.
Think of yourself as possessing
skills to amaze
with your original expressions of love
and fearlessness.
Every stroke you make on your canvas of life
is yours and yours alone. You're the one
who chooses the colors, the viscosity,
and the movement of the brush. It's you
making the art, nobody else.
Are you glad for the artist
I made you to be?
Are you thankful today that you're
one-of-a-kind, an original,
and that what you bring to the world
is wonderful?

MY WORDS TO HIM

Today, Lord Jesus, I'm going to think of myself as an artist.
I'm a painter preparing my life canvas
for a monumental invasion
of color, shape, and movement, creating
what the world has never seen.
Every stroke I make on my canvas of life reflects the essence
of my very being.
I'm the one who chooses the colors, the viscosity,
and the movement of the brush.
I'm creating the art of my life.
I'm glad to be the life artist you created me to be,
Lord. I'm so thankful today that my life
is one-of-a-kind, and I'm an original in your eyes.
You're the divine artist and I'm the little artist
who takes everything you give me seriously.
Together we make art.

It is God who works in you both to will
and to do for His good pleasure.

Philippians 2:13 NKJV

HIS WORDS TO ME

Block of Stone

Today, think of yourself
as a sculptor
facing your block of stone
and all ready to chisel out the beauty
locked inside.
A form in the stone has been waiting
to be set loose for centuries,
and My Father has sent you
to set the stone-trapped captive free.
You've been given the gift to see
into the hard interior of stone.
You're blessed with the consecrated skill
required to create beauty from ashes.
Trust your gifts today.
Trust Me who made you *who you are.*
Dare to chisel away
at your divinely appointed task
with dignity and holy pride.

Today, Lord Jesus, I'm going to think of myself
as a sculptor facing my block of stone with my chisel prepared
to carve out the beautiful life locked inside.
I'm going to discover the form in the stone that's been waiting
to be set loose.
Thank you, Father God, for sending Jesus
to set the stone-trapped captives free.
Thank you for the gift to see into the hard interior
of stone to create something beautiful.
I'll trust the gifts you've given me today and trust you,
King of kings, who made me who I am.
I'm going to dare to chisel away
at my divinely-appointed task with dignity and holy delight
sculpting my beautiful life for you.

Just as a person's body that does not have a spirit is dead, so
faith that does nothing is dead!

James 2:26 NCV

HIS WORDS TO ME

Drawing Board of Life

Think of yourself today
as an architect
at the drawing board of life
drawing your blueprints for a new environment
where learning, joy, and love will prevail.
See yourself flowing in your builder's gifts
moving forward with the dream
I put in your heart.
I tell you, create with confidence and enthusiasm,
and don't hold back.
I am with you to bring to pass
the results of what I've birthed in you.
Execute your plans with the skill
I've gifted you with,
and you'll receive approval and favor,
and many lives will be saved, enriched,
and prepared for the days to come.

Today, Lord Jesus, I'm going to see myself
as an architect at the drawing board of life,
drawing my blueprints for a new me
in a new environment where learning
and joy will prevail.
I see myself today
flowing in my architect's gifts
moving forward with the dream you've put
in my heart.
I'll create with confidence
and enthusiasm, Lord, and I won't hold back.
I know you're with me to bring to pass everything
you've birthed in me.
I'll execute my plans
for you as you grant me the skills to move ahead
with the dream you've given me.
I pray you'll receive my work with approval and favor
so lives will be saved, enriched, and prepared
for the days to come.

"I will look with favor upon you and make you fruitful and
multiply you; and I will maintain my covenant with you."

Leviticus 26:9 NRSV

HIS WORDS TO ME

Heaven's Music

Today,
think of yourself
as a musician
born to bring heaven's music
to a world weary of noise.
The beautiful song is yours,
yours alone to release into the atmosphere
of My creation
and to resound it against the raucous-topped mountains
and the sky's lustrous silver linings.
No gift of Mine is given without
the love of all heaven
as its back-up cheering it on.
A song without love is not found
in heaven's banks of hymnals and scores.
No recording's ever made it
to heaven's shopping cart without
My love.
So here's your question for the day:
As My personal adorable musician,
bringing music only you can make to a cacophonous world,
doing exactly as I created you to do,
and being exactly who I created you to be,
are you grateful you're you?

Today, Lord Jesus, I'm going to see myself
as a musician, born to bring heaven's music
to a world that's become weary of noise.
The beautiful song I want to bring forth is for you,
and you alone.
Help me to release your song into the atmosphere
so it resounds against the snow-topped mountains
and the sky's lustrous silver linings.
No gift of yours is released to the earth without heaven
observing. I can hear heaven cheering!
A song without love doesn't exist in heaven's concert halls.
Oh Jesus, I want to bring the ecstasy of your song
to the cacophonous world today!

Sing the praises of the LORD, enthroned in Zion;
proclaim among the nations what he has done.

Psalm 9:11 NIV

HIS WORDS TO ME

Annoying Bug Bites

I want you to love your life
and stop with the complaints and grievances
which are like annoying bug bites.
Discontent is a swollen itch
that you live with day by day,
and no swab of happy lotion will help.
You'll go on scratching through the nights
and finding even more to complain about.

I have a sweet contentment cream
like a warm massage to cover you
from head to toe, and mellow your heart.
This balm is all yours if you'll open the door
of your disenchanted mind
where I'm standing and knocking.
Let Me in!
I come with new comforting words
to replace the sore complaints that bristle and scratch
at you. I have beautiful things to tell you!
Let Me in and I'll restore your faith
and give you delicious peace today.

Oh Jesus, I'm going to stop with the complaints
and the grievances which are like annoying bug bites
to my soul.
Help me to possess sweet contentment
like a warm massage.
Mellow my heart, Lord.
I open the door of my disenchanted mind
and invite you in.
Come into my heart, Lord Jesus,
with new comforting words to replace
the sore complaints that bristle and scratch at me.
You have so many beautiful things to tell me.
Restore my faith today,
and give me the delicious peace you long for me
to possess.
I choose to love my life right now!

I will not die; instead, I will live
to tell what the LORD has done.

Psalm 118:17 NLT

HIS WORDS TO ME

Opening My Heart

I created you to go forward into this day
with great openness of heart,
and to embrace life fully.
If a dark moment emerges
in the sunlight of the hours,
breathe a prayerful thank you
and listen for My voice whispering
in your sweet ear:
It is well.
If an enemy of your peace strikes,
I'll give you a warrior's courage to rise up
and take a swing at the ugly thing in My name.
Don't lose a moment in discontent
or defeat today. Embrace goodness.
My Spirit embraces you.

Thank you, Jesus, for opening my heart to go forward
into this new month.
I'll enter life fully today,
and if a dark moment emerges in the sunlight
of the hours, I'll breathe a prayerful thank you
and listen for your whisper in my ear, *it is well.*
When the enemy of my peace strikes,
I'll seek within me a warrior's courage to rise up
and be strong in your name.
Help me not to lose one moment in discontent
or defeat today, Lord.
I'm going to embrace goodness!
Thank you for your Holy Spirit
embracing and comforting me.

"I will pray the Father, and he shall give you another Helper,
that he may abide with you forever."

John 14:16 NKJV

HIS WORDS TO ME

Life's Difficult Paths

Don't avoid life's difficult paths.
Experience the pain
and be complete. Be whole.
Exercise your muscles.
I'll not have you weak
and pampered like a fat rabbit.
Enter through the eye of hard work,
like the narrow hole
at the end of a needle.
Go through
singing and chuckling as you go.
Be wise. Be sympathetic.
Never be afraid of the thief in the night.
Be prepared.
Have a sense of humor.
Your faith is your armor.
Your wit is your relief.
Your courage is your strength.

Thank you, Jesus, for giving me the courage
not to avoid life's difficult paths.
Thank you for the experience of pain that teaches me
to be a complete human being, whole and able
to exercise my spiritual muscles.
I won't be weak in my faith, pampered like a fat rabbit
and expecting you to do everything for me.
Thank you for your Holy Spirit who guides me
and teaches me the path of spiritual maturity.
I want to enter through the eye of hard work
like the tiny opening at the end of a needle,
singing and happy as I go.
Help me to be compassionate and sympathetic,
and prepared with a sense of humor,
so my faith is my armor and my wit is my relief.
Give me wisdom so I'm never afraid of the thief in the night.
I'm so thankful for the courage and strength you give me.

Not that we are adequate in ourselves to consider anything as
coming from ourselves, but our adequacy is from God.

2 Corinthians 3:5 NASB

HIS WORDS TO ME

Sweet Urgings

Nothing is insignificant to Me.
Listen to the sweet urgings of My will
for this new day.
Quiet your heart.
Listen for our hearts to melt together
because I am in the silence,
and I want you to cherish the simplicity
of this moment.
I want you to observe the miniscule,
the almost imperceptible,
touch of My hand on the world
around you.
It's the restless, immature soul that demands
the grand, noisome, and monumental
at all times.
Cherish the simple
to keep from the fermentation of impatience.
Train your spirit to listen for Me
in the silent, desolate spaces.

Nothing is insignificant to you, Lord. Help me to listen
for the sweet urgings of your perfect will for this new day.
I'll quiet my heart and listen as our hearts meld together
because you live in the silence.
I want to cherish
the simplicity of this moment and observe the miniscule, the
almost imperceptible touch of your hand on the world around me.
Help me to overcome restlessness
and immaturity that demand the grand, noisome
and monumental stuff of life.
I'm making the choice now
to cherish the simple things in order to keep myself
from fermenting my mind with impatience and unmet demands.
Help me to train my spirit, Lord Jesus,
and to listen for you in the silent, desolate spaces.

"The LORD is in His holy temple.
Let all the earth keep silence before Him."

Habakkuk 2:20 NKJV

HIS WORDS TO ME

Let Go

You're giving too much time
to what is now gone.
The past offers you nothing but more of itself.
When you obsess about the past,
you give it power to rule the present
and you miss the glory of *this* moment.
To pine for yesterday's riches
is as destructive to the soul
as resentment for what's been robbed.
I tell you, today choose to appreciate
and open your eyes to the goodness in your life
as it is right now.
I use the past, both good and bad, as an instrument to create
a greater future.
I see your past as not only healed and delivered
from the gnawing teeth of the devil,
but as a scrapbook of success to add new pages to.
You're a living wonder today.
Think in terms of today, as I do,
and give the past in its many dimensions
to Me. I know how to turn everything to good.

MY WORDS TO HIM

Lord Jesus, today I'm making the decision to let go of the past.
Thank you for showing me that I'm giving too much time
to what's now gone.
I can see that when I obsess about the past, I give it
power to rule the present, and I miss the glory of this moment.
The past offers me nothing but more of itself!
I'm going to stop pining for yesterday and appreciate today!
Help me to open my eyes
to the goodness in my life as it is right now.
Thank you for using my past, both good and bad,
as an instrument to create a greater future.
My past is healed, and new pages are added
to my scrapbook of blessings.
I'm changing the way I think in order to think in terms
of today, as you do.
I'm handing my past with its many dimensions over to you
because you know how to turn everything to good.

Brothers and sisters, I know that I have not yet reached that
goal, but there is one thing I always do. Forgetting the past and
straining toward what is ahead.

Philippians 3:13 NCV

HIS WORDS TO ME

Living Wonder

Be strong today.
When things seem dreary
and without hope,
grab hold of the strength
I've poured into you.
The notion of hopelessness
doesn't exist in My Kingdom,
and I've given you the spiritual strength
to combat every wily scheme aimed at you
to discourage and tear down your faith.
The substance of everything you hope for
is positioned in your faith.
Be strong, I tell you.
Prove the power of My might today!

I'm a living wonder, Jesus. I'm amazed to see
the changes in me! I'm strong, I'm filled with hope!
The notion of weakness and futility doesn't exist
in your kingdom, and you've given me the spiritual
strength to combat every wily, discouraging scheme
that could tear down my faith. I'm rising up
as a new person inside and out!
Depression is no
longer my companion because I'm letting go
of a wounded heart and a litany of "don't have's."
Instead of disparaging about the thorns on roses,
I'm grateful for the roses on the thorns!
The substance
of everything I hope for is positioned deep within
my faith, and I'm discovering my life has meaning
and purpose beyond that of which I've been aware.
You've created this new person out of me, Father,
Son, and Holy Spirit. Thank you!

Blessed be the LORD,
who daily bears us up;
God is our salvation.

Psalm 68:19 NRSV

HIS WORDS TO ME

Sneaky Snake

Today, dear one,
the subtle taste of jealousy
may try to pinch your cheeks
and cause a grinding of your teeth,
but I want you to be prepared. Pull back
your shoulders and chop the temptation
away with the sword of My Word.
No temptation can grab you by the ear
and yank you into its dark hole
without your help.
Jealousy does more than cause sores on the tongue:
it's a killer.

Oh Jesus, today the sneaky snake of jealousy
nibbled its way into my life.
Help me to pull back
and chop the temptation away with the sword of your grace.
You've taught me that no temptation can grab me
by the ear and yank me into its dark hold unless I'm
willing to let it.
Jealousy does more than cause sores on the soul,
it robs the heart and creates horrible strife.
Peace goes right out the window.
When jealousy comes
at me from others, Lord, cast a balm of healing into
the atmosphere.
Help me to be gracious and not try to defend myself.
Oh Jesus, thank you for your compassion
and for your Holy Spirit in me
who constrains me to behave with a thoughtful heart.
Rescue me from a tendency toward toxic competitiveness.
Your generosity lives in me,
and I'll draw on that now with thankfulness.

Anger is cruel and fury overwhelming,
but who can stand before jealousy?
Proverbs 27:4 NIV

HIS WORDS TO ME

Anchor That Holds

I see you chartered on the open sea of faith
knowing My eyes are on you,
knowing My anchor holds in every storm
no matter the condition of your ship.
You're older now—you've sailed through
some furious storms with your mainsails tattered
and your weatherboard bruised and beaten.
And you've also cruised along the calm waters
of faith singing songs of deliverance and thanks,
knowing there's no storm that can
rip the fluke, pull up your anchor, flood your deck,
tear apart the bow, eat up the chine,
and swallow you whole.
I've kept you safe in the storm
and you'll stay safe all your life.

MY WORDS TO HIM

Thank you, Jesus, for being the anchor that holds tight
in every storm of life.
You've chartered me on the open sea
of faith with your eyes on me, and no matter what
the condition of my ship, you're at the wheel as the captain.
I've sailed through some furious storms,
my mainsails tattered and my weatherboard bruised and
beaten, but I'm still here!
I've cruised along the calm waters of faith,
singing songs of deliverance and joy.
Oh Lord, thank you for it all!
Thank you that there's no storm that can
rip the fluke, pull up my anchor, flood my deck, tear apart the bow,
or eat up the chine and swallow me whole.
You've kept this ship safe in every storm.
I don't ask you to remove the storms, but I ask you to give me
the courage and strength to bravely ride out and learn from them.
Each storm can be a tool for transforming me into the
beautiful, brave person of faith I was born to be.

For the LORD God is our sun and our shield.
He gives us grace and glory.
The LORD will withhold no good thing
from those who do what is right.

Psalm 84:11 NLT

HIS WORDS TO ME

Carry Me Through

Mark your calendar:
Today, I will not get upset.
I'm right at your side
with more than enough peace
to silence your emotional tsunami.
Think of yourself as a runner.
All of your hard work, practice, and sacrifice
is put to the test as you bring your very best
to the race of a lifetime.
But! Your opponent gains speed
in the final fifteen yards,
and crosses the finish line first.

When someone else succeeds
at nabbing the trophy you thought was yours,
find grace in your heart
to appreciate their success.
Contention and jealousy are evil cousins
who corrupt the minds of good people.
Always walk away from jealousy.
Tell yourself no one is less worthy than you.

MY WORDS TO HIM

Today, Jesus, I won't get upset. You're right at my side
with more than enough patience to carry me through.
Oh Lord, silence my emotional tsunami and give me peace!
I feel like the runner who's trained and sacrificed,
and at the race of a lifetime, her opponent takes off like a
bullet and crosses the finish line first. Ouch.
Jesus, when someone else nabs the trophy
I truly thought was mine,
give me grace in my heart to appreciate their success.
Save me from jealousy and self-pity.
And save me from self-condemnation: *I should have done—*
or *why can't I have—?*
Thank you for your gracious
spirit always leading and teaching me the generous mind and
heart of God.
I have all I need in you.
Thank you for showing me that
loss can simply mean a new beginning.

The Lord is near to all who call on him,
to all who call on him in truth.
He fulfills the desire of those who fear him;
he also hears their cry and saves them.

Psalm 145:18-19 ESV

HIS WORDS TO ME

Spiritual Discernment

I want you to learn when to contest
and when to keep your spiritual fists
to yourself.
I'm speaking to you of discernment—
spiritual discernment is a gift of My Holy Spirit
and it means you must give permission
for My will to cohabit your will
in penetrating light
that gives you clear vision on all sides
of what's before, behind, above, and around you.
There's a time to fight and a time not to fight.
The gift of discernment tells you when to speak
and when not to speak,
when to act and when to remain still.
The gift of discernment sheds light on what's true
and what's false.
The gift of discernment allows you to see through
the veil of unknowing and confusion,
and to recognize evil spirits.
Pray for, receive, activate, and put to use
My Holy Spirit's gift of discernment
today and every day of your life!

Thank you, Father God, for spiritual discernment.
Thank you for showing me by your Holy Spirit
when to contest and when to keep my spiritual fists to myself.
Thank you for giving me clear vision to see
on all sides of the matter, and to know there's a time
to fight and a time not to fight. Thank you, Jesus,
for the gift of discernment that tells me when to speak
and when to remain quiet, when to act and when to stay still.
The gift of discernment sheds light on
what's true and what's false, and I thank you for such protection!
Thank you for the gift that parts the veil
of unknowing and confusion, and opens spiritual insight
to recognize and separate evil with its many guises from
God's good.
Lord, help me to be fully aware and put to use
your Holy Spirit's gift of discernment each day of my life.

If you cry for discernment,
Lift your voice for understanding;
If you seek her as silver
And search for her as for hidden treasures;
Then you will discern the fear of the LORD
And discover the knowledge of God.

Proverbs 2:3-5 NASB

HIS WORDS TO ME

Passed Over

It may not be easy to watch someone else
walk off with the promotion or accolades
you deserve.
It may not be easy when another
takes possession of the blessings you've prayed for
and not received.
If you feel set aside and passed over when others
get the recognition and breakthrough,
rejoice for them. Be glad.
Remember, I look at your
heart, and it's your heart I love and promote.
I don't compare you with any living soul,
I see you as *you*. Never envy another.
Your day is coming.

MY WORDS TO HIM

Lord, I have to tell you that I feel ignored and passed over
when others get the breakthrough and blessings I've prayed for
and not received yet. I know your eye is always on me and
your plan for my life is perfect, yet it's not easy to stand in the
shadows watching and waiting as others
walk off with the blessings I'm praying for.
I've got to put an end to envy and feeling sorry for myself, Lord,
right now! I know your timing isn't my timing, and
your ways are much higher than mine, and so today I'm going
to make a new proclamation to be happy for others' success.
It may not be easy, but I'm making a promise to myself to
celebrate when others get what I want (or I think I deserve).
I'll be a much better person if I can keep
my heart pure and free from self-centered intrusions.
I know I'm loved. I know my day is coming.
I'll stop comparing myself with others and be aware of
the blessings I do possess.
I'm so thankful, Jesus, that you
don't compare me with any living soul, and you know
and cherish me enough to build deeper faith in me.
Thank you for seeing me.

A sound heart is life to the body,
But envy is rottenness to the bones.

Proverbs 14:30 NKJV

HIS WORDS TO ME

Attentive

My daily words to you
are meant to guide you
into My profound mysteries
and your assignment on earth.
I want you to be attentive to all I tell you.
Drink in My words
and become a simmering arrow
dipped in the fire of faith
that shoots a direct bull's-eye
into the heart of My purposes.
By My Word you can move mountains.
By My Word the sick are healed,
the lame walk,
the blind see.
Today, realize you were born
to do on earth as I did.

MY WORDS TO HIM

Thank you, Jesus, for talking to me every day!
I want to be attentive to all you tell me.
I want to drink
in your leading and become a shimmering arrow
dipped in the fire of faith that shoots a direct bull's-eye
into the heart of your purposes.
Thank you for the words you speak to me
to guide me into your profound mysteries and my
assignment on earth.
I know that by your Word I can move mountains,
and by your Word the sick are healed,
the lame walk, and the blind see.
Today, help me to follow your example
and to understand that as your child
I'm called to do the work on earth as you did.

"It is the Spirit that gives life. The flesh doesn't give life.
The words I told you are spirit, and they give life."

John 6:63 NCV

HIS WORDS TO ME

Worrying

You worry about the events in the world,
the horrors of the past with nation against nation,
and evil running rampant on the earth.
Listen to Me.
No atrocity performed on earth escapes My eye.
Man's inhumanity to man is not too heinous for Me
to break the neck of its master.
I alone hold the power
to destroy the powers of evil with My fist of judgment,
but this is *My* work, not yours.
You, My darling, pray
and do good in your sphere of influence.
I've shown you the power of goodness, and what I require
of you.
Love mercy, do justly,
and walk humbly with Me.
With these, you'll change the world.

Sweet Jesus, keep me from worrying
about the events in the world,
the horrors of the past with nation against nation and
evil running rampant everywhere.
Help me to listen
for your voice and your wisdom that tells me no atrocity
performed on earth escapes your eye.
Man's inhumanity is not too heinous for you
to break the neck of its master, the devil.
I realize it's your work to destroy the powers
of evil, not mine, for you have all the power of heaven and earth.
There's no power greater than you.
I'll continue to pray and do good in my sphere of influence.
Your instructions to me are to love mercy, to do justly,
and to walk humbly with you.
I trust you, Lord,
and not the events of the world.

He has told you, O mortal, what is good;
and what does the LORD require of you
but to do justice, and to love kindness,
and to walk humbly with your God?

Micah 6:8 NRSV

HIS WORDS TO ME

Sensitive to Your Presence

Be sensitive today to My presence
in the world around you.
Allow My Spirit to awaken your senses
to the sublime
and to all natural beauty.
Loving My world is a form of humility
as you set your inner conflicts aside
to communicate with life outside yourself.
Put your hands on the earth; experience its pulse.
Smell the rose with deeper appreciation, and dare to
watch the scurrying of the ant with greater amusement.

Delight in the dance of sunlight against your sleeve.
Be awed at the divine artwork a river of rain
makes as it slides across a window pane.
Feel the wind on your cheek
as the kiss of a friend you miss.
Don't lose out on the anthem of a sunset
because the drumbeat of worry has deafened you
to the wonders of your world,
and you fail to hear the sigh of My love.

Dear Jesus, teach me to be sensitive to your presence
in the world around me.
I want to allow your Spirit
to awaken my senses to the sublime and to all natural beauty.
I love your world, Lord, and I set aside my inner conflicts to
recognize and appreciate life outside myself.
When I put my hands on the earth to experience its pulse,
when I smell the rose with thankful awareness, and when
I watch the scurrying of a tiny ant, Lord, I feel a thrill.
Every day I discover something new created by you.
I'm learning the art of amazement and I thank you!

In the beginning God created the heavens and the earth.

Genesis 1:1 NIV

HIS WORDS TO ME

Unnatural for Me

To do one thing without Me is unnatural for you,
and exceedingly lonely.
I am He who fashioned the heavens.
I am He who stretched the waters into the seas,
and I am He who created you to be My *friend*.
The heavens tremble and the seas roar,
but with you, My child, I like to sit down
and relish a holy conversation.
I want to hear you speak of urgent earthly matters
and of your compassionate love
for the issues, troubles, and people I love.
I want to show you great and wonderful things
from heaven's storehouses of answered prayer.

Oh Jesus, to do one thing without you is unnatural for me!
You're the one who fashioned the heavens and stretched
the waters into the seas.
You're the one who created me
to be your friend!
The heavens tremble and the oceans roar,
but when we're together I can sense you relishing
our conversation. How amazing!
Thank you for caring about
the earthly matters, issues, troubles, and lives
of people I pray for.
Thank you for listening, and thank you
for showing me great and wonderful things from heaven's
storehouses of answered prayer!

Whatever you do in word or deed, do all in the name of the
Lord Jesus, giving thanks to God the Father through Him.

Colossians 3:17 NKJV

HIS WORDS TO ME

Your Voice

If you have ears to hear,
I'll speak to you now.
It's far easier to admire and make heroes
of those you've never met
than someone in your own midst whose foibles
you know only too well.
It's far more convenient to be kind
to a troubled stranger
than to be compassionate toward
an annoying soul of your own household.
Is there an aggravating, prickly someone
you might speak a gracious word to today—
someone you might make feel appreciated and less alone?

MY WORDS TO HIM

I'm listening for your voice now.
It's far easier to admire and make heroes
of people I've never met than someone
in my own midst whose foibles I know
only too well.
Open my spiritual ears
to hear your leading.
Help me to be kind
to everyone, Jesus!
Help me to treat all people
with respect.
Help me to speak a gracious word
to the people I come in contact with today
because surely the world needs kindness.
Help me to show compassion, Lord.
Thank you for the gift of love that comes directly
from your heart to mine.
And thank you for ears to hear as you guide me.

"He who has ears to hear, let him hear."

Matthew 11:15 ESV

HIS WORDS TO ME

Love Is the Root

Love is at the root of all I am,
and I want you to learn love's language.
I want you to spend time meditating
on My love
and in the practice of loving.
Love is not an accident
of good will or of genial pleasantries.
Love is deeply selfless,
penetrating through the heated,
throbbing core of every universe.
My holy love ignores no human being
nor any human suffering,
and I extend mercy which often the human eye
can't perceive.
Always know: love ignores no one,
insults no one,
takes no one for granted,
refutes no one,
crushes no one.
In the perfection of My love, there is perfect life.
There is nothing greater.

Love is the root of all I'm made of because love is the root of
all you are.
I want to learn love's language, Jesus. I want to
spend time meditating on your love.
Teach me to practice
loving as you love.
I understand that love isn't
an accident of good will or genial pleasantries.
No, love is deeply selfless, penetrating through the heated,
throbbing core of the universe.
Your holy love ignores
no human being, nor any human suffering.
You extend mercy
continually, offering what the human eye can't perceive.
Your love ignores no one, insults no one,
takes no one for granted, refutes no one, crushes no one.
Thank you, Jesus, for the perfection of your love,
for within the walls of your love all of life is perfect.
There is nothing greater.

He who does not love does not know God, for God is love.

1 Jon 4:8 NKJV

HIS WORDS TO ME

Heavy Burdens

I want to take the heavy burdens from you today.
I want to teach you the skills of *rest*,
and how to leap into My loving kindness
like plunging into refreshing cool waters
on a blistering hot day.

Don't ignore My offer to pass
your burdens and cares over to Me
because frustration and exhaustion
will come to sink your ship of hard work,
and you'll be too tired to send them away.
Come to Me now with every burden
and the pressures of your life's circumstances
will subside and recede into My care.

Rest, dear one. I'm reviving and energizing you.
In the midst of the storm, I'll give you peace,
sweet as honey, and its lovely taste
will revitalize your body, soul, and spirit.
Oh yes, rest.

Thank you, Jesus, for taking the heavy burdens from me today.
Thank you for teaching me the skills of rest
and relaxation when I leap into your loving kindness
like plunging into refreshing cool waters in the blistering hot
noonday sun.
Thank you for calling me to bring
the pressures of my life's circumstances to you so they'll
subside in the magnitude of your care.
Thank you for holy relief!
Thank you for sacred moments of
peace and stillness that nurture my daily life.
Thank you for reviving and energizing me.
In the midst of every storm, you give me your peace,
sweet as honey.
The lovely aroma of peace
revitalizes my body, soul, and spirit.
How I thank you.

Because he has set his love upon Me, therefore I will deliver him;
I will set him on high, because he has known My name.
He shall call upon Me, and I will answer him;
I will be with him in trouble; I will deliver him and honor him."

Psalm 91:14-15 NKJV

HIS WORDS TO ME

Your Word Stands

The grass withers, the flower fades,
but My Word stands forever.
My Word is eternal
and stands firm in heaven and on earth.
My Word is a magnitude of light
that enters you as you read,
and My Spirit pierces
into your mind, soul, and body.
My Word is My glory
in your hands as you absorb,
precept upon precept,
what I have to say to you.
Read. Understand.
I'll do more than guide you;
I'll caress you with the eye-opening embrace
of My wisdom and I'll feed you
with exquisite knowledge of who I am,
and who you are in Me.
My Word is the illumination you need
to travel the path of success
every day.

MY WORDS TO HIM

Thank you, Lord Jesus, that your Word stands forever.
The grass withers, the flower fades, but your words
are eternal and stand firm on earth and in heaven.
Your Word is a magnitude of light that enters me as I read.
Your Spirit pierces into my mind, soul,
and body with the living power of your written Word.
Your Word is glorious in my hands as I absorb precept
upon precept all that you have to say to me.
As I faithfully read your Word, you do more than
guide me; you caress me with the warm embrace
of your wisdom and you feed me with exquisite
knowledge of who you are and who I am in you.
Your Word is the illumination that all humans crave
to follow the path of a purpose-rich life.

The precepts of the LORD are right,
giving joy to the heart.
The commands of the LORD are radiant,
giving light to the eyes

Psalm 19:8 NIV

HIS WORDS TO ME

Illuminate Your Word

Today, pray for illumination
into My Word so the holy scriptures
will breathe new, fresh life into you,
and infuse your spirit, soul, and body
with understanding, revelation, and healing.
I'll multiply your faith like rain
as you devote time today to the study of My Word.
Treasure this time with Me
more than your daily bread.
My Word is the food
that never leaves you hungry.
Come, and I'll fill your heart like a cup
pressed down and running over with blessings.

Dearest Jesus, illuminate your Word within me
so the holy Scriptures will breathe new, fresh life
into me and infuse my spirit, soul, and body
with revelation, understanding, and healing.
Thank you for multiplying my faith like rain
as I devote time to the study of your Word.
I treasure the time with you more
than my daily bread! Your Word is the food
that never leaves me hungry.
Thank you for filling my heart with blessings
shaken together, pressed down, and running over!

Every word of God proves true;
he is a shield to those who take refuge in him.

Proverbs 30:5 NRSV

HIS WORDS TO ME

Beside Me

I see the troubles you're facing—
the problems that leap up
from behind the rise in the road,
the wolf poised to spring forth
to attack your flock
and devour your goods.
Oh, but dear one, you must remember,
whatever comes against you,
contends with *Me!*
Take your power today
and rebuke the devourer. Refuse to accept
the thrashing of the enemy's
spiked tail against the walls of your house
and your life.
Hurl the truth into the atmosphere
and strangle the lie
because your enemy is not flesh and blood.
I tell you, today use the fierce
and undefeatable weapon of *faith*
to combat the source of your troubles.

MY WORDS TO HIM

Thank you, Jesus, for being right beside me
as I face new trials.
Thank you for your Holy Spirit in me
guiding me with truth, wisdom, and goodness.
Thank you for peace beyond understanding.
Whoever comes against me must contend with you.
Today I take the power you've given me to rebuke the
devourer, the devil who wants to take me down.
I'll speak the truth into the atmosphere and squelch the lies of
the enemy because my enemy isn't flesh and blood.
Today, Lord, I'm going to fight a spiritual battle
with spiritual weapons and use the fierce and undefeatable
weapon of faith to combat the source of my troubles.
Thank you for empowering me!

They triumphed over him by the blood of the Lamb
and by the word of their testimony;
they did not love their lives so much
as to shrink from death.

Revelation 12:11 NIV

HIS WORDS TO ME

New Path

You're initiating a new path today,
so before you take your first brave steps,
lavish yourself in the balm of My love.
Breathe the aroma of My love
surrounding you; feel the squeeze of
My embrace, the warmth of
My hand in yours. Let My love ignite
love in your heart, in your eyes,
your voice, your touch.

Listen to the love
I've put in your heart, and trust
where I send you. Trust the task.
Trust the path.
My Spirit has gone ahead for you,
and you need not strive
for a single second. My love carries you
on its wings of sovereign favor.

Thank you for initiating a new path for me today, Lord.
Thank you for lavishing me in the balm of your love.
Thank you for the aroma of your tender heart surrounding me.
Thank you for the squeeze of your embrace,
the warmth of your hand in mine.
Your love ignites love
in my heart, in my eyes, my voice, and all I touch.
I trust where you send me, Lord.
I trust the task
you've given and I trust the path you've chosen for me.
Thank you for your Holy Spirit who goes ahead of me,
so I don't need to strive for a single second.
Your love carries me on its wings of sovereign favor.

You gave me life and showed me your unfailing love.
My life was preserved by your care.

Job 10:12 NLT

HIS WORDS TO ME

The Father's Purpose

Your age doesn't matter, dear one.
Never judge your life's worth
by the constraints of a calendar.
I was thirty years old before
entering My public ministry on earth,
and I ministered just three short years.
When I died on the cross, there were billions of souls
who remained unreached,
untaught,
unhealed,
but the shortness of My life didn't limit My Father.
A moment of time is as a thousand years
in heaven's economy, remember?
I fulfilled My Father's will
unrestrained by the boundaries of time on earth,
and your task is no different.
You will complete the will of My Father for your life.
Fix your heart to Mine.
Love Me.
This is what matters.

MY WORDS TO HIM

Jesus, when I realize that the shortness of your life didn't limit
the Father's purposes, I celebrate.
You could have lived to be a
hundred before being crucified on the cross,
but that wasn't the plan of God.
Thank you for showing me
that a life's worth can't be measured by the constraints
of a calendar.
Age isn't the issue, the purposes of God
is the issue.
Thank you that a single day is the same
as a thousand years in heaven's economy.
Thank you, Jesus, for fulfilling Father God's will perfectly,
unrestrained by the limits of your short time spent here
on earth.
Thank you, Jesus, for the assurance of completing
God's will in the time I have on earth perfectly,
just as ordained.

Beloved, do not forget this one thing,
that with the Lord one day is as a thousand years,
and a thousand years as one day.

2 Peter 3:8 NKJV

HIS WORDS TO ME

So Blessed

If you eat at a sumptuous banquet of delights,
or if you nibble on the floor at tasteless crumbs—
when you eat, eat for Me.
If you drink exotic elixirs from golden goblets
reserved for kings, or if you lap water cupped in your hand—
when you drink, drink for Me.
Whatever you do:
If you sleep til the noon sun bakes your bed,
or if you rise up early before the dew;
if you work around the clock, earning little except
the joy of your labor; if you dance with the moon,
sing with the stars; if you bring soup to the sick,
and grain to the poor; *whatever you do, do for Me.*
Work, play, laugh, cry—
love Me—
first.

MY WORDS TO HIM

Lord Jesus, I give to you all I do and all I think
and all I want. I'm so blessed! When I say "all for you,"
that includes eating.
I'm giving you my daily diet, Lord,
so I can honor you with the food that I choose to go into my body.
I want to be responsible for healthy eating so when I
eat, I'll eat for you, and drinking, I'll drink for you.
I know that if I do my part in living healthy, you'll do your part
to bless my efforts and my faithfulness.
Thank you for blessing me and helping me to see
the bright goodness of a healthy lifestyle.
I love feeling good physically,
and I have your Holy Spirit to thank for guiding me
as I make sound, healthy choices on my life's journey.

Listen, my son, and be wise,
And direct your heart in the way.
Do not be with heavy drinkers of wine,
Or with gluttonous eaters of meat;
For the heavy drinker and the glutton will come to poverty,
And drowsiness will clothe one with rags.

Proverbs 23:19-21 NASB

HIS WORDS TO ME

Dark World

Imagine the great cities of the world
in all their lighted splendor—
suddenly gone black.
The cities of the world may lose their light,
but not you.
You, My child, are the light of the world.
You're a city set on a hill
that can't be hid.
My Holy Spirit fills and ignites you,
and your light permeates
the spiritual atmosphere around you.
Everywhere you step your foot, you bring
My presence with you,
for I am the light of the world.
Demons hate the light and run screaming.
Walk with the authority of the Light.

MY WORDS TO HIM

Lord, you've said that though the world might be dark,
I won't lose the light of your presence and your love.
You've called me "the light of the world,"
and this is an incredible thought.
Your children
are a light of the world and cities set on a hill
that can't be lost from sight.
Your Holy Spirit fills
and ignites me, permeating the spiritual atmosphere
around me.
I proclaim that everywhere I set my foot I bring
your presence with me, for you are the light of the world.
Demons hate the light and run screaming from
its dazzling brightness.
Oh Jesus, thank you for
the authority of your light,
and thank you for shining through me!

"Let your light so shine before men, that they may see your
good works and glorify your Father in heaven."

Matthew 5:16 NKJV

HIS WORDS TO ME

Loved Ones

Today,
I want you to touch
the velvet crest of dawn
in the simple clasp
of a loved one's hand.
I want you to demonstrate your love
to those nearest you
with patience, thoughtfulness,
warmth, and prayer
even though you don't believe
they deserve it.
I expect this of you.
They need you.

Thank you, Jesus, for the friends and loved ones
you've given me today.
Thank you for all the people
you've given me to care for and love.
I'm so honored!
Help me to demonstrate my love with patience,
thoughtfulness, warmth and prayer.
I love my friends
and family, and I don't ever want to take a single
relationship for granted.
I don't want to neglect a person
in need when you're calling me to help them.
Keep my heart wide open, Lord, to love and be loved
like you want me to.

This is what God commands: that we believe in his Son, Jesus
Christ, and that we love each other, just as he commanded.

1 John 3:23 NCV

HIS WORDS TO ME

Hollow of Your Hand

I'm holding you in the hollow of My hand,
and here in this very private place
where no harm can touch you
you're *home*.
Rest here in the safety of My hand
completely covered, nestled securely.
You can fall asleep here,
and I'll fill your dreams with peace.

Did you know—to rest in My hand
is the longing of all humankind?
The human quest for love and safety
is a cry for *Me*.
My hand is open to you, dear child.
There's no safer, happier place than here with Me—
sheltered and completely loved.

MY WORDS TO HIM

Lord Jesus, I can sense you holding me in the hollow
of your hand, and here in this very private place where
no harm can touch me, I'm home.
I can rest here
in the safety of your hand completely covered,
nestled securely.
I can fall asleep here!
And you'll fill my dreams with peace.
I believe all
of humankind longs to rest in the palm of your hand like this.
The human quest for love and safety is a cry for you.
There's no safer, happier place than here alone
with you, sheltered and completely loved.
Thank you, Jesus, for your open hand to us!

You have given me the shield of your salvation,
and your right hand has supported me;
your help has made me great.

Psalm 18:35 NRSV

HIS WORDS TO ME

Cares That Rob

Live the winged life, beloved,
above the cares that rob your soul of flight.
Fly today! Soar to your waiting joys!
No longer count the scars,
but instead count the prayers I'm answering.
Come to My Word today;
wash yourself in My words of love.
How tender is the wound?
Let Me dress it for you. I'll clean out the infection
and apply My lovely salve of healing
to rejuvenate what's been damaged.
I'll pour on you the warm oil of My Spirit
to renew your strength. Be brave, dear one,
all shiny—clean and strong,
fire up your wings of faith and fly!
Your scars are the tail wind
to propel you higher.

I'm living above the cares that rob the soul of flight.
Oh Jesus, I live the winged life. I'm flying high today
in you! I'm soaring into joy!
No longer do I stand around
counting the scars of yesterday, but instead I count
the prayers you're answering.
You've dressed all my wounds
and cleaned out the inflection in my soul.
You've applied your lovely salve of healing
to rejuvenate what's been damaged in me.
I'm dedicated to your written Word today,
washing myself in your words of love.
Oh thank you for pouring on me the warm oil of your
Holy Spirit! My strength is renewed!
I feel brave, Lord, all
shiny-clean and strong. I'm firing up my wings
of faith today to fly higher!
My old scars are the tail wind
that propel me forward to my blessed future.

I press on to take hold of that for which Christ Jesus
took hold of me.

Philippians 3:12 NIV

HIS WORDS TO ME

Key to Happiness

The key to being happy when you feel depressed
is to praise Me.
Praise Me in silence and in awe.
Praise Me in thankful whispers.
Praise Me in noise.
Praise Me with instruments,
banners, and flags.
Praise Me with your creative gifts.

Look, I've opened My holy gates for you!
Enter as though you're leading
a long procession of jeweled and robed saints.
Pass the tall carved pillars
along the golden promenade,
and enter My sacred courts
with thanksgiving and more praise.
My house loves dancing, singing, and gladness.
Your praise fills My heart.

MY WORDS TO HIM

Jesus, thank you for the key to happiness.
Thank you that when I feel depressed
I can center my mind on praising you, and there's relief.
Thank you that the language of heaven is praise.
I'm choosing today to praise you with all my heart through all things.
You've opened your holy gates for me
and I'm going to enter as though I'm leading
a long procession of saints praising you.
I want to enter your sacred courts thanking you with all my heart.
Lord, I'll praise you loudly, and I'll also praise you in silence.
I'll praise you with instruments, banners, and flags,
and I'll praise you in the quiet hours alone in silence
and with awed whispers.
Heaven loves praise and I'll praise you as long as I live.
Thank you Jesus for the holy gift of praise!

Praise the LORD!
Let all that I am praise the LORD.
I will praise the Lord as long as I live.
I will sing praises to my God with my dying breath.
Don't put your confidence in powerful people;
there is no help for you there.

Psalm 146:1-3 NLT

HIS WORDS TO ME

Feeling Dejected

When you're distressed
and feeling dejected,
what should you do?
I say sing!
When the chains of disappointment
nip into the flesh of your heart,
and you're wilted with ennui,
give us a song! Yes, sing!
I've shown you that the turmoil of life
can't defeat you,
so come, sit on My shoulders,
and sing to Me.
The song of the dark hour of the soul
is significant, just as a rose after its bloom
is significant. The earth tries to devour you
with its sorrows, but I tell you, rise higher;
a new day is coming!
Feel it!
Sing through the forest of disappointment;
sing to the birthing of new things.
Sing, I say. Sing!

Lord Jesus, when I'm distressed and feeling dejected,
I'll open my mouth and start to praise you.
I'll sing songs of praise and play music that honors you.
I refuse to let the turmoil of life defeat me.
When I feel the chains of disappointment starting to
crush me, I'll come and sit on your shoulders
and sing to you.
You've shown me that the song of the dark
hour of the soul is significant, just as a rose after its bloom is
yet significant.
The world around me tries to devour me with
its sorrow, but I'll rise higher.
A new day is coming!
I can feel it!
I'll sing through the forest of disappointment and
sing to the birthing of *new* things.
Thank you, Jesus for a new song!

Oh sing to the Lord a new song;
sing to the Lord, all the earth!

Psalm 96:1 ESV

HIS WORDS TO ME

Face the Trials

Don't be afraid of the trials.
Oh, they'll come at you,
sometimes like arrows raining from the sky.
Trials strike without warning,
landing with multiple hits.
I tell you
get out of the rain; run to your battle station,
stand fast; hold your position!
Strike back; take the offensive!
Never retreat; fight the battle!
I'm your strength in the rumpus.
I give you power to overcome,
and I give you a holy army of helpers.
You have all the help you need.

Jesus, today I'm going to face the trials before me bravely.
I won't be afraid when the arrows rain from the sky
and trouble strikes without warning.
I'll get out of the rain
and run to my battle station.
I'll stand fast and hold my
position.
I'll take the offensive, never retreat; I'll fight
the battle of faith!
You're my strength in the war of disorder
and chaos, and you give me the power to overcome.
You also give me a holy army of helpers, your angels,
so I have all the help I need.
Thank you, Jesus!

He will give His angels charge concerning you,
To guard you in all your ways.

Psalm 91:11 NASB

HIS WORDS TO ME

Calming My Fears

You're oh so worried about the future, My child,
and worry is like a driving rain
beating down on a lone blossoming flower.
Soon the torrent will bow down the head
of the bloom, its fragrance crushed,
and the precious flower becomes
wilted,
soggy,
frayed,
and depressed.
Your storm of worry is not
engineered by Me.
Won't you end this tempest?

If you struggle to manipulate life's eventualities,
your efforts will frazzle you with worry
because you can't control the future.
You *know* the mind of Christ,
but you can't *control* the mind of Christ.
Leave tomorrow to Me, dear one,
and live for *today*.

Thank you, Jesus, for calming my fears of the future.
Thank you for showing me that worry is like a pelting rain
beating down on a lone blossoming flower.
The torrent bows down the head of the flower's bloom,
so its fragrance is crushed and the flower wilts.
You are not the author of worry.
Worry is never
engineered by you.
I realize I can't manipulate life's
eventualities, and my efforts to control the future
will only frazzle me in futility.
The Word of God
says I have the mind of Christ, but it does not say
I can control the mind of Christ.
I'll leave the future
to you, dearest Savior, and I'll live for today.

Wait on the LORD,
And keep His way,
And He shall exalt you to inherit the land.

Psalm 37:34 NKJV

HIS WORDS TO ME

An Important Day

The day you were born is an important day.
When I considered your birth,
I took into account the lives of those
whose world you'd share,
so I sent you to take your place among them,
and to live your days for Me.
I purposefully gave you the life you have
in order to fulfill the plans
I personally designed for you
in the world as you found it.
You were born perfectly on time.
I decreed the very day, hour, and moment
when you'd enter life on earth—
tiny, blinking, and wet. Can you still hear the angels
and the welcome song they sang over you?
My Father kissed you on the nose
and said, "It is good."
Honor who you are in this hour.

Thank you, Jesus, that the day I was born
is an important day to you.
When you considered my birth you took into
account the lives of those whose world I'd share,
so you sent me to take my place among them,
and to live my days for you.
Thank you, Jesus, for purposefully giving me the life
I have in order to fulfill the plans you personally designed
for me in the world as I found it.
I was born perfectly on time.
You decreed the very day, hour, and moment when I'd enter
life on earth.
Angels sang a welcome song over me,
and my heavenly Father kissed me on the nose and smiled.
Thank you for your love, and for the person
you've made me to be this hour.

"Before I formed you in the womb I knew you."

Jeremiah 1:5 NRSV

HIS WORDS TO ME

Robe of Courage

Awake, dear one,
and put on your robe of courage—
the beautiful gift I gave you
from My loving Father.
Wear your robe of courage
as you go forth into this day,
and take wisdom as your escort.
Courage and wisdom are powerful
weapons against the devil
who continually tries to bully you.
You need courage and wisdom
to stand against the devil, to stay strong
and not become prey to your emotions.
Wear your robe of courage and
hold tight the hand of wisdom.
Your eyes will be opened.
Your mind will bristle with insight,
and your spirit will be fortified.

Courage is like a robe I'm wearing as I go forward
into the new month.
Thank you, Jesus,
for the beautiful gift of courage.
Wisdom is my escort.
Courage and wisdom are powerful
weapons to keep me strong so I don't become prey
to my flimsy emotions.
I'm holding tight the hand
of wisdom with my eyes wide open as I head into
the challenges ahead.
My mind is alive and bristling
with the insight you're giving me.
Thank you, Jesus.
I'm fortified.

"Be strong and brave. Don't be afraid of them and don't be
frightened, because the LORD your God will go with you.
He will not leave you or forget you."

Deuteronomy 31:6 NCV

HIS WORDS TO ME

Lightened Burden

How heavy is your burden today?
Can you, beneath the weight
of your own troubles, help to lighten
the weary load of someone else?
Can you put your complaints on pause
for a moment?
You're never too boggled with care
that you can't help someone else.
You're never too lame to lift up one
who needs a hand.
You're never too blind to help another
see their proper path.
When the hurdles and obstacles
in your life numb you
to the omnipresence of
My loving kindness,
try showing love
to someone.

Thank you, Jesus, for making my burden light.
Thank you that now without the weight of my own troubles,
I can help to lighten the weary load of others.
Thank you for showing me how to put my complaints on pause,
and stop being boggled with care.
I want to reach out
to help with an open, giving heart.
Oh Jesus, save me
from being blind to another person's needs.
When the hurdles
and obstacles in my life become numbing, remind me
that your loving kindness is always with me,
and I can still reach out and show love to someone else.

"Take my yoke upon you and learn from me, for I am gentle and
humble in heart, and you will find rest for your souls. For my
yoke is easy and my burden is light."

Matthew 11:29-30 NIV

HIS WORDS TO ME

Surrounded by Goodness

At times your head may hang low
and your shoulders slump
like bags of laundry—
the weight of the world
is too heavy for you to tote!
I tell you,
look for the good in your life.
You're surrounded by My goodness.
My Father loves you
and is *good* to you.

No need to haul the world around
on your back.
Your life is centered in a glowing sphere
of heavenly *goodness.*
Look up and see your personal blessings.
I'm good to you.
In sweetness and in sorrow,
I'm good to you.
In life and in death,
I'm good to you.
Through every trial of the world,
see the good.

MY WORDS TO HIM

Thank you, Jesus, for surrounding me with goodness.
Thank you, Heavenly Father, for giving me Jesus
as my Savior.
Thank you for being so good to me!
My life is centered in a glowing sphere of heavenly goodness!
I see my blessings flying toward me day and night.
In sweetness and in sorrow, you're good to me.
In life and in death, you're good to me.
Through every trial of the world, you're good!
You're always good!

The LORD passed in front of Moses, calling out,
"Yahweh! The LORD!
The God of compassion and mercy!
I am slow to anger
and filled with unfailing love and faithfulness.

Exodus 34:6 NLT

HIS WORDS TO ME

Unlimited Power

Do you realize the power you have in Me?
You possess *unlimited* power when
you exercise your faith in who I am in you.
You honor Me and demonstrate
My authority in human lives and events
by confidently and assuredly
exercising your faith in Me.
Faith can only expand with use.
When things are difficult
your faith becomes a living illustration
of My power and grace.
Your faith can be as small as a mustard seed,
and it's sufficient to rattle mountains.
Today, put your faith to use as never before.
Enjoy the leading of My will
and pray the impossible.
Move mountains!

MY WORDS TO HIM

Thank you, Jesus, for the power you give me.
You give your children unlimited power when we exercise
our faith in you.
You are Master of my life. I honor you today,
Lord Jesus, and I'll demonstrate my love by confidently
exercising my faith in you.
Faith expands with use.
When things are difficult, my faith becomes a living
illustration of your power and grace.
You've told us that faith as small as a mustard seed
is sufficient to rattle mountains.
Today, Lord, I'm putting my faith to use as never before.
I love the leading of your will
in my day-to-day life.
Help me to pray with mountain-moving faith.

"Truly, I say to you, whoever says to this mountain,
'Be taken up and thrown into the sea,' and does not doubt
in his heart, but believes that what he says will come to pass,
it will be done for him."

Mark 11:23 ESV

HIS WORDS TO ME

Compassion at the Center

A heart of stone has no pulse,
and a person without compassion
has forged for himself a heart of stone.
Compassion is at the center
of My merciful heart.
Compassion doesn't repel or ignore
the inconvenient and messy needs of others.
Compassion doesn't turn sour
when things go awry. Compassion is never rude,
never judges harshly,
is never quick to condemn,
and is *always* loving.
A person without compassion is like a well
without water—a river of dust.
To be without compassion is to be
rotted fruit shriveled in sand.
You're called and chosen of Me, holy and beloved;
be compassionate in your choices today.

Thank you, Jesus, for showing me that compassion
is at the center of your merciful heart.
Compassion doesn't repel or ignore our
inconvenient and messy needs.
Compassion doesn't turn sour when things go awry.
Compassion is never rude, never judges harshly,
is never quick to condemn, and is always loving.
You are compassion.
Thank you, Jesus.
And thank you for calling and choosing me
to be compassionate like you.
I want to reflect your kindness and generous heart
in everything I do.
Show me the way of compassion
in all my choices today.

Do not let kindness and truth leave you;
Bind them around your neck,
Write them on the tablet of your heart.

Proverbs 3:3 NASB

HIS WORDS TO ME

Spiritual Refreshment

Come away with Me today,
and let's laugh and be free.
I'm offering you spiritual refreshment.
Let Me hug you with contentment
and a lovely sense of well-being.
Be My carefree child,
and let's go outside and play!
I not only love
the work you do in My name,
I love your recreation, too.
Think of taking time to play as a gift to Me,
and play with all your heart!
I delight in everything about you.

Thank you for spiritual refreshment today, Lord Jesus.
Thank you for laughter and rest.
Thank you for your
sweet peace that fills and grants me a tranquil heart.
Thank you for the wonderful sense of well-being,
for I know that the work I do in your name is good work.
I also know you love our time of rest and recreation.
Thank you for the gift of play and for this time
of feeling carefree and boundless with hope.
It's so good to pull aside for respite from the day's work
and its cares.
Thank you for delighting in me
because I delight in you!

He who has entered His rest has himself also ceased from his
works as God did from His. Let us therefore be diligent to enter
that rest, lest anyone fall according to the same example of
disobedience.

Hebrews 4:10-11 NKJV

HIS WORDS TO ME

Physical Exercise

Your body depends on you
to care for its needs.
You say, "But ,"bodily exercise profits little.'"
You quote Me wrongly.
Without exercise, you can't prosper
because your neglected body
will hobble along trying to keep up
with your enlightened spirit
and your rekindled soul. Weak and unused,
it shifts into neutral and goes stagnant.
Dear child, your body is your real estate.
It's home for your soul and spirit,
and you can't rent space elsewhere.
It's My Holy Spirit's temple.
Some live to glorify their body,
but I tell you to glorify Me *in* your body.

Thank you, Jesus, for physical exercise.
Thank you for showing me to take care
of my body's needs to exercise in order to
maintain muscle and bone health.
I realize it's important for my body
to keep up with my enlightened spirit.
I want to be strong for you because my body
is my real estate; it's home for my soul and spirit,
and it's your Holy Spirit's temple.
I've seen people
who live to glorify their bodies, but I choose
to glorify you in my body.

You should know that your body is a temple for the Holy Spirit
who is in you. You have received the Holy Spirit from God.
So you do not belong to yourselves.

1 Corinthians 6:19 NCV

HIS WORDS TO ME

Grace and Love

Don't be timid.
Today, bare your teeth
with grace, clench those fists
with love, and become
a sudden storm of godly authority.
Don't be intimidated
when jealous demons
with fingers like thorns
try to snap up your blessings.
Don't bargain with these devils,
or make a cowering effort to placate them.
Resist and stand against them!
When you're led by My Holy Spirit,
you can't be friends with the devil.
I realize you want to be nice to everyone,
but you can't pacify the destroyer
who wants to slap your soul to hell.
To function wholly and triumphant
in My kingdom, take off your shyness costume
with all the smiley faces,
and put on the My full armor
like the tough, smart warrior
I created you to be.

Today, Lord, I'm going to bare my teeth with grace
and clench my fists with love.
I'm going to become
a sudden storm of godly authority!
I won't be intimidated
when I'm met with unkind, jealous spirits eager to wipe out
my peace and composure.
I'm led by your Holy Spirit
and therefore, I won't play tag with the devil
who wants to slap my soul to hell.
I'm going to function
wholly and triumphantly today as a child of God.
I'm going to erase every vestige of spiritual shyness from me
with all my shy smiley faces.
I'm going to put on
my full armor and act like the smart, godly warrior
I'm called to be.

Little children, you are from God, and have conquered them; for
the one who is in you is greater than the one who is in the world.

1 John 4:4 NRSV

HIS WORDS TO ME

Extra Dose

Today, I'm giving you extra doses
of grace and wisdom
which you need.
Don't allow feelings of inadequacy to visit you
for one moment.
There's not a believer on the crust of the earth
who's inadequate for the tasks I assign.

You need grace to have the courage to relinquish
your jungle of responsibilities to Me.
Spiritually, you're empowered for greatness!
Don't surrender your glorious power in Me
for a sack of cheesy self-doubt.
I'm accomplishing My purpose in you,
and the choices you face today
depend on your brave, wise frame of mind.
Grace will bring you a caravan of rewards
when you least expect it.

MY WORDS TO HIM

Today, Lord, I need an extra dose of grace and wisdom.
I don't want to allow my feelings of inadequacy to take over
for one moment.
You've made me adequate for the tasks
you've assigned me.
Thank you for the grace and courage
to relinquish my jungle of responsibilities to you.
I'm empowered spiritually for greatness.
I won't surrender the glorious power
you've given me for a cheesy load of self-doubt.
You're accomplishing your purposes in me,
and the choices I face today depend on my brave,
wise frame of mind.
I'm fully aware of my need for surrender
to you because your grace brings me a caravan of rewards.

If you need wisdom, ask our generous God, and he will give it to
you. He will not rebuke you for asking.

James 1:5 NLT

HIS WORDS TO ME

Fountain of Mercy

When there's hardship
in your life, and your day
isn't going well, don't think
I'm the one throwing
sticks at the spokes of your wheels.
I'm not responsible
if things fall apart and don't go
as you planned.
I'm not evil.
I'm the goodness out of which
flows all goodness.
I'm the fountain of mercy
from which flows all mercy.
I am love.
Don't assign human suffering
as My perfect will.
Don't think I'm the one who
initiates poverty, disease,
destruction, failure, loss,
and misery of every stripe
in the world today.
*I have come to pour out life
in the world, and life more abundantly!*
I'm here to transform human suffering.
I'm here today to transform you.

510

Lord Jesus, you're the goodness out of which all goodness flows.
You're the fountain of mercy from which flows all mercy.
You are love.
I won't ever assign human suffering
as your perfect will, no, no, no.
You're not the one
who initiates hardship, poverty, disease, and misery in the world.
You came to pour out life to the world, and life more abundantly!
You're the Son of God who came to transform human suffering
and promote us to good lives of strength and courage.
Thank you for your love for all of humanity,
and forgive us for the misery we inflict on ourselves.
Forgive us, Lord.

O Lord, you are so good, so ready to forgive,
so full of unfailing love for all who ask for your help.

Psalm 86:5 NLT

HIS WORDS TO ME

Going Before Me

I realize your need for light
at the end of a seemingly endless, execrable tunnel,
but remember I go before you
to furrow out a clean, clear route to follow.
Don't think you're alone.
All I ask is you stay with Me,
close enough to feel My breath.

I'm leading you safely past dark
detours of temptation and doubt.
I'm showing you how to press on
in spite of foul air and emotional mudslides.
I'm leading you across fallen plans and
dashed hopes.
I'm preparing you for a new tomorrow
bathed in the Sonlight of My perfect plan,
and when you step your darling foot
on the threshold of your new life,
there'll be much celebration.

MY WORDS TO HIM

Thank you, Lord Jesus, for going before me, furrowing out
a clean, clear route for me to follow.
I'm not alone!
Thank you for knowing my needs better than I know them.
Thank you for keeping me close by you!
Sometimes, Lord,
I feel you so close, I can feel your breath on me!
How sublime is your love and your presence!
Thank you for leading me safely past dark detours
of temptation and doubt.
Thank you for showing me
how to press on in spite of my emotional mudslides.
Thank you for leading me across fallen plans and dashed hopes.
Thank you for preparing me for a new tomorrow
bathed in the Sonlight of your perfect plan!

God alone my soul waits in silence;
from him comes my salvation.
He alone is my rock and my salvation,
my fortress; I shall not be greatly shaken.

Psalm 62:1-2 ESV

HIS WORDS TO ME

Leading Me Today

Today, walk in the Spirit,
so you won't become entangled
in fleshy stuff of futile worldliness.
In order to stay vitally close to Me
and experience the myriad benefits I offer,
set your soul like a clock
and come to My throne more often.
Come with praise and gratitude;
come with your beautiful love and your faith.

Worship Me along with the legions of angels
who know that praise
is the fountain from which flow
all of My blessings.
You can beg and bargain,
but My holy ears respond to *faith*,
and faith burgeons when nourished
and trained by loving worship.
Set your soul like a clock and come to Me
knowing who I am,
and watch My favor explode over you.

MY WORDS TO HIM

Thank you, Jesus, for leading me today so I won't become
entangled in fleshly stuff of futile worldliness. Help me
to set my soul like a clock and come to your throne more often.
I praise you! I adore you! I love you!
And I worship you
along with the legions of angels who know that praise
is the fountain from which all of your blessings flow.
I can beg and foolishly bargain with you for answered prayer,
but your holy ears respond to faith, and faith burgeons
when nourished and trained by loving worship.
Oh what an honor to worship you!
I'm setting my soul clock
to worship you, and as I pour out my love, I thank you
for the favor I sense exploding around me.
You inhabit, actually live in, the praises of your people
and you're here! Now!

You are not like that, for you are a chosen people. You are royal
priests, a holy nation, God's very possession. As a result, you
can show others the goodness of God, for he called you out of
darkness into his wonderful light.

1 Peter 2:9 NLT

HIS WORDS TO ME

Things Above

Set your affections on things *above*,
and don't get side-tracked
by the racket you hear from below—
in the basement of life.
It's loud down there with the screaming
and yelling of your name.
I'm telling you, get on the
Holy Spirit elevator at once!
Groveling around in the dank,
window-less lower floors of life ruins your eyes.
You get snapped up in noise,
feeling your way around, blinded and stupid.
I'm up here in the holy penthouse!
The *top* floor. There's a rooftop garden
of delights up here, sweet, succulent,
happy, peace-fed.
Where are you?

Jesus, your Word tells us to set our affections on things above
and not below.
This means you're telling us to think
higher thoughts and not to get side-tracked by the racket
we hear from below in the basement of life.
I'm getting on
the Holy Spirit elevator now, and going up to a higher floor.
I'm moving on up to the holy penthouse where the sun
is brilliant and bright, and the smile of God fills the atmosphere!
I want to bask in the rooftop garden of your delights, Lord,
sweet, happy, peace-fed and beautiful.
Thank you, Jesus, for pulling me out of darkness
and high up into the light of who you are.

"I dwell in the high and holy place,
With him who has a contrite and humble spirit,
To revive the spirit of the humble,
And to revive the heart of the contrite ones."

Isaiah 57:15 NKJV

HIS WORDS TO ME

Never Doubt

Don't ever, for an instant, doubt Me.
I see all and I know all.
Today, I'm showing you more of the mysteries
of My kingdom.
Open the eyes of your spirit and listen with
your spiritual ears because
My ways are not a puzzle for humans to solve,
but a way of life that transports peace,
love, and joy into the human heart.
The hidden mystery I speak of isn't
revealed in the world but is embedded in heavenly
and divine power and wisdom.
If you continue to look for answers to what
concerns you in the breadbasket of the world,
you'll eat, but you won't be satisfied.
I've come to satisfy the longing soul,
to bring joy to the hapless,
hope to the wounded,
and inspiration to the thinker.
I've come with a banquet of mysteries explained
for you to feast on today.
Come and dine.

MY WORDS TO HIM

I won't ever for an instant doubt you!
You see all and you know all.
I open my heart to you, Jesus, to show me
more of the mysteries of your kingdom.
I open the eyes of my spirit and listen with my spiritual ears
because your ways are not a puzzle for humans to solve,
but a way of life that only your Holy Spirit can reveal.
You bring peace, love, and joy into the human heart, and this
is certainly a mystery.
The hidden mysteries of God aren't revealed in worldly pursuits,
ut are embedded in heavenly and divine wisdom from above.
Your Holy Spirit is my teacher.
If I continue to look for answers to the problems
of the human condition in the world itself,
I'll never know what's what.
You are creator of all there is!
In you is all knowledge!

"But only God has wisdom and power,
good advice and understanding."

Job 12:13 NCV

HIS WORDS TO ME

Eyes Haven't Seen

Human eyes haven't seen, nor have human ears heard,
and in fact, it hasn't even entered the heart
of any human being
the things I've prepared for My own
who love Me.
My Spirit searches the depths,
and the only way to know Me
is to be one with Me.
Toss out the icons of other gods. They are distortions
and powerless, pulp and mush.

Dear one, you haven't received the spirit of the world,
but the Spirit from Me!
I search all things, and *I know all things*.
I'm revealing My heart to you
and I really want you to listen.
I want you to know the things
that have been freely given to you by Me.
I want you to know more
than you thought possible to know.

I'm so grateful today, Jesus.
Human eyes haven't seen, nor have human ears heard,
and in fact, it hasn't even entered the heart of any human being
the things you've prepared for your people who love you.
Your Holy Spirit searches the depths of every person,
and I'm so grateful that I haven't received the spirit of the world,
but the Spirit of the living God!
You search all things,
and you know all things.
I've rejected the vain ideas and promises
of false religions and philosophies, Lord.
They're distortions of your majesty.
Thank you for revealing your heart to those who love you.
Thank you for filling the hungry soul.
Thank you for showing me so many of your free gifts.
I want to know more and more, Lord.
Open my heart and my mind to dedicate myself
to learning more of you, and who I am in you.

"Eye has not seen, nor ear heard,
Nor have entered into the heart of man
The things which God has prepared for those
who love Him."

1 Corinthians 2:9 NKJV

HIS WORDS TO ME

Aflame with Love

Allow Me to slip My hand
beneath your burden and lift it from you.
My love for you is of such intensity
that it's impossible to escape My watchful eye.
I'm glued to you.
We experience life together, dear one.
I'm not parked in a heavenly ramp
while you motor around down in the world on your own.
No no no. *I am with you always!*
You're precious to Me,
and those you love are precious to Me.
What concerns you concerns Me!
But remember, there's no fear in love,
and what frightens you escapes Me entirely.
I fear nothing

Child, you and I are *one* in the Spirit,
so if I fear nothing and I am all-knowing,
and all-powerful,
and present everywhere at once,
what are you upset about?
Pray in My name to dump the fear and the hassled mind.
Love Me and live!
I have wonderful things in store for you today.

MY WORDS TO HIM

I'm utterly aflame with love, Lord Jesus,
knowing your love for me is of such intensity
that it's impossible to escape your watchful eye.
I'm glued to you and you're glued to me!
We're one! I love knowing that we experience life
together because you're not somewhere up in the sky
while I'm down here doing life.
No, no, no.
You're with me always!
There's no fear in love,
how wonderful.
What frightens me escapes you
entirely because you fear nothing—and you live in me!
We're one in the Spirit! I'm dumping fear
and a hassled mind from me right now.
To love you, Jesus, is to live!
You have wonderful things
in store for me every day and I thank you
with every cell of my being!

"Whoever believes in me, as Scripture has said, rivers of living
water will flow from within them." By this he meant the Spirit,
whom those who believed in him were later to receive.

John 7:38-39 NIV

HIS WORDS TO ME

Move of Your Spirit

Listen. The move of My Spirit is like the roar
of the wind.
Evidence of My presence is all around you
and in you.
I've heard your prayers in the wind of My Spirit.
Your loving, gracious heart
has touched Mine;
our discussions have been recorded
and honored.
I'm fulfilling My Word in you today,
and blessings, like rain rushing to the earth,
are coming to you.
Take heart.

MY WORDS TO HIM

I'm listening for the move of your Spirit, Lord.
Evidence of your presence is all around me and in me.
I know you hear the prayers of your children
in the wind of your Spirit.
Your loving, gracious heart
leads me to goodness and happiness.
Thank you for fulfilling your promises in me today!
Blessings are rushing to the earth, aimed directly at your own.
I can almost hear the glorious roar of the mighty wind
of miraculous blessing on its way!
Thank you!
Like Hannah of old, I thank you in advance
of your blessings and answered prayer!

"My heart rejoices in the LORD!
The LORD has made me strong.
Now I have an answer for my enemies;
I rejoice because you rescued me."

1 Samuel 2:1 NLT

HIS WORDS TO ME

Teaching Discipline

Your choppy travels in self-gratification
have been derailed.
The folly train must stop
at the depot of discipline to refuel today.
Pause to look carefully into
the depot's mirror of My Holy Spirit.
Whose eye winks back at you?
Is it your own, outlined in pouting shadows?
Or is it the sweet reflection of
My Spirit in you?
To be content with your life's circumstances,
you need discipline.
I don't pamper you like damaged royalty.
I don't spoil you by catering to your many demands.
No, I build you—I form character and strength in you!
You'll never be happy without discipline.
I'm at the door of the depot of discipline,
welcoming you for your refueling.

Thank you, Lord Jesus, for teaching me discipline.
When I look into the mirror I want to see
a Holy Spirit-filled person smiling back at me.
Your Word teaches me that in order to be content
with my life's circumstances, I need spiritual discipline.
I must teach myself to think the way you think!
You don't pamper me, catering to my many demands
like a spoiled child; no, you teach me to be strong and live
with dignity.
Thank you for building character in me.
I'll never be happy without discipline,
and I'm so grateful that you never tire of teaching me.

I discipline my body and keep it under control, lest after
preaching to others I myself should be disqualified.

1 Corinthians 9:27 ESV

HIS WORDS TO ME

Every Hair

I know what you have need of.
I'm concerned about every hair
on your head.
You're concerned about such things as
what to fill your closet with,
and you lust for items in store windows
and on the pages of slick magazines.
You burden yourself with bills
to pay for the things you've bought
that make yourself feel richer
than you are.
Consider the lilies of the field, My love;
they neither toil nor spin,
and they're arrayed in outrageous beauty.
King Solomon, the richest king
in all the world, didn't wear clothing as beautiful
as a single lily.
You're concerned about clothing your body.
What about the wardrobe of your soul?

Jesus, it amazes me that you're concerned
about every hair of my head.
You're concerned about what I wear, what I eat,
what I do with my spare time.
You're concerned about my social life, my work, my teeth, my bills.
You're concerned about everything in my life!
It's thrilling to think that the Creator of the universe
is concerned about me.
You love the lilies of the field and clothe them
more royally than King Solomon in all his glory,
and you tell me you love me more than the lilies.
How beautiful! Lord, help me to adorn my soul
with such an array of outrageous beauty.

"The very hairs of your head are all numbered."

Matthew 10:30 NASB

HIS WORDS TO ME

Directly to My Heart

Don't be intimidated because
you lack knowledge in My Word.
Not to worry.
I'm speaking directly
to your heart today,
so you'll marvel at the reality
of My presence over you.
Sense the presence of goodness,
peacefulness, answered prayer,
and a Savior who loves you!
Though frustration has been
a constant irritant,
and you've felt inadequate in the past,
I don't want you to be intimidated
by those feelings any longer.
Come to My Word and absorb
into your heart the confidence and assurance
I freely offer you.
Let Me remove the fragments of uncertainty
because a vibrant connection with Me dispels negativism.
Don't worry. I understand you.

MY WORDS TO HIM

Thank you, Jesus, for speaking directly to my heart each day.
I marvel at the reality of your presence.
I sense the presence
of your goodness, your peacefulness and answered prayer, Lord.
Thank you for so much love.
I'm putting aside feelings
of inadequacies, and I'm coming to your Word to absorb
the confidence and assurance the Scriptures give me.
Thank you for removing the fragments of uncertainty from me.
A vibrant connection with you dispels negativism,
and this is what I aim for.
Thank you for understanding me
at all times, not just the good times, but all times.

By grace you have been saved through faith, and that not of
yourselves; it is the gift of God, not of works, lest anyone should
boast. For we are His workmanship, created in Christ Jesus for
good works, which God prepared beforehand that we should walk
in them.

Ephesians 2:8-10 NKJV

HIS WORDS TO ME

Person of Integrity

Always think of yourself
as a person of integrity—
a person who doesn't rely
on false pretenses.
You've no need to boast
or lie or fumble
with false inventions
to earn acceptance
or keep the peace.
Your integrity
doesn't muff responsibility
but delights in being loyal.
Words embroidered with flattery
and dishonest intentions
make an ugly pattern
to be kept hidden
in the cabinet of mistakes.
This is behavior you avoid.
I love honesty and faithfulness;
I love the wholesomeness and
the incorruptibility of your soul.

MY WORDS TO HIM

Thank you, Jesus, for making me a person of integrity,
a person who doesn't rely on false pretenses.
I have no need to boast, lie, or fumble with false
inventions to earn acceptance or to keep the peace.
My integrity doesn't shirk responsibility.
I delight in being loyal.
I avoid words
embroidered with flattery and dishonest intentions
at all cost.
I love honesty and faithfulness.
I love wholesomeness; I love living with
quiet faith and an incorruptible soul.
And oh, Jesus, I love you.

Your beauty should come from within you—
the beauty of a gentle and quiet spirit
that will never be destroyed and is very precious to God.

1 Peter 3:4 NCV

HIS WORDS TO ME

Without Complaint

Listen to your own words.
Can you hear the tedious grinding
when you complain?
When you complain, it's
living as a shadow scratching around
in the dark without substance.
Your grumblings are shadows and smoke.
They'll vanish in the light of My Word.
Take truth. Take substance. Take heart.
Take the blows. Take wisdom. Take the pain.
Take life!
Honor this day, beloved. Live it fully and cherish it
for everything it brings—everything.
Take the present with all it renders no matter what.
Live the present with all your wisdom, courage and
compassion.
Love the present with the magnificent power of your faith.

Forgive me for complaining, Lord.
I want to honor this day.
I want to live it
fully and cherish it for everything it brings—
yes, everything it brings! Good and bad!
Oh Jesus, today I take truth.
I take substance. I take heart. I take wisdom. I take pain.
I take the blows. I take life!
My grumblings are smoke
and they vanish in the light of your promises.
I'm going to take the present moment with all wisdom,
courage, compassion and live.
Thank you for exposing sin
when it needs exposing.
I've been complaining in my heart,
and I choose now to live by faith and stop complaining.
Thank you for freeing me from myself
and a pinched, self-centered mind.

Whatever gains I had, these I have come to regard as loss because
of Christ. More than that, I regard everything as loss because of
the surpassing value of knowing Christ Jesus my Lord.

Philippians 3:7-10 NRSV

HIS WORDS TO ME

Removing the Fragments

I know the betrayal you've suffered,
and I know how hard you've tried
to hide from your fears of being hurt again.
Dear one, let Me remove
the fragments of your wounded spirit.
You can face your fears!
In the humility of My love
and in the power of My Spirit,
proclaim the ascendancy of My Word
over your life
to permit the peace that has been stolen from you
to be restored.
True to My Word, *I restore your soul.*
I'll make you a beacon of honor,
but I need you to do your part,
so rise up and wash yourself
in the mist of glorious victory today.

Thank you, Jesus, for removing from me the fragments
of a wounded spirit.
Thank you for helping me to face
my pain and for giving me the inner strength to stand up
to the hurts I've experienced.
In the power of your Holy Spirit,
I proclaim the ascendancy of your Word over my life
to permit the peace that has been stolen from me
to be restored.
I'm rising up today to live in victory
over the past, and to become a beacon of honor in you, Lord.
I'm changing my self-talk to speak beautiful truths to myself,
words of healing and restoration.
You've given me everything I need
to open my heart to love again.

"I am the Lord who heals you."

Exodus 15:26 NKJV

HIS WORDS TO ME

Your Hand on My Life

My hand is upon you today.
Don't be discouraged or dejected.
You'll profit much this whole week if you
don't allow yourself to get faint-hearted
and droopy.
I'm revealing Myself
and My creativity to you
in exciting new ways.
I have a few new skies for you to fly,
steep valleys to zip-line across,
tall hills to climb—
and oh, you're going to love these challenges
because you'll see My hand on everything you touch,
and you'll bring My joy with you
wherever you go. I love you.

Thank you, Jesus, for your hand on my life today,
helping me to be all that I can be in you.
I won't be discouraged or dejected
because I know I'll profit much if I don't allow myself
to get faint-hearted and self-obsessed.
Help me to see what's inside me,
so I can go forward without personal hindrances.
Prepare me as you reveal yourself to me in new ways, Lord.
I know you have so much ahead for me to conquer
and to love—new skies to fly and steep valleys to ride across—
I know I'll love each challenge if my heart is right,
so today I'm choosing to absorb your joy
because you've said your joy is my strength.
Thank you for your joy which I'll bring with me
in every step I take, wherever I go.

The Spirit of God, who raised Jesus from the dead, lives in you.
And just as God raised Christ Jesus from the dead, he will give
life to your mortal bodies by this same Spirit living within you.

Romans 8:11 NLT

HIS WORDS TO ME

Proud Heart

Respect comes with a price.
Honor isn't free of charge.
Integrity is earned.
Those who strut about
with puffed up chests and noses pointed
like silos in the sky
will always annoy you.
You'll never make friends with
the proud unless you bend down to their
base status, and you could hurt
your knees squatting so low;
you could scrape your chin.
Forget about it.
Let the proud bury the proud.
You, dear one, walk with dignity
and humility and be glad
you're free.

Thank you, Jesus, for saving me from having a proud heart.
I know that if I strut about with a puffed up chest
and nose pointed to the sky,
I'll be walking in the lowest crevices of life.
Thank you for showing me that walking with dignity
and humility is walking on the higher road,
and in rejecting pride,
I'm free.

"If the Son sets you free, you will be free indeed."
John 8:36 ESV

HIS WORDS TO ME

Greater Than

Know My mind.
I'm greater than what you own.
I'm more than all your wants.
You can gather to yourself things—
cars, houses, trips, real estate, investments,
jewels, gold, and silver;
you may own castles in a few countries;
you may have avenues and islands
named for you;
but oh, beloved,
these things don't mean you're rich.
Detach yourself from what you own
and what you don't own.
See yourself as rising tall
above possessions, and be like a pillar of light,
rich in the glory of *My* unlimited resources.
In Me you have no lack
no matter what your bank account says.
I want you to enter the place
where your heart is free
and your mind is at peace,
the place of unending *spiritual* riches.

Oh Jesus, you're greater than my wants.
You're greater than my possessions.
I can gather up all that I have, but it means nothing
in light of the greatest possession of all—
being one with you.
Today, I detach myself from my possessions,
and I see myself as rising tall above
what I own and don't own.
I'm rich in the glory of your unlimited resources.
In you I have no lack, no unmet needs.
No matter what my bank account says,
I'm rich in you.
Today, I enter the place
where my heart and mind are free.
I'm at peace with who I am
and what I have.

Not that I speak in regard to need,
for I have learned in whatever state I am,
to be content:

Philippians 4:11 NKJV

HIS WORDS TO ME

Lackluster and Lukewarm

There's no place in your life for mediocrity.
Nothing about Me is inconspicuous
or lackluster; nothing about Me is secretive,
lukewarm, or wishy-washy.
If you bear My name,
you can't walk in the world unnoticed;
you can't live a tepid, bland life because
you'll never be invisible.
I am a holy, all powerful, omnipotent God,
and as My child you're on the earth
reflecting Me and the vastness of My personality.
Open your ears
and let Me speak to and through you.
Obey Me fully.
I'm not calling you to be a clanging bell,
a brassy symbol, a loud-mouth bore,
and religious threat, no.
It's our *relationship* that can be seen by all.
There's no substitute for My love for you,
and there's no substitute for your love for Me.
This in itself makes you and your faith
eternally unique.

Oh Jesus, nothing about you is inconspicuous or lackluster.
Nothing about you is lukewarm or wishy-washy. I'm yours;
I bear your name, and that means I can't walk around
in the world unnoticed.
I can't live a tepid, bland life
because with your Spirit in me, I'll never be invisible.
You're a holy, all-powerful God, and as your child I reflect you
and the vastness of your personality.
This is amazing!
Help me, Jesus. I know you don't want me to be
a clanging bell or a brassy cymbal.
You aren't honored if I'm a loud-mouthed know-it-all.
Or if I try to hide behind a false face of shyness and shame.
Oh Jesus, it's our relationship that should be seen by all,
and there's no substitute for your love.
Speak through me, Lord,
live through me!

I have been crucified with Chrst; it is no longer I who live,
but Christ lives in me; and the life which I now live in the flesh
I live by faith in the Son of God, who loved me
and gave Himself for me.

Galatians 2:20 NKJV

HIS WORDS TO ME

Gift of Wisdom

Wisdom wants to be your partner in life.
Wisdom wants to preserve your days
and give you good sense, perspicacity, balance.
Wisdom wants to make you discerning
and savvy.
Wisdom wants to teach you how beautiful
your life is, and how honored you are to be called
to live by faith.
Wisdom won't allow you to lament or pine away
for what's not yours,
and wisdom will show you that I made both
prosperity and adversity for your benefit.
Wisdom wants you to have My mind
and be glad.
Today, take wisdom by the hand
and don't let go.

Thank you, Jesus, for the gift of wisdom.
Thank you for making wisdom a partner in my life.
Wisdom wants to preserve my days and give me good sense.
Wisdom wants to give me balance and understanding.
Wisdom wants to make me discerning and savvy.
Thank you, Jesus, because wisdom has taught me
that my life is beautiful.
Wisdom has taught me how honored I am
to be called to live by faith.
Wisdom won't allow me to lament or pine away
for what's not mine, or what I don't have.
Wisdom shows me that both prosperity
and adversity are for my benefit.
Wisdom wants me to have your mind, Jesus, and be glad.
Today, I take wisdom by the hand,
and I'm not letting go.

Asking the God of our Lord Jesus Christ, the glorious Father,
to give you a spirit of wisdom and revelation
so that you will know him better.

Ephesians 1:17 NCV

HIS WORDS TO ME

Life Is Good

I tell you the truth;
your life is good,
and I'll always help you
through the storms of the world
as well as the storms of your mind.
I'll lift you out of every oppressive whirlwind,
and self-destruction will not be your master.
When you're weary, I'll pick you up in My arms.
I'll make you strong and put a new song in your throat.
Be at peace with yesterday
and look at the hope of *today*.
Beloved, look around you!
See the spring of life.
All is new, fresh. All is possible,
all is ours.

Oh my Lord and Savior, my life is good!
Thank you for always helping me
through the storms of the world,
as well as the storms of my mind
when it's misguided.
Thank you for lifting me
out of every oppressive whirlwind
and self-destructive behavior I might ignorantly choose.
Thank you for picking me up in your arms
when I'm weary.
Thank you for putting a new song in my mouth.
I'm at peace with yesterday
and I see the hope of today.
Oh Jesus, thank you for the spring of my life.
All is new, fresh.
All is possible; all is yours.

The LORD is good to all,
and his mercy is over all that he has made.

Psalm 145:9 ESV

HIS WORDS TO ME

Wonderful and Amazing

I want you to climb into the arms
of My goodness for this new month.
I want you to snuggle into the safety
of My love and mercy
and feel totally secure in My nourishing care.
I'm creating new passageways leading you
into the holy chambers of My heart.
Wisdom and knowledge are your lighted beacons,
I tell you, and the joy of life is yours.
I don't mislead and I don't lie.
I want you tucked in My sweet embrace
eating the fruit of contentment under My watchful gaze.
Oh, take what I have for you today!
Treasure these words.
All that I have is yours.

Oh how wonderful, how amazing,
how true and good you are!
I'm yours and you're mine, Lord.
Bless this month and make it yours!
On the first day of this month, I want to snuggle
into the wonder of your love and mercy
where I'm totally secure in your nourishing care.
Thank you for creating new passageways
leading me into the holy chambers of your heart.
Wisdom and knowledge are my lighted beacons.
The joy of life is mine!
You'll never mislead me, and you don't lie.
I'm living in the interior of your sweet embrace,
and I'm eating the fruit of contentment.
I have an identity! I know who I am and whose I am.
Thank you, Jesus, for giving me an eternal identity.
Today, and all this month, I'm going to be
open to everything you have for me.

The LORD looks down from heaven
on all mankind
to see if there are any who understand,
any who seek God.

Psalm 14:2 NIV

HIS WORDS TO ME

Looking for Approval

In the past you've looked to people
for approval.
You compared yourself with others
and were snared
in the unstable notions
of inferiority and superiority.
I put you on the earth to be a star
in My kingdom and to glorify Me.
When you put Me first,
and your ways please Me,
I'll make even your enemies
to be at peace with you.
Put Me first today and you'll experience My favor
to accomplish your calling
with dignity and success.

Oh, Jesus, I've always looked for approval from people.
I've worked hard to earn self-worth
by attaining goals and doing good.
I compared myself with others and became
snared in the unstable notions of inferiority and superiority.
You put me on the earth to be a star in your kingdom
and to glorify you.
Today I'm going to concentrate on pleasing you first,
so I might experience your favor.
I want to honor you above my own wants,
and be true to my calling as your child.
I'm constrained by love.
It's for love I lose myself in you,
and it's for love I say goodbye to chasing goals
for human gain and approval.
It's for love I renounce the habits seeking vain self-benefit.
Thank you for showing me the way to accomplish
my calling with dignity and success.

We can make our plans,
but the LORD determines our steps.

Proverbs 16:9 NLT

HIS WORDS TO ME

Stop Comparing

Can you stop comparing yourself
with others and start living
for *My* approval?
Oh the blessings and delights
that wait for you!
Here with Me you'll discover
lasting joy—the kind that doesn't up
and evaporate at the first whisper
of an emotional drought or heat wave.
The joy I give you disdains
the behavior of fair-weather friends
and the hollow physiognomy
of fake heroes.
When you discover
your own immense value to Me,
you'll stop comparing yourself
with others and start believing in
the person I've created you to be.
Your confidence will inspire and draw
many to Me.

Thank you, Jesus, for helping m
to stop comparing myself with others.
I want to discover lasting joy—
the kind that doesn't evaporate at the first glimpse
of someone else's success.
Lasting joy is deep and unshakeable, and it's what I crave.
Help me to discover and believe in the immense value I have in you,
so I'll stop comparing myself and my life with others and start
believing in the person you created me to be.
I want to be a person of steadfast confidence and deep inner joy,
and then be an inspiration to others,
even to those who reject you.

Whatever gain I had, I counted as loss for the sake of Christ.

Philippians 3:7 ESV

HIS WORDS TO ME

Reaching Into My Needs

Dear one, I'm here.
I reach into your need eagerly!
Swiftly!
Like pulling a rabbit from a snare,
I'm here to free you from the hunter's trap.
I see all the dangers you're unaware of;
I see the traps set in wait,
yet your foot won't be seized between their teeth
because My promise to keep you safe
is iron-clad and hewn in solid rock.
Stay close to Me. I'm your fierce,
protective barrier against all dangers.
I'm here to show you how to maneuver
the quick-tempered tsunamis when they hit.
The missiles of doubt, anger, and fear
hurtling everywhere won't hit you
when you're in My arms.

Thank you, Jesus for reaching into my needs today
and protecting me from myself.
Thank you for going
speedily before me and keeping me from plummeting
into deceitful traps.
I'm like a rabbit who trips into snares,
but you're right there alert to all the dangers I'm unaware of.
You see the deceptions set in wait for me, yet I won't be
seized by them because your promises to keep me safe
are iron-clad.
You're here now to show me how to maneuver
my quick-tempered tsunamis when they hit.
The missiles of doubt, anger and fear hurtle about me,
but they won't entrap me when I choose your ways.
How I thank you for the relief and peace I now feel.

He will rescue you from every trap
and protect you from the deadly disease.

Psalm 91: 3 NLT

HIS WORDS TO ME

Saint without Sorrow

When your anxious thoughts multiply in you
like mice chasing crumbs,
and when your week is consumed
with the polluted air of worry and doubt,
pause for a moment and look for Me.
Can you find Me
in the nighttime of your mind?
Your gnawing fear is more deadly
than the serpent's fangs,
more menacing than
the hungry lion on the hunt.
Your anxious thoughts are thieves
meant to slam you,
to bruise and break your dignity.
Don't give fear another minute.
It's the call of the jackal,
the drool of the sluggard.
Be brave!
There's never been a saint without sorrow,
never been a hero without impediments.
Today, trample the venom of fear
and take your place of strength and honor with Me.

MY WORDS TO HIM

Thank you for reminding me that there's never been a saint
without sorrow, never been a hero without impediments,
and never been an act of greatness without the necessity
to conquer human weakness.
When the pollution of doubt and insecurity assail me,
I must pause to breathe in your Holy Spirit and your words of life.
Be still and know that I am God.
Thank you Jesus, that when anxious thoughts
run through my mind like mice chasing crumbs,
you're right there to calm me down.
I've got to remember to stop and listen
for your sweet, loving voice telling me all is well.
You're never honored in a job accomplished
through stress, or one that's fraught with hassles.
Anxiety bruises my dignity in you.
Today I choose to take my place of strength
with renewed faith in your faithfulness,
and I choose to release my anxious thoughts
at the foot of the cross.

He shall be like a tree planted by the waters,
Which spreads out its roots by the river,
And will not fear when heat comes;
But its leaf will be green,
And will not be anxious in the year of drought,
Nor will cease from yielding fruit.

Jeremiah 17:8 NKJV

HIS WORDS TO ME

Patience and Trust

You've been waiting for answers to prayer,
and you've been patient.
Don't let doubt bite you on the neck
when you've come this far trusting Me.
Doubt will strip you of your faith
simple as peeling an orange.
I told you I would never leave you,
and above the shouts of confusion
know that I'm here with you as you wait.
I'm answering you—
but in *My* time.
Let Me carry you to the place
that is *best* for you.
Let Me bring the *best* to you.
Let Me multiply My *best* for you.
Isn't the *best* worth waiting for?
Endure a little longer, dear one.
Endure with triumph.

Thank you for patience, Jesus.
Thank you for the trust you've placed
in my human spirit by your Holy Spirit.
Doubt comes along and strips me of faith
like peeling an orange, but you've told me
you'd never leave me, so above the shouts
of confusion around me in the world,
I know that you're here with me
and I can trust you.
You're answering me
and showing me the exact best for me.
Multiply your best in me, Lord.
I'll endure a little longer,
and I'll endure triumphantly.

"By your patience possess your souls."

Luke 21:19 NKJV

HIS WORDS TO ME

Divinely Appointed

Today is the day
for you to take your place
in My divinely appointed school of the brave.
Today is the day to take your seat
and be strong and confident in who you are!
As an initiate in the school of the brave,
you'll no longer be able to mope and grovel unprepared
for weekly tests, probes, and exams.
You won't be permitted to oversleep
with no light to guide you to the moment of truth
where you rise up victorious against fear and shame.
Here in the school of the brave you'll
value your gifts while singing the school song,
Let the weak say I am strong!

MY WORDS TO HIM

Today is the day I'm taking my place in your
divinely appointed School of the Brave.
Today is the day I'm taking my seat in the front row
as a person who's strong
and confident in my identity in God.
I won't concern myself about the tests and exams
because I have a light to guide me and a holy, divine teacher.
I'm no longer someone who mopes, worries,
oversleeps, and fiddles around with vain philosophies
that bear some of the truth, but not all of it.
All truth is found in you, Jesus.
Thank you for showing me how to rise up victorious.
I value the lessons I'm learning,
and I'm singing the school song
loud and clear:
Let the weak say I am strong!

Watch, stand fast in the faith, be brave, be strong.

1 Corinthians 16:13 NKJV

HIS WORDS TO ME

Deadly Enemy

Fear of the future is a deadly enemy with nothing
but vapors as ammunition. It insults your
spiritual integrity to worry about the future
when I AM your future.
No pestilence will overtake you in spite of
your worries and fears.
I've given you abundant life to appreciate and be grateful for!
Open your heart and mind
to receive the wonders of it.
Pause today and meditate on "abundant life" and what
this means to you at this moment.
Consider the hours, days, and years ahead,
then see them spilling over with abundance,
with blessing,
with prosperity,
with love,
with joyfulness.
It's all yours.

Thank you, Jesus, for saving me
from the deadly enemy of doubt.
Worry insults my spiritual integrity.
Forgive me for worrying!
You're the entirety of my future
and I'm safe in that knowledge.
You've given me a rich,
abundant life to appreciate and be grateful for!
I'm opening my heart and mind now
to receive the wonders of your gifts.
I'm going to meditate all day on the words,
"abundant life" and what that means to me
at this very moment.
I refuse to embrace negative fears and concerns
that you died to save me from.
I am going to
purpose to see the hours, days, and years ahead as
spilling over with abundance, with blessing, with goodness,
with love, and with inner happiness.
This is how I choose
to think and how I choose to believe because you've given me
everything I need by your death and resurrection.
How can I thank you?

Happy are the people
whose God is the Lord!

Psalm 144:15 NKJV

HIS WORDS TO ME

Resist Temptation

Today, I'm empowering you
to resist the temptation
to return to your old ways of thinking.
I'm empowering you to renounce
self-pity and self-aggrandizing
because your heart
was meant to soar freely
with exuberant joyfulness!
Don't let yourself flip-flop back into
the dialogue of demons with dreary,
depressing self-talk that squashes out faith
and happiness, slamming shut the blinds
on the glorious panorama of My creative plan for you.
Poor me is not an expression
heaven recognizes.
Snap open the blinds of truth today
and shut up those ungodly thoughts.
Why allow your best to be captured
and your strengths paralyzed?
You're My faith-child;
tell yourself the *truth*.

MY WORDS TO HIM

Thank you, Jesus, for empowering me
to resist the temptation to return
to my old ways of thinking.
Thank you for empowering me to
renounce self-pity and self-aggrandizing.
My heart was meant to soar freely
with exuberant joyfulness.
I don't want to flip-flop
backward into dreary, depressing self-talk
that squashes out faith and happiness,
and closes the doors on the glorious panorama
of your creative plan for me.
"Poor me" is an expression heaven doesn't recognize.
Today I'm shutting out ungodly thoughts
and telling myself the truth!
I'm loved, I'm favored, I'm safe, I'm strong,
I'm a cherished child of God.

"You shall know the truth, and the truth shall make you free."
John 8:32 NKJV

HIS WORDS TO ME

The World's Story

When you look only for blessings
and answered prayers
as the assurance of My love,
you limit your experience of Me.
My gift to you is the full vocabulary
of life's poetry.
My gift is all life's literature,
even the discordant phrases
and passages that are difficult and tragic.

When your prayers and desires
are centered only on worldly blessings and rewards,
and not Me,
discouragement will become your buddy.
I'm here to give you the full measure of life's gifts,
but understand that trials can be gifts.
They're meant to change you to become brighter,
more beautiful, and more like *Me*.
Can you be as content with life and its stony paths
as you are with sunshine and flowers?
The greatest gifts I've given you are the ones
you carry within you!

If my prayers and desires are focused on
the world's story and not on the Author of the story,
I'll always fall short of the truth
and be discouraged and disheartened.
You're at the center of all life,
and you're here to give me
the full measure of life's gifts,
even when they're in the form of trials.
You're the author of humanity's story,
which doesn't eliminate discord or tragedy
because you're at the center.
I won't succumb to fear and worry.
Trials are meant to charge a fire in me
to become a brighter more beautiful person,
and more like you.
I'm going to be content with my life
and its stony paths, as well as those lined with sunshine
and flowers!
The greatest gift you've given me
is the story I carry within me.

The God who equipped me with strength
and made my way blameless.

Psalm 18:32 ESV

HIS WORDS TO ME

Called

Do the work I've called you to do today.
Be brave, be strong!
Pull down the strongholds.
Fight the good fight.
Resist the devil.
Power is yours.
Wisdom is yours.
Courage is yours.
Peace that passes understanding
is yours.
Let Me be the loving guide and friend
who enables you in everything
you're called to do today.
Observe with the mind of Christ,
and in every word you speak
and all you do,
let Me be the inspiration.

Thank you, Jesus, for the work
you've called me to do today.
You're my loving guide and friend
who enables and empowers me
for everything I'm called to do.
I'll fight the good fight of faith
and carry my wisdom and courage
within me as a golden badge.
I have the mind of Christ,
and in every word I speak
and in all I do,
you're my love and my inspiration.

"This is the work of God,
that you believe in Him whom He has sent."

John 6:29 NASB

HIS WORDS TO ME

Deliverance from Evil

In the Prayer I modeled for you,
I taught you to pray for
deliverance from evil. The evil
I want you to think about today
is your own tendency to agree with,
and team up with, the devil
who is the master of evil.
There's not a human being without
the tendency to sin, so I'm telling you today
to be aware and on the alert
for your own desire to slither backward
into such traps as jealousy, greediness,
and a critical spirit.

I've given you Holy Spirit power
to transform each nettled nest of discord in your heart
into a clean, polished, welcoming home for Me.
Look into your heart now.
I promise to relieve and deliver you from everything
you acknowledge and confess to Me.

In the Lord's Prayer, you said to pray for deliverance
from evil.
The evil I want to be delivered from today, Lord,
is my tendency to be negative and think negative thoughts.
In being negative, I'm unknowingly agreeing with the devil
who pours out hatred and condemnation on human beings
like hot coals on the eyes.
I'm fully aware of the tendency
to sin and displease you, so help me, Jesus, to be aware
and on the alert for the fire of a critical spirit.
You've given me
your Holy Spirit to transform each hot, nettled nest
of discord in me, and create something beautiful for God.
I'll look into my heart now where you live, and I'll receive
your promise to deliver and recover me from the consequences
of my negative choices.
I know you're at work in me,
and I thank you, Jesus, for forgiving me
and renewing my heart and mind today.

Being confident of this very thing, that He who has begun a good
work in you will complete it until the day of Jesus Christ.

Philippians 1:6 NKJV

HIS WORDS TO ME

Temptation to Sin

Don't ever assume I'm the cause
of your temptation to sin.
I *never* lead you into temptation to sin.
I don't come at you with urgings
of wrongdoings. Never!
I want you to understand that temptation
and testing are two different things.
Abraham was not led by *temptation* to offer
his son, Isaac, as a sacrifice to Me.
He was *tested with the test of obedience,*
to refine and build his faith, and he was therefore
hugely blessed.

The test of obedience is not the same as temptation to sin.
The *devil* tempts you to sin.
I set you free from sin!
I'll initiate tests of faith to strengthen and draw you
closer to Me. I want you empowered with wisdom,
courage, and inner fortitude. I want you
to rise up with character, dignity, and genuine godliness.
Trust Me.

Jesus, you never lead us into temptation to sin.
You don't come at me with urgings to do wrong.
Never! I understand that temptation and testing
are two different things.
Abraham was not led
by temptation to offer his son, Isaac, as a sacrifice
to you.
He was tested with the test of obedience
to refine and build his faith, and he was
subsequently hugely blessed.
Thank you, Jesus, for initiating tests of faith
to strengthen me and draw me closer to you.
Help me to rise up with character, dignity,
and genuine godliness through
every test of obedience.
I trust you, Jesus.

Then the Lord knows how to deliver the godly out of temptations.

2 Peter 2:9 NKJV

HIS WORDS TO ME

Hearing My Prayers

Never stop praying!
But I want you to understand that
your prayers can be hindered by an attitude
that's more self-centered than Me-centered.
No human being is entitled to take credit
for answered prayer.
Answered prayers are *Mine.*
It's not a *person* who answers prayer and performs
the miracles, it's *Me!*

Place the desires of your heart inside the desires of My heart
and lift them up to Me.
Pray *believing* I'll answer.
When your fervent, faith-rich prayers
are funded with love's currency,
I'll send My answers zinging into your holy mail box
like gold lightning.

MY WORDS TO HIM

Thank you, Jesus, for hearing my prayers.
I'll never stop praying!
I realize that my prayers can be hindered by an attitude
of self-centeredness, but I'm placing the desires of my heart
inside the desires of your heart today,
and I'm lifting these desires up to you to bless.
I know and believe you'll answer.
My fervent, faith-rich prayers are funded
with love's currency, I know you hear.
You send your answers zinging
into my holy mailbox like gold lightning.
How I worship and thank you, Lord Jesus!

One thing I asked of the LORD, that will I seek after:
to live in the house of the LORD all the days of my life,
to behold the beauty of the LORD, and to inquire in his temple.

Psalm 27:4 NRSV

HIS WORDS TO ME

No Hurt Too Trivial

I want you to see Me quietly caring
for the hurting, the desperate, and the poor.
I want you to see that nothing escapes My eye.
No hurt is too trivial and no dilemma too small
to command My care.
I'm the God of kings, and I'm the God
of the sparrows and lilies.
Hannah of old prayed for years
for a son. I heard her the first time, of course,
but I answered in My time, not Hannah's.
She didn't give up, but continued to cry out to Me
because her will and Mine were *one*.
She wanted what I wanted!
Hannah lifted up My desire with her own,
and ultimately, her prayer was for My honor.
We both wanted a son for her,
and the prayer was answered.
Her story, and the birth of Samuel,
is to encourage you to search your heart for My heart
when you pray, and to not give up.
Trust My purpose, trust My caring,
and trust My timing.

Thank you, Lord, that no hurt is too trivial
and no dilemma too small to escape
your loving concern.
Thank you for quietly caring
for the hurting, the desperate, and the poor.
Thank you for seeing every need and every tear
that's spilled. You're the God of the sparrows
and the lilies.
Thank you for showing me not to stop
praying when I don't receive answers.
Your timing
is perfect and I trust you.
Thank you for your purpose
in all things, and thank you for showing me that
it's your purpose I need to connect with.
I'm confident in your loving care for me
and all you've given me to do.
I trust your timing in all things.
Thank you, oh thank you, Jesus.

Let them give thanks to the LORD for his unfailing love
and his wonderful deeds for mankind.
Let them sacrifice thank offerings
and tell of his works with songs of joy.

Psalm 107:21-22 NIV

HIS WORDS TO ME

No More Worry

I won't let you fall,
don't worry.
I've always been here to hold you up
to guide and protect you,
and I'll *always* be here. I'm not eons away
out in space; I'm *in* you.
Yes, I hold your hand, but I also hold your heart.
If I'm *in* you that means by your choice,
you can fuse your thoughts with Mine.

Your dreams, your longings, your passions,
are not separate from Mine when we're one.
Today, I want you to transcend
from the worldly grip on your life that comes and goes
like a moth beating at the window.
Be fixed to *Me* and we'll fly together
to your divine destination.

MY WORDS TO HIM

Thank you, Jesus, for not allowing me to fall.
I don't worry anymore because you've always
been here to hold me up and guide and protect me.
You're always here, not eons away out in space,
you're in me.
Your Spirit lives in my spirit!
You hold my hand, but you also hold my heart.
You're in my heart, Lord Jesus, and therefore,
my thoughts can be fused with yours.
My dreams, longings, and passions aren't separate
from yours when we're one like this.
Today help me to transcend the worldly grip on my life
that comes and goes like a moth beating at the window.
I'm fixed to you on my way to my divine destination.

God is working in you, giving you the desire
and the power to do what pleases him.

Philippians 2:13 NLT

HIS WORDS TO ME

Each Facet

You're precious to Me;
never forget that.
Never lose sight of these sheltering words.
I am fully aware of each facet of your
character. I know your choices,
your strengths, your flaws, and your glories.
I know you better than you know yourself.
Your aims in life are too low, however,
and your target unfocused.
This is why your confidence is shallow.
Open your eyes of understanding today,
and stop permitting the clouds of sin
and self-reproach to waste your energy.
I give you your breath,
and I number your days.
Take charge of your choices today,
and make Me Lord of absolutely
everything.

MY WORDS TO HIM

I know you're fully aware of each facet of my character.
You know my strengths, my flaws, and my glories.
You know me better than I know myself.
At times, Lord,
my aim in life seems too low and my target seems unfocused.
I realize this is when my confidence becomes shallow.
Today, I open the eyes of my understanding.
I'll stop permitting the clouds of self-reproach to waste my energy.
You give me my breath and you number my days.
I'm taking charge of my choices today,
and installing you as the permanent Lord
over absolutely everything in my life.
Oh Jesus, thank you for making me feel valuable to you.
You tell me in your Word you love me.
I don't ever want to lose sight
of these empowering and sheltering words.

He brought me to the banqueting house,
and his banner over me was love.

Song of Solomon 2:4 ESV

HIS WORDS TO ME

Who I Am

I know you're in need of help,
and I'm answering you,
but first
I want you to see yourself
as *one* with Me. We aren't separate and apart.
You aren't stationed on terra firma while I'm
up the clouds with a pair of holy binoculars and
a yellow legal pad taking notes.
Understand that My Spirit is *in* you.
We're united from *inside*;
are you listening? I'm here now!
We're spiritually connected
in a divine, miraculous fusion making us *one spirit*.
What's born of the flesh is flesh,
but My Spirit fused with your human spirit
has created a new life in you.
Right now. Here and now. This minute.
When you ask for My guidance, don't fancy Me
yanking your sleeve or holding onto your foot
yelling, "This way!"
Darling, I'm *in* you. Listen with your *heart*,
and you'll hear Me.

Thank you, Jesus, for helping me to see myself
for who and what I am.
Thank you for showing me I'm one with you,
and that I'm not my own.
We aren't separate and apart.
You've given my life value.
Thank you for paying for my worthiness
with your own blood.
Thank you for changing and renovating me
to resemble you on the inside.
As I meditate on this truth and practice the living power
of your words in my life,
I'll begin to look more and more like you!
Thank you for the Holy Spirit who lives in me.
Thank you for transforming me
into a loveable person and leading me
to my divine destiny.

"They will be Mine," says the LORD of hosts,
"on the day that I prepare My own possession."
Malachi 3:17 NASB

HIS WORDS TO ME

Burden Exchange

You're carrying a heavy burden today,
and you may feel worn out and depressed.
Oh, dear one, I, too, carry a burden,
but My burden is *light*.
Would you like to exchange the heaviness
of your burden
for the lightness of Mine?
When your attachments oppress you
and you feel weighted and over-extended,
come and be yoked with Me
where you'll find rest,
relief,
ease,
and refreshment.
Let Me teach you the easy rhythms of grace.
The lightness of My burden can be yours,
easy to be borne,
comfortable,
blessed
because *together* we can handle anything.

Thank you, Jesus, for your light burden
that you exchange for my heavy one.
Thank you for taking weariness
and depression from me.
I love to be relieved
and refreshed by you.
When the situations
in my life oppress me and I feel weighted
and over-extended, I come to you to be yoked
with you where I always find rest, relief, ease
and encouragement.
Teach me today the rhythms of grace.
The lightness of my burdens
when I'm yoked with you
are easy to bear, and I'm comfortable
in my skin, and blessed, because together
with you I can handle anything.

Cast your burden on the LORD,
And He shall sustain you;
He shall never permit
the righteous to be moved.

Psalm 55:22 NKJV

587

HIS WORDS TO ME

Your Generosity

You call yourself generous
and so you are.
You're a giver.
You love to give,
and I love it that you love to give.
You give nice things to people.
You shop, buy things,
you send flowers, you remember birthdays.

Today, I want you to remember to give to Me
before you wrap that next present.
When you buy a gift for a person,
think of it as a gift for Me.
Give your greeting cards, your good deeds,
your heart to Me.
If you give because it feels good
and because giving earns attention,
it becomes self-centered giving.
I gave you your giving heart
for Me-centered giving.
Give your gifts to Me first.
I love you.

Thank you, Lord, for your generosity.
Your generosity makes me generous.
You've given me a real and earnest love
for giving.
Today I want to give you a gift.
I want to give every good deed to you that I do.
It feels good to give, Lord.
I give because you've placed
a loving, giving heart in me,
and I can't help myself.
You gave me your life on the cross,
and I can't give less than my life in return.

Let each one give as he purposes in his heart,
not grudgingly or of necessity;
for God loves a cheerful giver.

2 Corinthians 9:7 NKJV

HIS WORDS TO ME

A Gift's Value

A gift is measured by the effort and love
it took to give it, and every gift you give wings to
goes to your heavenly savings account
where nothing is calculated by numbers but by
integrity.
I want you to see the divinely appointed
authority of the gifts you give to people.
When you give a gift through effort, grief, sacrifice,
sorrow, hardship ,and joy,
it bears powerful authority.
Start to proclaim the authority of your gifts,
for such gifts aren't mere charitable
niceties; they're kisses from Me!

The gifts you give from a selfless heart
go to Me first, and then to your recipients.
No matter how simple or grand, freely give,
whatever the cost,
because it's the heart of the giver
that multiplies itself
and only what you give from the heart
is truly yours
and Mine.

Lord Jesus, you measure the value of a gift
by the love it took to give it, and every gift
you give wings to goes to my heavenly savings account
where nothing is calculated by numbers, but by integrity.
When I give a gift through effort, sacrifice, hardship and joy,
it bears powerful authority and results in joy
to the giver. I pray for precious fruit for the kingdom of God
to be birthed through the gifts I give to others
because the gifts you give me to give
aren't mere charitable niceties,
they're kisses from you!
Thank you for showing me
you love a selfless heart that gives all gifts to you first,
then to others.
No matter how simple or grand,
I'll freely give, whatever the cost, because it's the heart
of the giver that multiples itself.
Only what I give from the heart is truly mine.

The gifts and the calling of God are irrevocable.

Romans 11:29 NRSV

Gifts to Share

The closer we are,
the easier it is for you to accept being loved
by others.
Love is not something you earn.
You're loved because you're flat-out loveable.
I've given you many gifts to share,
and as you fill your heart and mind
with growing closer to Me,
you'll want to reach out
to accept the love of those around you.
They have much to give you.
Truly be, and let yourself be loved.
Fill your whole heart with My words.
Fill your whole mind with My mind.
Fill your body with My enabling health.
Fill your soul with the knowledge of My will.
Dear one, a refreshing new creative spirit
is about to explode in you.

MY WORDS TO HIM

Thank you, Jesus, for the many gifts you give me to share.
As I fill my mind and heart with you and your ways,
I find myself wanting to reach out
to others more and more.
I'm making it my purpose
to fill my whole heart with your words
and my whole mind with your mind.
I'm filling my body with your enabling health,
and my soul with the knowledge of your will.
You gave me the gift to see beneath the surface of things
and to give voice to a unique vision and passion.
I love this exciting, creative gift bursting in me
to be released.
Lead me in wisdom and discernment
as I reach out to touch the world today.

Since you are eager for gifts of the Spirit,
try to excel in those that build up the church.

1 Corinthians 14:12 NIV

HIS WORDS TO ME

Opening My Heart

Heaven's currency is *love*.
Let's look at your heavenly bank account today.
Have you tallied the expenditures and deposits
made this month in your heavenly bank account?
How much have you drawn out compared to
what you've put in?
You opened your heavenly account with *love*.

Love is more than a human feeling and doing nice deeds—
it's an expression of who I am.
I AM LOVE.
If only you realized how your heavenly account multiplies
and expands when you make regular love deposits.
You store up treasures that multiply and gather interest
each time you make your love deposits.
If only you knew how happy you make all of heaven
when you pour out your love for Me because only then
can you distribute the immensity of your wealth
in loving others.

Thank you, Jesus, for opening my heart to accept love.
You teach me that your love isn't something I earn,
but something that you give freely without hesitation;
I'm loved because I'm loveable to you. You love me!
This is a revelation to me, and it's changing my life.
Heaven's currency is love, and I have a heavenly
bank account that's not empty!
Love is an expression of who you are,
so your love for me exemplifies you.
Help me to realize how my heavenly account multiples
and expands when I make regular love deposits for you
and when I love myself as your child.
I'm storing up treasures that multiply and gather interest
each time I make a love deposit.
If only I could grasp how happy it makes
all of heaven when I pour out my love for you
because only then can I distribute the immensity
of my wealth and give love to the world around me.

Beloved, let us love one another, for love is of God;
and everyone who loves is born of God and knows God.

1 John 4:7 NKJV

HIS WORDS TO ME

Kingdom Emissary

I watched a poor widow
place her last two coins into the temple treasury,
and her humble offering
is still honored today as a precious gift—
yet the glamorous gifts of the indifferent rich
of the day are long forgotten.
You're hired as chief financial officer
of My money as it comes to you.
You approve the bills and sign the checks.
How much or how little filters into your hands
is not important. What matters is the dedication
to multiply generosity and faith.
Be an emissary for My kingdom
and assign authority to your gifts and tithes.
Appropriate My money with dignity
from your high position
in My holy banking system.
It's not frugality I honor;
it's wisdom and faith.

Dear Jesus, make me an emissary for your kingdom.
Honor my tithes and offerings and cause them to multiply
where I send them to bring much fruit to your kingdom.
I know that as your child I'm the chief financial officer
of your money as it comes to me.
It's my responsibility
to manage my money and distribute my tithes
and offerings as spiritual seed to help nurture a harvest
of glory for your sake on earth.
What matters to you
is the dedication I exhibit to multiply generosity and faith.
Help me appropriate your money with dignity to uphold
your holy heavenly banking system.
It's not frugality
you honor, it's the wisdom of a Spirit-kissed generous heart.

It is more blessed to give than to receive.

Acts 20:35 NIV

HIS WORDS TO ME

Designer of Emotions

Don't be afraid of bad feelings.
Respond to the feelings of your heart
honestly and openly here in the light of My love.
Don't let your irritation and unresolved anger
get stuffed under the bed and behind closed curtains
because anger is a wily devil. It'll turn on you
and punch you until you're its victim.
Come into the light with Me.
Let's see clearly and listen carefully, so
facing your feelings will reveal
what you need to know about yourself.
Know you're loved
and safe. You're empowered
and forgiven. You're on the brink of
something wonderful. Nothing can take you down—
unless you let it.
I give you the power and authority of My name
to cast every evil hindrance out of your life.
Replace the strangling tentacles of anger
with the healing nectar of mercy.
Freedom and peace are yours.

Thank you, Jesus, for understanding my feelings.
You're the designer of human emotions, and you knew
at the beginning some human emotions would miss
the godly mark.
Thank you for showing me
not to be afraid of bad feelings, or to condemn myself
when a bad feeling shows up in my emotional storage tank.
I'm coming against irritableness and unresolved anger,
so I don't stuff them under the bed and pretend they're not there.
Thank you for the bright light of your Spirit that shines
through me to reveal what I need to know about myself.
I know this: I'm loved. I'm safe. I'm empowered. I'm forgiven.
I also know I'm on the cusp of something wonderful in my life.
I won't permit foolish reckless emotions to stand in the way
of the breakthrough I'm about to experience in you!
Nothing can take me down without my permission.
Thank you,
Jesus, for the insight you give to identify, remove, and replace
ungodly emotions with the healing nectar of your mercy
and grace.
Thank you for the wisdom you give me
to understand my emotions and to control them.

You were dead in your trespasses and sins, in which you formerly
walked according to the course of this world.
Ephesians 2:1-2 NASB

HIS WORDS TO ME

The Way I Am

I know the reasons for your behavior.
You need love, and you long
to be relevant and appreciated.
I want you loved, relevant,
and appreciated too!
I want you to walk in favor.
When your ways please Me, you'll have favor!
(Run off on your own without Me,
and you're a pawn of chance.)
I have greatness ahead for you—
respect, appreciation, love, and relevance—
everything you long for.
It's not in the milk of self-centeredness.

Thank you for creating me just the way I am.
You know the reasons behind all of my behaviors.
You know my need for love and how I long to be
relevant and appreciated in this world.
You want me loved, relevant, and appreciated too!
Thank you, Jesus! You want me to walk in favor,
and when my ways please you, I have favor.
Your Spirit lives in me and I know there are
great blessings ahead for me along with respect,
appreciation, love and relevance—everything I long for.
These are not found in the mud of self-centeredness,
but in the truth of perfect love.
Fill me with your Holy Spirit,
so I can live in perfect love, Jesus,
so I never falter in my pursuit of you above all else.

Now hope does not disappoint, because the love of God has been
poured out in our hearts by the Holy Spirit who was given to us.

Romans 5:5 NKJV

HIS WORDS TO ME

Entangling Situation

You think you're bogged down with a situation
that's impossible to get out of, but I'm here to crank open
the lid of the box and set you free.

I can work miracles in your life if you'll let Me.
You can stop fretting and scratching your chin with worry.
My name is Deliverer. My name is Healer.
I'm in you by My Spirit, and I am guiding you by My Spirit,
turning things around for you, opening pathways
to set you free. I'm your divine physician.

Don't concern yourself with sins of the past. You're forgiven.
I've forgotten the things you keep mentioning.
If you've been foolish, remember I've told you
that the foolish will confound the wise, so sanctify your heart
and make it beautiful in Me!

Let Me cauterize the situation. Let Me be the miracle worker,
and you…you proclaim My authority and power,
and be My trusting child.

No entangling situation is impossible to get out of
because you're here to set me free. Jesus, you can work
miracles in my life if I'll hush up long enough to let you
do your work as you've promised to do.
Sometimes I'm
so busy praying I don't hear you when you answer!
I'll stop fretting and scratching my chin with worry
when I call on your name: Deliverer and Healer.
You and I are one by your Holy Spirit and you're
guiding me right now by your Spirit to lift me up
to a higher place.
You're my divine lawyer
and you're my divine physician.
You said
you'll use the simple to confound the wise,
so I'm sanctifying my heart now to make it beautiful for you.
Cauterize the situation I'm facing, Lord,
and be the miracle worker in me.
I'll proclaim your greatness forever.

Let us, then, feel very sure that we can come before God's throne
where there is grace. There we can receive mercy and grace to
help us when we need it.

Hebrews 4:16 NCV

HIS WORDS TO ME

The Wrongs

Today, put out of your mind the wrongs others have done to
you.
The evil-doing of others has no power over you
unless you foolishly give them that power.
Resentment will lead you to futility and misery,
and I'm telling you, don't squander another moment
on what you can't change.
It's time to push the offenses
out of the cupboard of your beautiful mind
because bitterness kills
like rats ravaging a dung heap.
Bitterness will shut you off
from the Sonlight of My Spirit
and make you a prisoner in your own head.

I'm asking you to trust Me
to bring new and fabulous blessings
into your life.
I want you to humbly rely on Me
so you can face the calamities you've endured
with courage, no longer traumatized,
but with holy confidence and perfect peace.

MY WORDS TO HIM

Today I'm putting out of my mind the wrongs
others have done to me. The evil-doings of others
have no power over me any longer.
Resentment only leads to futility and misery,
and I don't want to squander another moment
on what I can't change.
Thank you, Jesus, for removing the offenses
I've stored in my mind.
They're like rats on a dung heap.
Thank you for showing me to trust you to bring
new and wondrous blessings into my life as I let go
of the grievances and hurts I've suffered.
I'm humbly relying on you, Jesus, so I can face
the calamities I've endured with courage,
no longer traumatized, but with holy confidence
and perfect peace.

He drew me up from the desolate pit, out of the miry bog,
and set my feet upon a rock, making my steps secure.
He put a new song in my mouth, a song of praise to our God.
Many will see and fear, and put their trust in the LORD.

Psalm 40:2-3 NRSV

HIS WORDS TO ME

Age Discrimination

I'm calling My seasoned generals out of seclusion,
calling them out into the heat of My final battle.
I'm calling My seasoned veterans who worry they're too old—
out of their quietude,
out of their repressed jobs in the back yards of the young
and ambitious,
out of their backseats
and basement positions in the churches,
out of their gratuitous jobs
and unsung ministries.
I'm calling My seasoned veterans
into the forefront of My 21st century campaign
to shift the atmosphere of the entire planet.
Be ready!

MY WORDS TO HIM

Thank you, Jesus, that in your economy
there's no age discrimination.
You're calling your senior saints out
into the heat of your final battle.
You're calling the seasoned spiritual veterans
who've been made to feel they're too old
out of the shadows of their quietude.
You're putting these great saints of God
on the front lines and the forefront of your
21st century campaign to shift the atmosphere
of the entire planet.
We must prepare and get ready!
Your spiritual generals will go before us as leaders
in this generation.
Thank you, Jesus,
for calling your generals out of seclusion.

They will still bear fruit in old age,
they will stay fresh and green,
proclaiming, "The LORD is upright;
he is my Rock, and there is no wickedness in him."

Psalm 92:14-15 NIV

HIS WORDS TO ME

Glorious Light

Here at My holy beauty spa,
where life makeovers are the specialty,
I'm doing a great work.
The treatment begins with My calling you
out of darkness, and then with a gentle heave-ho
you're placed in the hot room
of My glorious light where you see yourself
for who you are.
Do you need the total Holy Spirit makeover today?
First, the amazing cleansing process
purifying the pores of the soul, a complete
body-soul spirit bath where you dump your sins
and foibles down the condemnation drain and emerge
golden in forgiveness.
Don't let old-fleshy yesterday keep you from
your divinely appointed, healthy new-life look today.
I am Jesus. I love you,
and here at My holy beauty spa,
I work miracles.

Thank you, Lord, for doing a great work in me
and setting me in your glorious light,
where I see myself as a person who can be strong
in the presence of evil.
Thank you for showing me
when I need a divinely appointed, healthy new surge
of courage.
Thank you for bringing out strong points
in me that I can be pleased about.
Thank you for keeping me in your watchful, loving eye
giving me wisdom and power in the Holy Spirit.
Thank you for showing me to praise and thank you
because the devil and his demons can't bear it
when your children worship you with thankful hearts.

Submit yourselves therefore to God.
Resist the devil, and he will flee from you.

James 4:7 ESV

HIS WORDS TO ME

Heaven Sings

All heaven is behind your success.
The words I speak create life
and power, so today, take My Word
as your authority,
your strength, your shield, and your oxygen.
If you'll see truth in all that I tell you,
your faith will intensify, and your success will
burgeon beyond human ability
to the point where you'll bring to pass that which is not
by contending and speaking it out.
Haven't I told you whatever you ask in My name
I'll answer?
Isn't it written that faith is the substance
of things *unseen?*
In Me you have the good success I ordained
for you from the beginning.

Thank you for the words you speak that create life.
All heaven sings at the sound of your voice.
You're my strength and my shield.
I can see truth
in all that you tell me, and my faith intensifies
at your Word.
I know success will burgeon beyond
my human ability to the point where I'll bring to pass
that which doesn't even exits at this moment by contending
and speaking it out.
You've told me that whatever I ask
in your name you'll answer.
It's written that faith
is the substance of things unseen, and I know that
you'll bring to pass everything you ordained for me
from the beginning.

We do not look at the things which are seen, but at the things
which are not seen. For the things which are seen are temporary,
but the things which are not seen are eternal.

2 Corinthians 4:18 NKJV

HIS WORDS TO ME

I Am Yours

You were born at an exact perfect moment in time.
I called you into being
for such a time as this.
I have every one of your days before
My eyes.
Each moment and each breath
is important to Me.
There are no mistakes on heaven's holy calendar,
so today, I'm calling you to be grateful
and to honor the days and months and weeks and hours
and minutes
I've given you
in the world.
Your life is always before Me.
Cherish the moments as holy events.
Cherish today.

Bless this month and make it a joy to you.
Thank you, Jesus, for bringing me into the world
at the exact perfect moment.
Thank you, Jesus.
You called me into being
for such a time as this.
You have every one
of my days before your eyes, and each moment and breath
I take are important to you.
There are no mistakes
on heaven's holy calendar and I'm deeply grateful
that you honor and bless the days and months and weeks
and hours I'm in the world.
My life is always before you
and I cherish each moment as a holy event.
I cherish this day,
and this new month.
I pray I'll be a blessing to you
and bring you glory as I live each day for you.

"Everyone who is called by My name,
And whom I have created for My glory,
Whom I have formed, even whom I have made."

Isaiah 43:7 NASB

HIS WORDS TO ME

Lifter of My Head

Heaven rejoiced at your birth,
and rejoiced again when you gave
your heart to Me.
Angels sing at the altar
of the repentant heart.
I'm your shield, your glory,
the one who lifts your head.
Listen for My voice today.
I'm leading you in a new path,
and you'll hear Me in the stillness
and in the quietness of your mind.
Hinge your thoughts
to My gentle guidance.
Can you feel My kiss on your forehead?

MY WORDS TO HIM

Jesus, you're my shield and protector.
You're the lifter
of my head and my heart's delight.
Thank you
for the love song the angels have been singing over me
since the day I was born.
Thank you for the new life
you gave me when I was born again! I gave my life to you and I
truly became a new person.
Thank you for filling my life with good things
and too many blessings to count.
Today I'm going to
quiet my mind and hinge my thoughts completely
on you. I'm going to study your Word and delight
in the Scriptures so I can to learn exactly
what you want me to hear from you.
I love your Word, Lord. I love studying
and meditating on its precepts.
I love how
you show me the way to live a beautiful, fulfilled life
and I can only fall on my knees in gratitude
and worship you with all my heart, soul, and mind.

All Scripture is given by inspiration of God, and is profitable
for doctrine, for reproof, for correction, for instruction in
righteousness, that the man of God may be complete,
thoroughly equipped for every good work.

2 Timothy 3:16-17 NKJV

HIS WORDS TO ME

Good to Myself

Be good to yourself today.
Be tender-hearted, kind, and merciful
toward yourself as I am merciful to you.
The wrongs done to you have hurt and angered you,
and I know you've suffered.
I tell you, darling one, these afflictions will produce
an eternal weight of glory if you let Me
take your hand and lead you to inner freedom.
You have the power to forgive within you,
and when you forgive,
the sins done against you lose their prominence
on the walls of your memory,
and the stains on your heart will evaporate.
I don't want you to go on hurting and
giving the devil your time and attention.
Forgive and be free. The pain is temporary;
the glory is eternal. Let the glory rise within you.
Be good to yourself.
Forgive them.
Forgive yourself.
Forgive life.

MY WORDS TO HIM

Thank you, Jesus, for teaching me how to be
good to myself.
Thank you for showing me
to be tender hearted, kind, and merciful
toward myself, as you are merciful to me.
The wrongs done to me have hurt
and angered me in the past but you show me
that these afflictions will produce
an eternal weight of glory in me
when I take your hand and allow you
to lead me to inner freedom.
Thank you for the ability to forgive, Lord.
When I forgive the wrongs done against me
they lose their saturation in my memory.
The wounded stains on my heart evaporate.
Thank you for pulling me out of the swamp of hurt feelings
and showing me the path of forgiveness and healing.
All pain is temporary. Glory is eternal.
Today I'm permitting your love to rise up in me
and I'm going to be good to myself.
I forgive others. I forgive myself.

You were made free from sin,
and now you are slaves to goodness.

Romans 6:18 NCV

617

HIS WORDS TO ME

Author of Love

I'm the author of love
and its rule on earth.
All creation was formed by love.
When you absorb yourself in My love,
vibrating with its intensity,
you then begin to exude love back to Me
and the world around you.
This is the life force between us—you and Me—
a power greater than anything on earth.
It's the essence of eternity.
Today, allow your love to be pure and selfless,
and make every effort
to give and receive with a generous heart.
Your single purpose
is to love and be loved by Me.
I delight in you.

MY WORDS TO HIM

Oh Jesus, you're the author of love and its rule on earth.
All creation was formed by love.
When I absorb myself
in your love, vibrating with its intensity, I begin to exude
love back to you and the world around me.
This is the life force
between us, Jesus—a power greater than anything on earth.
Love is the essence of eternity.
It's the essence of all beauty
and everything good.
Today, Lord, help me to love
with a pure and selfless heart.
I'm going to make
every effort to give and receive with a generous heart.
My single purpose is to love and be loved by you.

I delight to do your will, O my God;
your law is within my heart.

Psalm 40:8 NRSV

HIS WORDS TO ME

Many Decisions

So many decisions.
Shall you go this way or that?
Shall you go left or right? With this one or that one?
Oh, what should you do?
When in the valley of decision
and you can't seem to find direction,
too often your decisions are based on
what you think will make you happy
and what will be most advantageous for *you*—
and later, when you're eating the bitter fruit of your choices,
choking on the bad taste, you'll blame Me
for not stopping you.
Haven't you learned by now?
The valley of decision is a test
to ponder what would be best
for you and Me both.
Ask yourself what would honor
My kingdom?
That which honors Me will always
honor you.

I have many decisions to make today, Lord,
and when I'm in the valley of decision I always
turn to you for help.
I don't want to make decisions
based merely on what I think will make me happy
or what will be most advantageous for me—
I want to listen carefully for your guidance.
I need your wisdom, Lord Jesus.
The decisions
I make must be for your benefit, not mine alone.
I want to do what will honor the kingdom of God
because I know that which honors you will always bless me.

All this also comes from the LORD Almighty,
whose plan is wonderful,
whose wisdom is magnificent.

Isaiah 28:29 NIV

HIS WORDS TO ME

My Plans

When you leave Me out of your plans and decisions,
I don't interfere. I'm very considerate.
If you choose to lie down with dogs
in the mud holes of life, you're free to do it.
If you choose to chomp on contaminated meat,
I won't stop you.
I didn't jump in shouting protests at Adam and Eve,
"Stop right there, you two! Put that apple down!"
did I?
They had, as you do, the gift of choice.

I gave you the gift of free choice not
to do whatever you want to do;
I gave you the gift to choose to obey Me
and do what is good in My eyes.
I gave you free choice to make glorious,
earth-shaking decisions to bless and make beautiful
your world.
Today, you have choices to make.
What will you do?

Lord Jesus, I never want to leave you out of my plans
and decisions.
You set me free to make all my choices
and that's why I'm so thankful I can turn to you and ask
for your guidance.
You don't interfere with my plans
because you're very considerate, but you're always ready
to help and guide me by your Holy Spirit.
If I make
decisions without considering you, I can't blame you
for the consequences.
I think of Adam and Eve
when they disobeyed you and made the terrible decision
to eat the forbidden fruit in the Garden of Eden.
You didn't jump up and shout, "Stop! Put that apple down!"
They had the gift of choice and so do I.
It's a gift from you
that's beyond beautiful because it shows how much
you honor your creation.
It shows that you respect us
as our Creator. Knowing this takes my breath away.
I ask you for spiritual ears to always hear your gentle guiding!

You guide me with your counsel,
leading me to a glorious destiny.
Psalm 73:24 NLT

HIS WORDS TO ME

World to Cherish

Did I create the apple
for its own sake?
Did I create the sweet peach
to bless itself?
The rose?
The pineapple?
The fig?
No, I created these for *you*.
Within each fruit are seeds that multiply more
of its kind, and so it is with the gifts I've given you.
My Holy Spirit lives in you as the supernatural
kernel of life that generates more of Myself
so the world might be blessed through you.
There's never been a peach
plucked from a tree for its own sake.
And you, darling, alive and thriving
from My tree of life, bearing the beautiful savor of heaven,
are multiplying more of Me right now.
Right where you are.

Oh Father God, thank you for this beautiful world
you've given us to cherish.
Your Holy Spirit in me
is the supernatural kernel of life that generates
more of yourself so the world might be blessed
through me.
Help me to make excellent choices
that honor you in all I do.
Free choice isn't a gift
to do whatever I want.
You gave me the gift of choice
to choose to obey you and do what is good in your eyes.
You gave me free choice to make decisions to bless
and make the world a better place.
Thank you, Jesus,
for partnering with me in the decision-making process.
I worship and adore you for your enormous loving heart.
Thank you for the chance to be a blessing today.
Multiply more of yourself through me!

Blessed be the God and Father of our Lord Jesus Christ,
who has blessed us with every spiritual blessing
in the heavenly places in Christ,

Ephesians 1:3 NKJV

HIS WORDS TO ME

You Are Great

Dear one,
greatness is My job, not yours.
I ask only for your love.
Works without love mean little to Me.
Do you remember reading about
My encounter with the Samaritan woman
at the well at Sychar?
I was thirsty and the dear woman not only gave Me water,
but at My words, she arose in a flutter of praise and love.
What about you? I'm thirsty for your *love*.
Before you fast and sacrifice your goods to Me,
check the purpose.
My living flame transforms
your soul into the very soul of love.
It's who I am.
Today, walk in your own flutter of praise and love.

Thank you, Jesus.
You are great and all that you do
is great.
I'm awed every day that you were sent
by God the Father to come down from heaven
and die on the cross for insignificant and unworthy me.
Such shocking love shows me I'm significant to God.
Because you rose up from the dead
and released your Holy Spirit to the world, I'm alive
with the fire of God in me.
It's so amazing, so incredulous,
and so wonderful, I can hardly stand it.
The living flame of your Spirit in me has transformed me.
I'll thank and praise you forever, dear blessed Lord.

He rescued us from the domain of darkness, and transferred
us to the kingdom of His beloved Son, in whom we have
redemption, the forgiveness of sins.

Colossians 1:13-14 NASB

HIS WORDS TO ME

Taking My Sins

When you need a physical healing,
come and gaze intently at the cross
where I bore your sicknesses and your sins.
In My Word I've told you
that you'd know the truth
and the truth would make you a free person.
Hug these words to your heart today—
Truth = Free.

Fully open yourself to receive what I've told you.
Think about, believe, and love the truth
that sets you free from your physical ailments
and every adverse entanglement you encounter.
Proclaim My Word to be true
to your beautiful body.
Love your body as I do,
and be healed.

MY WORDS TO HIM

Thank you, Jesus, for taking my sins on your own body
when you were tortured on the cross.
Thank you for taking
my punishment for me.
Thank you for your sacrifice which,
by faith, has set me free to live a beautiful Spirit-led,
guilt-free life.
Thank you for sending your Holy Spirit
to fill me and create in me a new heart.
Thank you
for the physical healing your death on the cross
accomplished for your children.
Thank you for the gift
of prayer so I can pray for healing knowing my body
is yours.
Today I'm fully open to receive the words
you've spoken to me, and to love the truth
that sets me free from sin and sickness
and every adverse entanglement I encounter
on earth.
Thank you for loving me, Jesus,
for loving all of me, spirit, soul, and body.

My heart is glad,
and my glory rejoices;
my flesh also will rest in hope.

Psalm 16:9 NKJV

HIS WORDS TO ME

Word Speaks Life

Today, I want you to see how precious
your body is to Me.
I've told you that My Word is life to you
and health to your whole body.
This means I love your *entire being*,
no matter what shape,
size, age, or condition.
Soak yourself in this truth.
Put this truth on as a coat. Swallow it as fruit.
My Word is life and health
to your body.
Today, absorb what I'm telling you.
Set aside time in your schedule
to find My words of healing and health,
and make them yours.
Yours!
I'm the Lord who invigorates, heals,
restores, and renews your youth like the eagle's.
Believe this today, and honor your body.

Thank you, Jesus, for your Word that speaks life and health
to my complete being, spirit, soul, and body.
Thank you for loving me in my total self,
no matter what shape, size, age, or condition I'm in.
I'm wearing truth today as an expensive coat.
Your Word is life and health to my body.
That's the truth!
I am absorbing what you tell me
in your Word and I'm setting aside time in my schedule
to learn more.
I'm going to keep your words of healing
and health and make them mine!
You are the Lord
who invigorates, heals, restores, and renews my youth
like the eagle's.
Today I will honor my body as you do.

You were bought at a price;
therefore glorify God in your body
and in your spirit, which are God's.

1 Corinthians 6:20 NKJV

HIS WORDS TO ME

Through Every Season

Don't underestimate the relevance
of your tears.
I've gathered and counted each one, My darling.
My heart is large enough
to hold your hurts.
I'm with you in lack, in plenty, in joy, and in sorrow;
I'm with you in tears and in laughter—good and bad.
You may be tempted to think that affliction
comes from Me, but I have not treated you badly.
I don't afflict you. I save you!
I never turn My head when danger comes your way,
though you may not sense My presence.
I don't leave you when things go wrong in your life,
nor can My love for you waver for an instant.
I catch your tears in My hand,
and turn each one to diamonds for your crown.

MY WORDS TO HIM

Thank you, Jesus, for being with me
through every season of life.
Thank you for being with me in good times and bad,
lack and plenty, joy and sorrow.
You're with me in tears and in laughter,
in youth and old age.
Thank you for never turning your head
when danger comes my way
even if I may not sense your presence.
Thank you for not leaving me
when things go wrong in my life.
Thank you for a love that never wavers.
You never afflict your children,
nor do you treat your children badly.
You are all love!
You love to give good gifts!
Everything you give your children is for their good!
I'm completely in love with you.

Let no one boast about human leaders. For all things are yours,
whether Paul or Apollos or Cephas or the world or life or death
or the present or the future—all belong to you,
and you belong to Christ, and Christ belongs to God.

1 Corinthians 3:21-23 NRSV

HIS WORDS TO ME

Find Me

If you lose your way,
you can always count on Me
to come find you.
Heaven's holy taxi service
will be right there to transport you
where you belong.
Your home is in the very specific center
of My will, My dear,
one with Me, sound and found.
With Me you'll glow with health,
your bones vibrating with life.
But off-course without a map
you become shaky, unstable;
you can't see the way.
Oh, dear one, don't wait for a second.
Call heaven's holy taxi service
and I'll bring you right home.

MY WORDS TO HIM

Precious Lord, if I lose my way,
I can always count on you to come find me
and set me back on the right path.
Thank you, Jesus!
I love my home when it's in the very specific center
of your will and I'm one with you.
I feel myself glow
with health as my bones vibrate with life.
I'm drawing
nearer to you, loving and cherishing you as Lord
of my life.
Without you at the helm of my life,
I'm off-course and my way becomes a broiling,
dust-ridden desert.
I can't see clearly without you.
Your written Word is a road map for me to see
my way with my eyes focused on the wonders
you present me with each day.
How I love my life
in you!
Thank you from my heart.

The one who gets wisdom loves life;
the one who cherishes understanding will soon prosper.

Proverbs 19:8 NIV

HIS WORDS TO ME

Penalty of My Mistakes

I'll never let you bake in the oven
of your mistakes.
If you've taken some wrong paths
and gotten yourself tangled
in relationships you'd like to get out of,
I'm here to help.
I have plans for you—plans to prosper you and
to open doors of possibility.
So come to Me openly,
honestly, and let's make a new start.

I'll remove the hot glare from your life,
and I'll place you in your sweet destiny.
Put your faith in Me.
Be strong and trust Me.

MY WORDS TO HIM

Thank you, Jesus, for saving me from the penalty
of my mistakes.
I'm so thankful!
Thank you for being there when I've taken wrong paths
and gotten myself tangled in relationships
that I shouldn't have.
Thank you for helping me through difficult times
and protecting me from myself.
Thank you for the plans
that you have for me, plans to prosper me
and to open the doors of possibility and blessing.
I come to you today openly and honestly
to make a new start.
Remove the dust and soot from my life, Lord,
and place me in my sweet destiny.
I'm putting all my faith and trust in you.

"God sent his Son into the world not to judge the world,
but to save the world through him."

John 3:17 NLT

HIS WORDS TO ME

Reliable Sources

Don't doubt your faith, My child.
Doubt your doubts.
Your feelings and emotions aren't
reliable sources for you to base
important decisions on. In Me you have
the guidance you need
because I have the plan for your life.
I've numbered the hairs
on your dear head. I've calculated
the breaths you've breathed
and stored them in golden containers
to celebrate a life being lived
for *Me*.
You are close
to My heart.
Never doubt My love. Never doubt
who you are in Me.
Make your decisions with Me.

Thank you, Jesus, for showing me
that my feelings and emotions
aren't reliable sources for me to base
important decisions on.
Thank you for showing me not to doubt
my faith.
I'll doubt my doubts instead!
In you, I have the guidance I need
because you have the perfect plan for my life.
You've numbered the hairs on my head
and calculated the breaths I'll breathe.
I love living close to your heart.
I won't leave you out when I make decisions.
I won't doubt your love, Jesus,
and I won't doubt who I am in you.

Let him ask in faith, with no doubting, for the one who doubts is
like a wave of the sea that is driven and tossed by the wind.

James 1:6 ESV

HIS WORDS TO ME

Written Word

My power is working in you
mightily today.
My Word has made you alive,
and the power of heaven is right now
yanking you up out of the muck
of the world and its mess of temptations.
Darling, you're going to experience victory
over the situation you've been going through.
Begin to think of the problem as dissolved.
Be relieved.
Set your dear foot on your new path
with glad expectation.

Thank you, Jesus, for your written Word that lights up my life
and my way through life.
Thank you for the victory
I'm going to experience today because of your loving care
and guidance.
Thank you for victory over each trying situation
I encounter.
Thank you for helping to dissolve problems
as I confront them today.
Everything you do for me
is a miracle.
I'm filled with glad expectation and delight
knowing you're here with me, and your glorious power
is working in me mightily.
Thank you, Jesus!

In the word of truth, in the power of God; by the weapons of
righteousness for the right hand and the left.

2 Corinthians 6:7 NASB

HIS WORDS TO ME

The Way to Flourish

Pause for a moment, take a deep breath,
allow your shoulders to relax,
and be still.
Let the following words reach into your
heart and mind:
The righteous shall flourish as the palm tree.
Palm trees live long, dear one.
Many species live over a hundred years.
The palm tree flourishes happily
producing fruit in its season and is
a source of beauty to the world.
My child, you are beautiful to Me,
and your days are in My hands.
Take another deep breath
as you bring the word *flourish*
into your heart and mind.
Now, gently and sweetly,
close your eyes and believe.
Today, flourish.

Thank you for showing me how to flourish
in the same way the palm tree flourishes.
Palm trees live many years and produce fruit
in their season.
They're a blessing to the areas
where they're planted.
I want to be a blessing
where I'm planted, too.
My days are in your hands!
I want to flourish and keep on flourishing.
I want to be a blessing to you and your kingdom.
I'm taking a deep breath and calming
my heart to be still before you as you nourish me
by your Word.
Nourished, I flourish!

In His days the righteous shall flourish,
And abundance of peace,
Until the moon is no more.

Psalm 72:7 NKJV

HIS WORDS TO ME

Time for All Things

There's a time for all things.
Keep yourself, My love
and you'll understand.
You can't live in self-absorbed flesh
and at the same time be available
to My Spirit.
Today, set a deliberate choice of your will
to obey My Word, to worship Me,
and to walk in wisdom.
Take authority over your choices
and set your heart on the greatness of My
wisdom and knowledge.
I know what you're up against.
Your clever strategies without Me
will tire you out. Can you trust
My will for your life today?

Thank you, Jesus, that there's a time for all things.
I'm keeping myself in your loving care to understand
more about the importance of the timing of my choices.
A selfish heart isn't prepared to hear the gentle guiding
voice of the Holy Spirit.
Today I'm setting a deliberate
choice of my will to obey your Word, to worship you
and to walk in wisdom.
I'm taking responsibility
for my choices and for honoring the time, and not
rushing ahead of you.
I'm setting my heart
on the greatness of your wisdom and knowledge.
You're ever aware of the struggles I'm up against
and my own clever strategies and hasty, flash conclusions
won't work; in fact, they only cause chaos.
I'm turning
everything over to you and your leading, Jesus.
I trust you, and I totally submit my gifts and talents
for you to manage with your holy will now and always.

Depend on the LORD;
trust him, and he will take care of you.

Psalm 37:5 NCV

HIS WORDS TO ME

Love Song

When the fury of life and the fears of the day
get to you and cause your throat to tighten,
your stomach to flinch,
listen for the song I'm singing to you.
Be very still and hear the music,
more luscious than human ears can bear.
Honey-smooth and fragrant
is My love song to you.
Shudder with joy at the melody
inside the noise of the storm around you
and rest your wonderful self in Me.

Thank you, Jesus, for your love song over me.
When the fury of life and the fears of the day
get to me and cause me to get anxious and upset,
I listen for your sweet song of love.
If I become very still I can hear the music
in my heart, and it's so freeing and sublime,
I want to dance!
I shudder with joy
at the music of heaven in the midst
of the raucous noise
of the human storms
surrounding me.

"Break forth together into singing,
you ruins of Jerusalem;
for the LORD has comforted his people,
he has redeemed Jerusalem."

Isaiah 52:9 NRSV

HIS WORDS TO ME

Central Moving Force

It pleases Me
when you refuse to allow your ego
to be the central moving force in your life.
It pleases Me when you don't stress
over the trifling opinions of others.
Wisdom has shown you to stop
driving yourself to impress the world.
I'm pleased when you zap your lust
for approval and rest in *My* love and approval.
I delight in you when you tell Me
the life you're living now is no longer all about you,
and you're living by faith in *Me!*
Willingly I gave My life for you
to see you vibrate with glory
and to hear you speak these words to Me.

MY WORDS TO HIM

Thank you, Jesus, for helping me to set my ego aside
as the central moving force in my life.
Thank you for helping
me avoid stressing out over the trifling opinions of others
and the actions I dislike in others.
Thank you for wisdom
that shows me to stop driving myself to impress the world,
and thank you for zapping my lust for approval.
I'm resting
in your love and approval, Lord.
I love to know you delight
in me when I come to you unbound by my ego.
My life
is no longer all about me. I'm living by faith in you!
I'm complete in you!
You gave your life willingly
on the cross for me so I could live my life unselfishly
and gloriously full.
I'm going to shimmer and bask
in the glory you give your children and exclaim
to the world how much I love you.

The fear of the Lord is the beginning of wisdom;
all who follow his precepts have good understanding.
To him belongs eternal praise.

Psalm 111:10 NIV

HIS WORDS TO ME

Selfish Pleasures

Eyes stuck to the world and its fickle rewards
will confuse you and make it difficult
to repent, change, and gloriously move forward.
If you crave pleasure and are driven to
escape discomfort, avoid pain,
and narcotize hurtful memories,
you'll be blinded to the blessings
I have for you of spiritual strength.
Dear one, it takes courage to be truly happy,
and temporary pleasures will never
satisfy you. I want to give you a clear mind today,
like gazing out a clean window.
want you to be brave and face the world
with all its trials and unpleasantness,
but look for *goodness and mercy*.
Goodness and mercy are right there in plain sight.

I don't crave selfish pleasures, Jesus, and I'm asking you
to keep me from trying to escape discomfort, to avoid pain
or narcotize hurtful memories.
When my eyes are stuck
to the world that functions without knowing you,
there are few rewards, and what's there is fickle and empty.
Outside your boundaries it's difficult to repent and ask forgiveness
because I don't think I've done or thought anything wrong
or ungodly.
Help me, Jesus. I want to be strong in you and
I want you to be pleased with me.
I want to see myself
as a spiritually strong person, one who lives with the courage
to be truly happy without making demands that the world
around me do as I wish.
Temporary pleasures never satisfy.
Oh Lord, give me a clear mind today to bravely face
the world around me with all its trials and temptations.
I'm going to look for signs of your goodness and mercy
everywhere I go and in all I do today.

Let the Holy Spirit guide your lives.
Then you won't be doing what your sinful nature craves.

Galatians 5:16 NLT

HIS WORDS TO ME

Need for Joy

Open your spiritual ears,
and listen to the gold-toned nectar
of perfect harmony that lives in you.
Listen for heaven's voices in concert,
open wide your wonderful heart,
and sing along.
Angels' voices are lifted up in praise
for their Creator.
They're singing a song of happiness.
They're making the beautiful music of
love, joy, peace,
patience, kindness, goodness
gentleness, faithfulness, self-control—
Will you sing along?

MY WORDS TO HIM

Thank you for recognizing my need for joy.
When I experience spiritual hunger
and feed on earthly, perishable food
and its entertainments, I remain hungry.
I have no joy.
But I live in fullness of life
with your perfect joy flowing in my veins.
You died on the cross to give me the gift
of your joy and I'm so thankful!
You came to satisfy the longing soul,
to bring joy to the hapless, hope to the wounded,
and inspiration to the thinker.
Lord Jesus,
I'm placing all my needs into your hands.
I'm placing the concerns of my heart
and mind into your care.
The Scriptures tell me
that my real treasure is located in my heart.
Today I'm going to reach out
from my heart and experience joy!

The meek shall obtain fresh joy in the LORD.
Isaiah 29:19 ESV

HIS WORDS TO ME

Give and Receive

Why do you suppose I told you
that it's more blessed to give than to receive?
Wouldn't you think it would be more blessed
to be on the receiving end?
Oh, but hear Me today.
You *are* on the receiving end when you give!
I want you to grab hold of this principle right now
so you never forget.
When you give from the heart,
directed by Me for My purposes,
you are really *receiving*.
When you give sparingly, worried about your little self
and your little needs, that's exactly what you get back.
Little.
When you give as I give—bountifully, joyfully, richly—
that's exactly what you'll receive in return,
and the bountiful blessing return is yours!
Perhaps the question is, darling, *where* you should give.
There are always those with the palms of their hands
waving at you in the face—so I tell you, *listen to your heart*.
When you're thrilled with the pleasure of giving
there'll be no room for coercion, duty, obligation, or guilt.
Let's give together.

Thank you, Jesus, for showing me
it's more blessed to give than receive.
I discovered I'm actually on the receiving end
when I give!
When I give from the heart
directed by you for your purposes,
I'm really receiving.
When I give sparingly,
worried about my little self and my little needs,
that's what I get back—little.
You gave everything
for me, Jesus, and when I give I want to give
bountifully and joyfully in honor of you
and all you give to me.
Show me where to give,
and how to be wise in giving.
I'm so thrilled
with the joys of giving, I make no room
to be taken advantage of or obligated.
Because of you, my divine giver,
giving is not a duty; it's a holy privilege
for which I am so grateful!

"He who sows sparingly will also reap sparingly,
and he who sows bountifully will also reap bountifully."

2 Corinthians 9:6 NKJV

HIS WORDS TO ME

Religious Sanctimony

I don't want you addicted to religious sanctimony
or efforts trying to prove how holy you are.
I don't want My children galloping about
with banners of false righteousness.

I want you to see Me with My arms open
to all of My creation, and especially
to those of My own household.
I want you to understand how precious is
each person and each breath of life.
I want you to be *in love with Me*
and to love one another.
I live in the deep, abiding passion
of eternal, omnipresent *love*,
and I ask you to live in that love too,
because religious addiction will never
love you back.

MY WORDS TO HIM

Thank you, Jesus, for delivering me from
religious sanctimony and efforts to prove
how holy I am. Whew!
You're not blessed
with your children galloping about with banners
of smug pious self-righteousness.
Your arms
are open wide to all of your creation, and especially
to those of your own household, and you ask us
to walk humbly with you with genuine, purity
of heart and soul. You want your children
to understand how precious we are to you,
for each breath of life is vitally important
to you.
You want us to fall in love
with you and to love one another.
You live
in the deep abiding passion of eternal,
omnipresent love, and all you ask is we live
in that sweet, non-self-serving love, too.
Help me, Jesus, to love you from my heart
purely and wholly, with no other agenda
but to know you, to love you, and to love others.

"A new commandment I give to you, that you love one another;
as I have loved you, that you also love one another."

John 13:34 NKJV

HIS WORDS TO ME

Things to Ponder

When you glue your mind to a thought
or idea, that thought or idea
takes root in you, and whatever is rooted in you
overtakes you, which is why
I've told you to glue your precious mind
to the things that are true, honorable,
just, pure, lovely, kind, and gracious.
Fill your mind with such thoughts,
and they'll grow in you until
they become a part of you.

I want you to think and ponder on the things
of Me, and put an end to the stomping and trampling
of heavy, profane thoughts in your head.
Rebuke your mind's wandering to dark places
and insert *My* mind in you.
You'll grow closer to Me every day,
and you'll experience a beautiful life
of ultimate freedom and peace.

MY WORDS TO HIM

Today, Lord Jesus, I ponder on the things
you tell me to think about.
You tell me to think about things
that are true, honorable, just, pure, lovely,
kind and gracious.
I want to fill my mind
with these thoughts so they'll grow in me
and become a part of me.
I'm going to put
an end to thinking dreary, profane thoughts
and mind-wandering into dark places
where I shouldn't go.
It's your mind
I want alive in me.
Help me to grow closer
and closer to you every day, dear Jesus,
because I love my beautiful life of ultimate
freedom and peace.

Whatever things are true, whatever things are noble, whatever
things are just, whatever things are pure, whatever things are
lovely, whatever things are of good report, if there is any virtue
and if there is anything praiseworthy—meditate on these things.

Philippians 4:8 NKJV

HIS WORDS TO ME

Great Eternal Plan

Patience, My child, be patient.
You're an important part of My great eternal plan,
and not as an almost-winner, or as a once-was
or as a coulda-been, you're *it*.
You're the right-now, in-the-game, authentic child of Mine.
I've sent you out with My anointing and blessing
to practice My presence everywhere and in all things.
Conquer frustration.
Accept the time that real achievement takes.
Make patience your friend. Be ready for anything.
Today, think about finding happiness
as you wait. Persevere in the upward climb—
in the struggle and the thankless hours.
Let your soul expand and grow,
not squirming out of problems
as frustration would have you do.
I want you strong in character,
and complete in Me.
Suffering is a portion of triumph.
Remember that.

Thank you, Jesus, for self-control.
Thank you
for making me an important part of your great
eternal plan.
Thank you for giving me
an authentic life of blessing and value.
Thank you for showing me to practice
your presence everywhere and in all things.
Thank you for helping me conquer frustration.
I accept the time that real achievement takes
and I've decided to make patience my friend.
Today I choose to think about finding happiness
while I'm in a period of waiting.
I'll wait with patience.
I'm persevering in the upward climb and I praise you,
Jesus, that my soul expands and grows in my patience.
Thank you for helping me cast frustration aside
and to show up strong in character before your throne.
Thank you for showing me that suffering is a portion
of triumph. I'm complete in you!

Rejoice in hope, be patient in suffering, persevere in prayer.

Romans 12:12 NRSV

HIS WORDS TO ME

Giving Me Insight

When you're alone and uninterrupted,
you have the holy privilege to see yourself
with clear, honest eyes minus all outside influence.
Don't be afraid to spend time alone.
Alone you have the opportunity to listen to yourself
and to carefully observe the way you're living.
It takes daring and boldness to pull down the veil
of neutrality and take a good, piercing look
at yourself in the light of My Word.
Do you see yourself continually captivated by Me?
Have you brought Me into all situations?
All activities? All relationships?

Thank you for the time spent alone
when I have the holy privilege to see
and think with clear eyes minus all outside
influence.
There was a time in my life
when I hated to be alone,
but you've taught me the exquisite joys
of solitude. Thank you!
Alone I have
the opportunity to listen to myself
and to carefully observe the way I'm living.
I'm daring to be bold and courageous enough
to pull down the veil of neutrality
and take a good, piercing look at myself
in the light of your Word.
I can see
my desperate need to keep you front and center
in all of my activities and my relationships.
Oh Jesus, here in my solitude
I'm captivated by you.

Search me, God, and know my heart;
test me and know my anxious thoughts.
See if there is any offensive way in me,
and lead me in the way everlasting.

Psalm 139:23-24 NIV

HIS WORDS TO ME

Pick Up the Pieces

Each new day I give you
the opportunity to drink from the fountain of joy
and to flourish like a prize-budding rose.
I don't want you to lie gasping
on the blistered ground of yesterday.

Pick up the pieces of your life
and take a good look at them.
Where does each one belong?
Should any pieces be thrown away?
Which pieces will you repair?
Where are the pieces that fit
perfectly together?
You're not in the mouth of a drought.
The worst is never the worst.
I've called you to flourish
with every piece of your life in place.

Thank you, Jesus, for helping me
pick up the pieces of my life
and take a good look at them.
Thank you for showing me
where each piece belongs.
You show me which piece
needs to be repaired, which one needs
to be thrown out, and then
you show me how all the pieces
of my life fit together.
Each new day
you give me an opportunity to drink
from the fountain of your joy.
Thank you
for a flourishing life, one with
every piece in its place!

You yourself must be an example to them by doing good works
of every kind. Let everything you do reflect
the integrity and seriousness of your teaching.

Titus 2:7 NLT

HIS WORDS TO ME

The Banquet Before Me

I'm preparing a banquet of wondrous treats
for your beautiful soul today.
Come and have a feast with *Me*—
feast on our friendship.
Experience the delight of a refreshed soul.

I want you to recognize your need for joy.
When you groan with spiritual hunger
and feed yourself with earthly foods,
bread, wine, gooey stuff, sweets,
empty chatter, and entertainments—
you'll stay hungry.
You can't *fully* live without My perfect joy
flowing in your veins.
I died on the cross to give you the gift of My joy.
Today, let's
be joyful *together*.

Thank you, Jesus, for the banquet
you prepare before me
each day, a banquet of holy delights.
Just knowing you is the greatest delight
of my life!
Thank you for the feast
of your presence!
I can't get over
you calling me your friend.
It's such a sublimely mysterious thing
to think about.
Me, a friend of Jesus Christ,
the Savior of the world!
I live with
the delight of a refreshed and astonished
soul every day in the knowledge
that I'm your friend.

You are my friends if you do what I command you.

John 15:14 ESV

HIS WORDS TO ME

Gift of Faith

I treasure your faith.
Your faith in Me is built on love,
and it's monumental enough
to move mountains,
heal the sick,
bring hope to the hopeless,
and give courage to the feeble.
From faith springs every good thing,
giving the authority to overcome evil
and to charter unknown seas.
Without faith it's impossible to please Me.
I want you to understand the immensity
of one miniscule mustard seed of faith.
Understand that one beautiful act of faith in Me
has the power
to change the course of human history.

Thank you, Jesus, for the gift of faith.
Thank you for faith that's built on love
and trust, monumental enough
to move mountains, heal the sick,
bring hope to the hopeless,
and give courage to the feeble.
Thank you for faith that brings forth
every good thing and gives power
to overcome evil.
Faith gives courage
to go into unknown land and to charter
unexplored seas.
You've said that
without faith it's impossible
to please you. Oh Jesus, increase my faith!
The immensity of one miniscule mustard seed
of faith can actually move mountains.
Thank you that one act of faith in you
has the power to change the course of human history.

"Because of the littleness of your faith; for truly I say to you,
if you have faith the size of a mustard seed, you will say to this
mountain, 'Move from here to there,' and it will move; and
nothing will be impossible to you."

Matthew 17:20 NASB

HIS WORDS TO ME

Life-Giver

My Spirit, the life giver,
breathes new spark into your endeavors today,
and produces fresh vitality into what was
asleep. You're being blessed with freedom
to accomplish new things. Arise, shine,
for your light has come!
My glory is all over you.
You're radiant!
Oh, what a day this is!
Joy, the mother of enthusiasm,
fills you.
Arise I say,
and go ahead, dear one, shine!

Thank you, Jesus, for the Holy Spirit,
the life-giver, who breathes new spark into my life
each day.
I'm filled with fresh vitality today, Jesus,
and I thank you!
I'm blessed with freedom
to accomplish new things and move ahead
following your call, "Arise! Shine! For your light
has come!"
Yes, I know that my light has surely
arrived and I feel radiant.
Oh, what a day this is!
Joy, the mother of enthusiasm floods over me.
Thank you, Jesus, for your call to arise because
I'm going to live this day alive and lifted up
and shining in the light of your glory!

Then Jesus spoke to them again, saying,
"I am the light of the world. He who follows Me shall not walk in
darkness, but have the light of life."

John 8:12 NKJV

671

HIS WORDS TO ME

Fabulous Journey

You're on a fabulous journey, dear one,
so don't get frustrated.
This intruder, frustration, will cause you
to grab for immediate rewards,
will yank you down a slippery hill
to avoid the slow, steady upward climb
of the unpaved highway I've set you on.
When you encounter difficulties,
the nasty blubbering of frustration
takes over your thoughts
and it's time to pay a visit
to My Holy Spirit's traveler's aid station
for sweet rejuvenation.
My Spirit will show you
that the challenge of the roughest path
on life's sojourn, the one
few people choose,
is by far the most rewarding.

Thank you, Jesus, for this fabulous journey I'm on.
The unholy intruder called *frustration* always
gets me off track, and I'll grab for immediate rewards
and lose my way. Not today!
No, Jesus, today
I'm calling on your Holy Spirit to rejuvenate
and inspire my faith.
Thank you for your Spirit
who shows me that the challenge of the roughest path
on life's sojourn, the one few people choose,
is by far the most rewarding.
Thank you for such
an exciting life that's even filled with challenges
and bumpy roads.
I love the journey
because we're on it together.

Yet I will rejoice in the LORD.
I will joy in the God of my salvation.

Habakkuk 3:18 NKJV

HIS WORDS TO ME

No Problem Too Great

Is there a problem too great
that My Word doesn't cover?
Is there a situation I can't handle?
Did I leave something out when I laid the
foundation of the earth?
Did I forget something when I took your
sins, burdens, and cares on My body
on the cross?
My child, I hear your complaints
and your grievances, but you're forgetting
I'm bigger than they are.
Cast your cares upon Me, I tell you,
it's of no advantage to complain
when you can pray and proclaim with confidence
that I am the strength
of your life.
Today, gather your fears and doubts in one heap,
deposit them at the foot of the cross,
and proclaim the victorious power of My Word
over every situation you face.

MY WORDS TO HIM

Jesus, there's no problem too great that the Word of God
doesn't cover.
There's no human situation that heaven
is unfamiliar with.
When you laid the foundation
of the earth, Jesus, you left nothing out.
And then you took my sins, burdens and cares
on your body on the cross.
I know you hear
my prayers.
You hear the concerns of my heart,
and you're bigger than my concerns.
You said
to cast all my cares on you and proclaim
with confidence that you're the strength of my life.
Lord, today I'm gathering my fears and doubts
in one lump and depositing them at the foot of the cross.
I'm proclaiming the victorious power of your Word
over every situation I face.

The peace of God, which surpasses all understanding,
will guard your hearts and minds through Christ Jesus.

Philippians 4: 7 NKJV

HIS WORDS TO ME

Holy Spirit's Nudging

I hear you when you say
you don't have enough time to do everything
you think you must get done.
Would you like to know the truth of the matter?
I'll tell you if you listen.
You've been afraid of self-denial, of saying no
to yourself; you're afraid of not being appreciated,
of disappointing someone; you're afraid of failure, of being
unimportant, of being out-done.
The problem is not lack of time, dear one,
it's lack of discipline.
There are enough hours in the day.
I'm here to give you a heavenly boost
and a divine nudge to help you recognize
your need for discipline and sustained dedication to a task.
I never give you more than you can handle.
There is nothing to fear.
I've given you the ability to do all things well!

Thank you, Jesus, for your Holy Spirit showing me
that I make myself busier than I need to be.
Thank you for opening the eyes of my understanding
so I can recognize inside me the fear of saying no.
Oh Jesus, I see the kind of thinking that's all about me,
and not about what you're calling me to do or be involved in.
Thank you for showing me my out-of-balance need for appreciation.
I can see now that fear of failure or rejection
motivates me to take on more responsibility than you
ask me to.
I understand, Lord, that my problem hasn't been
a lack of time, but a lack of spiritual awareness and discipline.
You're showing me now that there are
enough hours in the day according to your design to accomplish all
I'm called to do.
You're here to give me a heavenly boost
and a divine nudge to achieve discipline and sustained dedication
to the tasks only you give me to accomplish.
You never give me
more than I can handle.
You've gifted me with
the ability to do all things well—that is, that which you assign me.

I will instruct you and teach you in the way you should go;
I will counsel you with my eye upon you.

Psalm 32:8 ESV

HIS WORDS TO ME

A Mountain to Climb

You want to climb a mountain today,
but have you considered
that I may be asking you
to *descend* the mountain?
Have you considered
that I may be waiting for you
down below in the valley of humility?
Your strength is in *humility*
not in your conquests.
You aren't the master,
I am.
The valley of humility is a place
of glory and honor.
It's a place where you see who I am
and who you are in Me.

Thank you, Jesus, for giving me a mountain
to climb up, and also a mountain to climb down.
I thank you for the descent, as well as the upward trek.
I'm so thrilled to know that on the way down you're waiting
at the bottom for me.
You call it the valley of humility.
It's the mountain that teaches me that spiritual strength
is found in humility.
Conquests are wonderful when
I make you the master of my life.
The valley of humility
is a place of glory and honor where I see the greatness of you
and the smallness of me.
Lord, I want to know you
for who you are in all your greatness!
The struggles up
and down the mountains of life reveal you to me in every step.

Humble yourselves in the presence of the Lord,
and He will exalt you.

James 4:10 NASB

HIS WORDS TO ME

Strength to Overcome

Pray for My strength to rise up in you
and overtake your inclinations
to act according to your *feelings*.
My servant Peter depended on
the fervor of his feelings
instead of relying solely upon
My supernatural strength and courage,
so he sank in the stormy water
when he could have walked without a problem.
You're stronger than you think,
and you have boundless courage in you.
Reach inside and draw out
more of the power of My Spirit
to meet your needs, help others,
and walk on your stormy waters.

Thank you, Jesus, for strength to overcome
my inclination to act according to my feelings.
Your supernatural strength and courage is enough
for me.
Peter couldn't walk on the stormy waters
with you because he depended on the fervor
of his feelings instead of relying solely upon you.
You've made me stronger than I realize.
I have boundless courage.
I'm reaching
inside today and drawing out more of the power
of your Spirit to meet my needs.
I'm going to walk
on stormy waters trusting solely in you.

My God shall supply all your need
according to His riches in glory by Christ Jesus.

Philippians 4:19 NKJV

HIS WORDS TO ME

Drained of Energy

If you feel empty and drained of energy,
I understand.
I'm here.
I'm here to revive you.
My Spirit is in you to lift you up
and restore your soul
to an even happier and more energetic you.
When you're weary and without
strength to carry on, take a deep breath,
fix your thoughts on Me,
and let Me love you.
When you feel you have nothing to give,
give Me that nothing.

Thank you, Jesus, for being here
when I become drained of energy.
Thank you for being here to revive me.
Your Spirit is in me to lift me up
and restore my soul to an even happier
and more energetic me.
When I'm weary and without strength
to carry on, I fix my thoughts on you,
and let you love me.
I proclaim
your strength in me.
I take a deep breath now
and know that though I may think
I have nothing more to give at this moment,
it's not true.
In you I can do all things!

I can do all things through Christ who strengthens me.

Philippians 4:13 NKJV

HIS WORDS TO ME

Doing Good Work

When you're caught up in your dizzying plans,
demanding projects, and driving goals,
eventually you'll find yourself frazzled
and wondering why you can't
seem to manage your life without stress.

I don't want you to wear yourself out doing good work;
I want you to celebrate the *process*.
I want you to be energized by your
conversations with Me, so your creative
gifts will unfold and flower.

Notice how your energy is spent. Notice
where and when you find yourself
drained and exhausted.
Notice where and when you're happy
and joyfully alive.
Notice where you need to make
some changes.

Dear Jesus, I realize I can easily wear myself out
doing good work that I think is honoring you,
but is it? I can become caught up in dizzying plans,
demanding projects, and driving goals thinking I'm
serving you while I'm frazzling and stressing myself out.
I know you don't call me to wear myself out.
There's a time to work hard and a time to not work.
Give me the wisdom to know which is which.
I choose to celebrate the process, and to be energized
by my conversations with you so my creative gifts
unfold and flower.
Thank you for teaching me
to observe how I spend my energy, and to recognize
when I'm foolishly drained and exhausted.
Thank you for helping me to focus on you
and your Word and the art of being joyfully alive.
And thank you, dear Lord, for showing me
when it's time to make serious changes in my life.

He satisfies the longing soul,
And fills the hungry soul
with goodness.

Psalm 107:9 NKJV

HIS WORDS TO ME

Know the Truth

You'll love what you know
when you love the truth.
When you act according to what you love,
you become like the truth you love.
Think about it.
You were created for more truth
than you can carry in your natural mind,
and you were created for much more love
than you reach for.
If your only reality is confined within
the impulses of your human nature,
your identity can't soar higher than your limitations.
You're stuck!
Today, realize your entire identity
rests in Me.
I want you to enter
your gorgeous, fully-formed identity,
mounted and framed in the truth.
I want you fully alive in *Me* today
as you've always been meant to be.

I was born to know the truth
and carry the truth in my natural mind.
I was created for much more love
than I've reached for.
I love what I know
when I love the truth. My reality is based on
knowing truth, not on the impulses
of my human nature.
My identity soars
higher than my limitations each day
my heart and soul are solidly focused on you.
I have no identity without you.
Today I enter my gorgeous, full formed
identity mounted and framed in the truth
of your Word.
I am alive in you
as I was born to be.

The grass withers and the flowers fall
But the word of our God endures forever.

Isaiah 40:7 NIV

HIS WORDS TO ME

Courage to Live

Have the courage today
to live as I meant you to live.
Have the courage today to partner with Me
for your beautiful life.
Your true being is in Me.
Allow Me to convert your shrunken world
for My vast, endless eternity.
Allow Me to convert your selfish human will
to the glories of Mine.
Your struggle against temptation
divides you against yourself
with conflicting loyalties and
and wants.
I'm calling you to enter your true identity,
the one I formed before you were
in your mother's womb.
I called you, named you, and loved you
from the moment I first thought of you.

Thank you, Jesus, for the courage today
to live as I was meant to live.
Today I'm partnering with you
as I live my beautiful life.
My true being
is in you.
Thank you for converting
a shrunken personal world
into your vast, endless eternity
of delights.
Thank you for converting
my selfish human will for the glories
of your perfect, omnipotent will.
Thank you for holding out your hand
to me each time I struggle against temptation.
Thank you for calling me to enter
my true identity, the one you formed
before I was in my mother's womb.
You called me, named me and loved me
from the moment you first thought of me.

You made all the delicate, inner parts of my body
and knit me together in my mother's womb.

Psalm 139:13 NLT

HIS WORDS TO ME

Power within Me

Don't be upset at that thorn in your side.
I'll pull it out.
In the meantime, be glad
that the power within you
is greater than any struggle or hassle
on the surface and surrounding you.
A thorn is not a sword. An annoyance and nuisance
is not a catastrophe (though it may feel like it).
I'll cause the voice of My authority to be heard.
The majesty of My voice and the strength of My arm
will be known!
My voice will carve flames of fire
in the conscience of all opposition to My will.
Be still and trust Me.

MY WORDS TO HIM

I'm so glad the power within me
is greater than any struggle or hassle
annoying me.
Thank you for the thorn
in my side that I'm trusting you to pull out
because a thorn is only a nuisance
and an irritation.
It's not a catastrophe,
even though it may feel like it.
Jesus, cause the voice of your authority
to be heard and known today.
The majesty
of your voice and the power of your will
must be known!
Your voice will carve
flames of fire in the conscience of all
opposition to your will.
And your voice
will yank out the troublesome thorn
as smoothly as a drop of rain
slips to the ground.

"Instead of the thorn shall come up the cypress;
instead of the brier shall come up the myrtle;
and it shall make a name for the Lord,
an everlasting sign that shall not be cut off."

Isaiah 55:13 ESV

HIS WORDS TO ME

Perfect Day

I'm peeling from you the unnecessary
and the banal.
I'm pouring My thoughts into you.
I'm climbing upon the pinnacles
of your finest hours.
Listen.
My voice shakes the wilderness—
your wilderness.
This is a new day for you and a time
to increase!
Be glad and expand the pegs of your tents.
I'm going to cause
your good deeds to multiply.

MY WORDS TO HIM

Thank you, Jesus, for this new day.
It's a day designed perfectly for me to focus
my attention on my relationship with you.
It's a day for me to increase my faith.
Thank you, Jesus, for your voice that shakes
the wilderness.
Your voice shakes the wilderness
within me, and I'm moved to take inventory
of the empty spaces in my soul.
Today I'm proclaiming "I believe." I believe
I've been delivered from spiritual drought.
Lord, I worship you and I believe
you've called me to walk a higher walk.
I believe you've called me to know you
intimately, and to live in complete freedom
from emotional stress.
I claim my happiness in you,
my Savior, now.
Right now.

I press toward the goal for the prize
of the upward call of God in Christ Jesus

Philippians 3:14 NKJV

HIS WORDS TO ME

Gladness and Gratitude

Receive all you have as a gift from Me,
and honor what you have.
I especially want you to respect the currency
I entrust to you, even if it's less than you desire.
Gain understanding and financial integrity,
and allow Me to prosper you *My* way.
If you're given to whim and an urge to possess things,
you'll clutter up your destiny.
I'm watching what you do with My gifts.
One piece of gold or one million are the same to Me.
Both require prudence and conscious management
to multiply and do good for My kingdom.
Humility multiplies riches,
but ignorance will diminish My blessings.

Oh heavenly Father, I'm filled with gladness
and gratitude today.
I'm thrilled with knowing
that my entire life is in your hands.
I'm amazed that I'm considered righteous
in your holy judicial system because
it's through your glorious righteousness
that I can be cleaned up and made a new person
who's now righteous with an honest heart
and pure mind.
Your wisdom and strength
are an unending support and source of joy.
I can't keep silent about what you've done for me
because if I kept silent the very rocks would cry out
with the story of salvation.
I praise and worship you
today because you've given me this wonderful day
and you've given me a wonderful future
to look forward to in this life and the next.
You've given me a wonderful forever!

God made him who had no sin to be sin for us,
so that in him we might become the righteousness of God.

2 Corinthians 5:21 NIV

HIS WORDS TO ME

Against Me

When it seems everything is against you,
and you don't think anyone's listening
to you; when the world around you collapses
at your doorway in heaps of nasty insults
and contention,
that's the precious moment to turn to Me—
to dive into Me, hang on tight,
and don't let go. Cling! Hold on!
When you feel like you're in the pits,
I'm in there with you.
Wrap yourself around Me;
I'll pull you out.

When everything seems against me
and I don't think anyone is paying attention
or listening to me, and when the world
around me collapses at my doorway,
these are the critical moments when
I turn to you. I turn to you, Jesus,
to dive into you and the power
of your love and presence.
It's time to
hang on tight to you and not let go.
I know for sure that I can do all things through
your strength in me, and I also I know
I can do nothing without you.
It's a wonderful freedom you've given me
to rise up above myself.
Thank you, Jesus.

Let the weakling say,
"I am strong!"

Joel 3:10 NIV

HIS WORDS TO ME

Know My Soul

I know your soul,
and I know how to restore your soul.
If you're weary,
disappointed, or bored,
I know what will perk you up.
When you need a holy lightning jolt
of energy and creative breath,
immerse yourself in things you love.
Take Me with you and listen to good music,
read a great book, work out, go for a walk, dance.
Fully engage in what is beautiful and
inspiring to your thirsty soul.
Be restored as a holy lightning jolt
of love and peace overtake you and lead you
to peace, new energy, and inspiration.
I'm with you.

Thank you, Jesus, for knowing my soul even better
than I do.
You know every aspect of me
and you know exactly what is necessary
when my soul is in need of restoration.
I can't do
the restoring alone.
You, author of my existence
and all that I am, work out the restoration process,
and I thank you!
If I'm weary, disappointed, or bored,
you know what will perk me up.
When I need
a holy lightning jolt of energy and creative breath,
all I have to do is immerse myself in you
and your Word.
I pray and I proclaim today
to be the person you created me to be
with a restored and wholesome
body, soul and spirit!

He restores my soul.
He leads me in right paths
for his name's sake.

Psalm 23:3 NRSV

HIS WORDS TO ME

Renewed Faith

Today, seize the opportunities I've placed before you
because when I make a promise to you.
My words aren't mere sounds or nice platitudes;
each syllable is breathed from My holy mouth
ordained to reach and teach you.
You'll succeed because I've said so.
My words over you are forever
settled in heaven!
My words infuse you with ability
that can't be counterfeited.
You'll succeed at your task
as I have planned it.
I'll never let you plunge headlong
into collapse.
When you believe and trust Me,
you become a golden thread
in the fabric of My perfect will.
There's no higher calling.

When I feel like I'm in the pits,
I know you're in there with me.
I wrap myself around you,
and you always pull me out into
the light again.
I'm healed and made new
over and over again because of your
compassionate love and mercy.
And because of the courage and strength
you infuse into me, I'm alive and filled
with hope and renewed faith.
Thank you, Jesus.

Whoever is wise will remember these things
and will think about the love of the LORD.

Psalm 107:43 NCV

HIS WORDS TO ME

Moving Life

All that lives, moves.
The smallest microbe throbs, pulses, breathes.
A bird of flight, a deer running,
a skittering insect—
leaves in trees bristle and flutter,
then shiver and float to the earth.
Clouds jostle the landscape of the sky,
and the wind shakes like
restless fringes across the earth.
All that lives moves,
but *fear* paralyzes,
turns the bones stiff and the breath stale.

My soul takes no pleasure
in the one who shrinks back, benumbed
and deadened with fear
because I've given you the power and courage
to be free, to move!
Will you kick your fears
into the caravan of My love now?
I can't guide and motivate you
if you're not moving.

MY WORDS TO HIM

Thank you, Jesus, that all that lives moves.
Thank you for the smallest moving microbe
that throbs, pulses, and breathes.
Thank you
for all living creatures: the bird, the deer,
the skittering insect.
Thank you for the leaves in trees bristling and fluttering
and the clouds jostling the landscape of the sky.
Thank you for the wind shaking like restless fringes
at the hem of a skirt. All that lives has movement,
but one deadly emotion can paralyze and turn the bones
stiff, and the breath stale — and that's fear.
Oh Jesus, save me from the grip of fear
on my life.
You've said in your Word that your soul
takes no pleasure in the one who shrinks back,
benumbed with fear, because you've given us
the power and courage to be free from fear
and to move in authority and courage.
Today, Jesus, I claim my freedom from fear
in all its guises, so your strength will guide
and motivate me in all I do. I want to be free
like the wind in the joy of your Spirit .

Such love has no fear, because perfect love expels all fear. If we
are afraid, it is for fear of punishment, and this shows that we
have not fully experienced his perfect love.

1 John 4:18 NLT

HIS WORDS TO ME

Hard Work

You're worried that your hard work
might not produce the results you desire.
You're worried you'll lose precious time,
and you wish you could see into the portals of tomorrow
to be positively certain you'll succeed.
Such thoughts form mushy lakes in your head,
your feet become buried in weeds,
your dreams wander like smoke.
Awake I say!
No energy spent in My kingdom is wasted.
No time is ever lost in a labor of love.
My rewards aren't temporary fireworks.
I'm forever!
I bless your soul.
I enrich your heart.
I kiss your spirit.
Listen to Me: you'll succeed
as you invest in a life of faith
trusting that I'll do through you
My good pleasure.

MY WORDS TO HIM

Dear Jesus, save me from worrying that my hard work
won't produce the results I desire.
Set me free to simply
love the work, do my best, and leave the results to you.
When I lose precious time worrying about tomorrow
and whether I'll succeed or not, please stop me.
Wake me up from such thinking because it creates
mushy lakes in my head so I can't enjoy what I'm doing!
No energy spent serving you is wasted.
No time is
ever lost in a labor love.
Your rewards aren't
temporary fireworks.
You are forever
and so am I! I'm created as an eternal being
to love you and serve you forever.
Thank you
for blessing my soul and enriching my heart.
Thank you for your Holy Spirit's kiss
on all my work.
I choose today to invest
in a life of faith works, trusting that through me
you'll do your good pleasure.
I'm yours
and all I do is yours.

The wage of the righteous leads to life.
Proverbs 10:16 ESV

HIS WORDS TO ME

More Creativity

Today, I'm drawing more creativity out of you.
Dip into the source
of all that is life-inspiring,
and be My mind and My heart.
Discover joy in sorrow,
create beauty out of ashes,
learn strength through weakness,
make something wonderful out of nothing.

Find the music in the storm,
see the colors of a thousand rainbows
in confusion's murky gray.

Consider life's simple treasures
to fill your home.
Multiply blessings, and prosper
in the adventure of loving.
All that you do in love
will create more love.
Discover this and
see how truly creative
you are.

Thank you, Jesus, for drawing more and more creativity
out of me.
Thank you for stretching me!
Thank you
for showing me to dip into the source of all that is
life inspiring. I know you want me to live with your mind
and your heart guiding me to discover joy in sorrow,
and to create beauty out of ashes.
Thank you for teaching me strength
through weakness.
Thank you for showing me
the sound of music in the storms of life, and the colors
of a thousand rainbows in the world's confusing murky gray.
Today I honor life's simple treasures as you multiply
my blessings and prosper me in the adventure of loving
all that you've made both great and small.
Thank you for teaching me that
everything I do in love creates more love.

We have come to know and have believed the love which God has
for us. God is love, and the one who abides in love abides in God,
and God abides in him.

1 John 4:16 NASB

HIS WORDS TO ME

Walk of Integrity

Walk in your integrity today.
Walk with Me.
Iron sharpens iron,
and I am the friend who sharpens you.
I draw from the depth of you
where I've planted strength
for every purpose.
I've given you a heart
to recognize, understand
and be acquainted with My ways.
I'm your *best* friend.
Your whole heart fits within Mine.
Your soul is knit with Mine,
making your presence a gift to the world
and a joy to Me.

Thank you, Jesus, for a walk of integrity.
Iron sharpens iron, and you are the immortal
friend who sharpens me.
Thank you for drawing out
the best of me of me and planting new strength
into me.
You've given me a heart to recognize,
understand and be acquainted with your ways.
You're my best friend!
My whole heart fits
within your huge heart, and my soul is knit
with yours.
Oh Jesus, as your friend,
I want to be a joy to you,
and a blessing to the world.

As iron sharpens iron,
So a man sharpens the countenance
of his friend.
Proverbs 27:17 NKJV

HIS WORDS TO ME

Business of Healing

I don't send sickness on you
as punishment or to get
your attention.
I'm in the business of *healing lives.*
I'm your healer and deliverer.
I command My healing
and it's done.
I want you to understand that I know
what I'm doing, and that
no matter what you see or hear,
be a mighty prayer warrior.
As My child,
you have authority to decree
and proclaim My Word, and I want you
to focus your heart and mind
on what I've taught you of redemptive
healing. *Take your authority*
and proclaim My will for healing
and deliverance.
I embrace *all* your needs.

Thank you, Jesus, that you're in the business of healing
our bodies as well as our souls.
You're my healer
and deliverer.
I thank you that you command healing
and it's done.
I trust you because you're on the throne,
and you answer prayer.
You're God, and you'll always
have your way.
Today I commit myself to prayer.
I want to be a mighty prayer warrior with authority
to decree and proclaim your will.
I'm focusing
my heart and mind on what you've taught me
of redemptive healing.
I proclaim your will for healing
and deliverance.
You embrace and care for all my needs,
body, soul, and spirit.
How I rejoice at knowing this!

Bless the Lord O my soul;
and all that is within me,
bless His holy name!

Psalm 103:1 NKJV

HIS WORDS TO ME

My Future

I'm your future.
I'm removing the struggle.
I'm cleaning you up
from the inside out.
I'm removing old habits and
filling you with a higher vision.
The devil's honey-laced voice
feeds you sweet poison tasty on your palette,
but it's death to your soul.
I'm here to strip the ugly things off you
if you'll let Me.
A full, happy life awaits you—
a future with no more secrets.

Thank you, Jesus.
You're my future.
You're my everything!
Thank you for removing
the struggles of my life and cleansing me
from the inside out.
Thank you or removing
old habits and filling me with a higher vision.
I'm through listening to the devil's honey-laced voice
feeding me sweet poison.
I'm taking a stand against
fault-finding and self-pity.
I'm stripping off
the grip of worry and doubt.
Thank you, Jesus,
for the full and happy life you've prepared for me
and a future with no unfulfilled secrets.

"For I know the plans I have for you,"
says the LORD.
They are plans for good and not for disaster,
to give you a future and a hope."

Jeremiah 29:11 NKJV

HIS WORDS TO ME

Your Glory

I'm standing at the door of your heart
quietly calling.
Hear My voice and open the door.
I'll come in to you,
hold you, and tell you
wondrous things you need to hear today.
We'll share the feast of life together,
you and I,
We'll be one.
Hear Me.
Come to Me.
Open to Me.
Our time together is heaven-blessed
and holy.

Thank you, Jesus, for the earth
filled with your glory. Holy are you!
God Almighty, glorious and wondrous
in power and might! I adore you!
Thank you for standing at the door
of my heart calling to me to be loved
and guided by you.
Every day you tell me
wondrous things that I need to hear.
It's so beautiful to share the feast of life
with you, Lord, to be one with you,
to hear you and know you personally
is the most beautiful thing I could ever
hope for.
You're so good to me, Jesus,
how I worship you!

Ascribe to the LORD the glory due his name;
worship the LORD in the splendor of his holiness.

Psalm 29:2 NIV

HIS WORDS TO ME

New Creation

Today, in this Christmas season,
you have an opportunity to be generous
and you may be tempted to withhold,
to draw back,
but I tell you, pause and listen to your heart.
If you hold back, a vacuum of loss is created
that blocks My blessings and your joy.
Remember I've said the generous soul will be made rich,
and the one who waters will also be watered.
I'm a giving God, abundantly generous, and it's
My Spirit who lives in you prompting you to give.
Lavish your gifts of love and kindness.
Give these without reservation and with holy generosity.
To live the honored life, don't hesitate
to give your love.

I worship you in this Christmas season, Lord Jesus.
I thank you for the opportunity to be generous
and express your love to others.
Help me to birth new life
through generosity at this time when we honor
your physical birth on earth.
Joy and happiness
surge through my veins as I contemplate how secure
and anchored I am in you.
You have my destiny
in your hands.
My heart swells with the velvet goodness
of divine peace flowing into every cell of my being
as I meditate on what I've become in you.
I'll never be the selfish person I used to be.

The one sitting on the throne said,
"Look, I am making everything new!"
Revelation 21:5 NLT

HIS WORDS TO ME

Abundantly Generous

How do you feel
knowing that I am the God of the universe,
and I have your destiny in My hands?
Do you have a huge sense of relief and joy
rushing through your veins
as you contemplate how secure,
sheltered, and anchored you are in Me?
Does your heart swell with the velvety goodness
of divine peace flowing into every cell
of your being as you meditate on your elevated
position in the heart and mind of the Almighty?
Are you overcome with genuine love and
holy gratitude knowing all is well?
Are you pleased to know your destiny
is having a wonderful time
in My hands?

You're a giving God, abundantly generous,
and it's your Holy Spirit who lives in me
showing me how to give.
You said in your Word
that the generous soul will be made rich
and the one who waters will also be watered.
I want to lavish my gifts of love and kindness
today on you and everyone I meet!
I'll give without reservation and with holy generosity.
My only desire is to live a holy life,
honored by you, Jesus,
so worthy are you to adore!

The generous soul will be made rich,
And he who waters will also be watered himself.

Proverbs 11:25 NKJV

HIS WORDS TO ME

Happy Birthday

Listen for Me today.
I want you to hear My voice.
Can you describe My voice
like the rush of many waters
over your soul as the King of glory comes in
whispering, chanting, loving?
I'm the voice inside the storm clouds
that paint the sky.
I'm the thundering storms;
I'm the voice in the somber wake
of the earthquake, and I'm the consuming fire
you can't name.
Today, as you celebrate My birth,
listen for My voice.
My voice is great and covers
the entire expanse of the earth;
yet, I speak in a voice hushed and small,
imperceptible to the non-spiritual ear.
I'm the voice in the still garden,
and I'm the voice
walking the hallways of your mind
right now.

Happy Birthday, Jesus!
Today as we celebrate your birthday
I want to listen for your voice.
I want to hear your response to the world you created
with our Father on this day.
I want to hear your voice: to know how you think
and what's in your heart on this day of days.
Your voice is like the sound of the rush
of many waters over all existence.
Oh, King of glory, come!
Your voice is a consuming fire.
Today as we exchange gifts, feast, and worship you,
I'll listen for your voice, great and powerful,
covering the entire expanse of the earth—
your voice gently calling to all of humanity
to look up because you're so near to us.
Yours is the gentle voice in the still garden,
and the voice echoing in the hallways
of my mind right now.

For unto us a Child is born, unto us a Son is given;
and the government will be upon His shoulder.
And His name will be called Wonderful, Counselor,
Mighty God, Everlasting Father, Prince of Peace.

Isaiah 9:6 NKJV

HIS WORDS TO ME

Heroic Heart

Before you aim for experiences,
aim for a pure, heroic heart.
Before you chase miracles,
chase a faith-filled life
based on love.
Before you fight for attention,
have faith enough to be quiet.
I'm revealing more of Myself to you
one step at a time.
Your faith will grow from a grain of sand
to a field fit for battle.
Faith multiplies with use,
and faith is at the front line
of all your scrimmages.
Faith is the real hero in your life.

Before I aim for experience above knowing you,
I'll aim for a pure, heroic heart.
Before I chase miracles,
I'll chase a faith-filled life based on your eternal values.
Before I fight for attention, I'll exercise faith enough
to be quiet and listen.
You reveal more of yourself to me
when I'm paying attention.
You lead me one step at a time,
and my faith grows from a grain of sand to a field fit for battle.
Faith multiplies with use, and faith is at the front line
of all my scrimmages.
I choose more faith today
because it's the source of all greatness.
How can I thank you, Jesus?

Now faith is the substance of things hoped for,
the evidence of things not seen.

Hebrews 11:1 NKJV

HIS WORDS TO ME

Your Throne Room

Today, I'm ushering you into My throne room
where you'll open your spiritual eyes and see
unimaginable glories. You'll see yourself as I see you,
perfect and whole, and shining in My image.
I wash you with My Word and I chasten you
with My holiness.
As you prepare your week remember
where you've been and who you are.
You live in My presence;
you bring Me wherever you go
and into whatever you do.

MY WORDS TO HIM

Today, dear Jesus, usher me into your throne room
where I'll open my spiritual eyes to see more of your glory.
I want to see you in your splendor, in the natural wonders
of the world which you created, and in the miracle-working
power of your love in your children.
Thank you for revealing
exactly how you see me so that I can keep myself
washed clean in the blood you shed for me on the cross.
I want to remain bathed in your Word day by day.
You chasten
and correct me by your sweet compassion and your holiness.
As I prepare for the close of this year I'll remember
where I've been and who I am.
I live in your presence
and I bring you with me wherever I go and into whatever I do.

You will show me the path of life;
in Your presence is fullness of joy;
At Your right hand are pleasures forevermore.

Psalm 16:11 NKJV

HIS WORDS TO ME

Eternity Apart

Be willing to live by My time, not yours
because your works are set
by the holy clock of My perfect timing.
All things happen
in the appropriate time, dear one.
There's a time for laughter
and a time for crying.
There's a time for sorrow
and a time to be carefree.
There's a time for plenty
and a time for lack.
All of time
is in My hands.
Time is designed by Me to serve you.
Fix your agenda according to Mine,
not yours,
and watch how your plans, intentions,
schemes, and systems
will each fall into place finding their
perfect timing.
Today, fix your schedule according
to the holy clock of My perfect timing
and find yourself at peace.

Oh Jesus, I realize your time and my time
are an eternity apart.
All of your works and intentions
are set by the holy clock of your perfect eternal timing.
All things on earth happen in their appropriate earth time.
You've taught us there's a time on earth for laughter
and a time for crying.
There's a time for sorrow
and a time to be carefree.
There's a time for plenty
and a time for lack.
Since all of time is in your hands,
it's only reasonable that I give my time to you.
Time is designed by you to serve you.
I'm fixing my agenda
according to your time, not mine, and then I'll notice
how my plans and intentions fall into place
finding their perfect timing.
Today I'm fixing my schedule
according to the holy clock of your perfect timing
and I'm at peace.

The Lord isn't being slow about his promise, as some people
think. No, he is being patient for your sake. He does not want
anyone to be destroyed, but wants everyone to repent.

2 Peter 3:9 NLT

HIS WORDS TO ME

Creating a New Heart

I'm creating a new heart in you.
The sweet ecstasy of union with Me
transforms you—
creates all things new
in you.
I'm elevating you above the thick fog
of vanity,
and I'm setting you free
from the futile pursuit
of seeking your own best.

Thank you, Jesus, for creating a new heart in me.
Thank you for the sweet ecstasy of union with you.
Thank you for transforming me and creating all things new.
You're elevating me above the thick fog of vanity
and struggling to find my place in the world.
You've set me free!
I'm free from the futile pursuit
of seeking my own best.
Now I seek your best
because you know what's best for me.
Thank you for your faithfulness
because now I'm living and thriving in your best!

Trust in Him at all times, you people;
Pour out your heart before Him;
God is a refuge for us.

Psalm 62:8 NKJV

HIS WORDS TO ME

Prospering in Every Area

I've called you to prosper
in every area of life.
I want you to give and invest in others,
for this is wisdom.
Humility and faith are your banners
and your guides. Goodness and mercy are your
accomplices. Joy and prosperity
are your rewards.
I'm calling you today
to give more of yourself to others.
As the year comes to a close,
consider multiplying your gifts,
and invest in lives as never before.
I'll guide you,
and you'll ride the heights of glory
rejoicing.

Thank you for prospering me in every area of my life
this year. Thank you for guiding me to give and invest
in the lives of others.
Thank you for wisdom, humility,
and faith as my banners.
Goodness and mercy are my accomplices.
Joy and prosperity are my rewards.
Thank you for calling me today to give more of myself
to others.
Multiply my gifts and help me to invest
in others as never before.
Guide me, Holy Spirit,
and I'll enter the new year riding the heights of glory
with rejoicing and profound hope.

Praise the LORD!
Give thanks to the LORD, for he is good!
His faithful love endures forever.

Psalm 106:1 NLT

HIS WORDS TO ME

New Vision

I placed a boundary for the sea with sand,
and though the waves of the sea toss and shake,
they can't prevail against the fortress
of simple grains of sand ordained for My purposes.
When your plans and My plans
are united in a single, beautifully ordained divine plan,
no storm will prevail against us.

I know your dreams,
and I'm familiar with your plans.
I hear the daily orchestration of your thoughts.
You have no secrets from Me.
I know all things,
and I want you to know My deep, intricate ways.

I want you to know My omniscience.
Pause now and allow the secrets of your heart
to fall into My compassionate hands
where I can gently hold them.
I have wonderful plans for you,
and at this year's end, let Me supply you with
a new vision.

Be thankful for this departing year and embrace the new.
I'm in all your tomorrows.

MY WORDS TO HIM

Here we are at the end of the year, Lord Jesus.
Supply me with new vision, for I'm so thankful
for this departing year.
Thank you for knowing
my dreams and my plans for each year we live
together.
Thank you for listening to the daily
orchestration of my thoughts.
I have no secrets
from you.
You know all things. Oh Jesus,
I want to know your deep, intricate ways
so I can bring you much honor in the coming year.
I want to know your omniscience and allow
the inner workings of my heart to reach into
your compassionate heart to know your will
and your purposes for me and the world.
Thank you for the plans you have at this year's end.
I now embrace the new.
Thank you for being with me in all my tomorrows.

Be filled with joy, always thanking the Father.
He has enabled you to share in the inheritance
that belongs to his people, who live in the light.
Colossians 1:11-12 NLT

New York Times best-selling author of over
thirty books, MARIE CHAPIAN passionately
seeks the heart of God as she writes and
ministers to people from all walks of life. Her
previous devotional books written in the voice
of the Lord were among the first of their kind.
Today she continues to touch and empower
millions of lives around the world with the
words God loves to speak to His children.

BroadStreet Publishing® Group, LLC.
Savage, Minnesota, USA
Broadstreetpublishing.com

Walking with Jesus
© 2017 by Marie Chapian

978-1-4245-6443-9 (faux)
978-1-4245-6466-8 (e-book)

Design by Chris Garborg | garborgdesign.com
Editorial services by Michelle Winger | literallyprecise.com

Printed in China.

21 22 23 24 25 26   7 6 5 4 3 2 1